Choctaw Women in a Chaotic World

Choctaw Women in a Chaotic World

The Clash of Cultures in the Colonial Southeast

Michelene E. Pesantubbee

University of New Mexico Press ▪ Albuquerque

©2005 by the University of New Mexico Press
All rights reserved. Published 2005
Printed in the United States of America

Library of Congress Cataloging-in-Publication Data

Pesantubbee, Michelene E., 1953–
Choctaw women in a chaotic world : the clash of cultures in the colonial Southeast / Michelene E. Pesantubbee.
p. cm.
Includes bibliographical references and index.
ISBN 0-8263-3333-8 (cloth : alk. paper) — ISBN 0-8263-3334-6 (pbk. : alk. paper)
1. Choctaw women—History. 2. Choctaw women—Social conditions. 3. Indians of North America—History—Colonial period, ca. 1600–1775. 4. Southern States—History—Colonial period, ca. 1600–1775. 5. France—Colonies—America. I. Title.
E99.C8P48 2005
305.48'897387076'09033—dc22
2004028693

Design and composition: Melissa Tandysh

In memory of my mother,
Annie Mae (Cricklin) Barrows,
a truly beloved Choctaw woman.
Yaiya

Contents

List of Illustrations	viii
Acknowledgments	ix
Introduction	1
Chapter One In Search of Beloved Women	9
Chapter Two A Violent Landscape	34
Chapter Three The Novel World of the Jesuits	59
Chapter Four Struggle for Survival	86
Chapter Five When the Dancing Stopped	115
Chapter Six Restoring Balance to the World	144
Conclusion: The Legacy of Corn Woman	168
Notes	179
Bibliography	192
Index	204

Illustrations

Fig 1. Distribution of Tribal Groups in 1700   17
Fig 2. Frontal view of Keller Figurine   118
Fig 3. Side view of Keller Figurine   119
Fig 4. Frontal view of Birger Figurine   122
Fig 5. Rear view of Birger Figurine   123

Acknowledgments

Many people have contributed to the realization of this work, and in the reciprocal fashion of Southeastern native people I offer thanks and gratitude: to Marcia Westkott, dear friend and colleague who cheerfully spent her Saturdays at the Women Studies Cottage to provide mentorship and humor during the writing process; to Patricia Galloway, who although we never met generously shared her vast knowledge of Choctaw culture and history; to Joel Martin, who with wonderful Southern tact directed my attention to ideas and texts that warranted attention; and especially to Mary Churchill, who deserves much recognition for her unwavering support of my work and who shared my excitement and frustrations throughout the entire process. I am thankful for the time each of them dedicated to reading my manuscript and for their encouragement. My appreciation also goes to Loriliai Biernacki, Laura Donaldson, and Clara Sue Kidwell for reading and commenting on my work.

As is often the case for scholars, I presented papers on various aspects of my book in different forums from which I benefited greatly. I want to thank the members of the Society for the Study of Native American Religious Traditions, the steering committees of Native Traditions in the Americas Group and Women and Religion Section of the American Academy of Religion, and Inès Hernandez-Avila and the planning committee for the

Indigenous Sovereignties Hemispheric Convocation who made it possible for me to share my work in progress in intellectual forums. I also want to acknowledge the Women's Studies in Religion Program at Harvard Divinity School. I had the good fortune to be in residence with five wonderful supportive scholars: Joan Branham, Anne Lapidus Lerner, Vijaya Ngarajan, Emilie M. Townes, and Ann Braude, director of the Women's Studies in Religion Program, who provided a nurturing intellectual space in which to share our work. Not least of all I want to thank the native women pastors of the United Methodist Church in Oklahoma and the native women from the Southeast Jurisdictional Women's Retreat of the United Methodist Church for inviting me to share my research on Choctaw women's traditional leadership roles. Their excitement of learning about traditional women's roles is what makes a project like this so worthwhile.

Special thanks also goes to Inès Talamantez, my mentor since graduate school; David Carrasco and Philip P. Arnold, who introduced me and my work to publishers; the excellent staff in the Interlibrary Loan Office at the University of Colorado who tenaciously tracked down some obscure materials for me; the staff at the Western History Collection, University of Oklahoma; the librarians at Andover Library, Harvard Divinity School; Christopher Schmidt for translating French documents for me for the sheer joy of working with the language; Lillie Roberts, the Choctaw language Internet class instructor, and Abe Frazier, Choctaw language instructor, for their translations and interpretations; and Paula Gunn Allen for stimulating conversations on popular and scholarly depictions of native women.

This work was completed with the help of research grants. The research phase of this work was supported in part by an IMPART grant from the University of Colorado. A fellowship from the Women's Studies in Religion Program, Harvard Divinity School, provided much-needed time and research facilities to complete my manuscript.

I extend my deepest thanks to the Choctaw women of Oklahoma and Mississippi who shared their stories with me. This book was conceived of as a result of the time I spent among Choctaw Protestants in Oklahoma while researching culture retention in Choctaw churches. Two Choctaw women in particular have had a deep impact on my work: Juanita Jefferson, tribal judge for the Choctaw Nation of Oklahoma, and Billie Nowabbie, United

Methodist pastor. Finally, I want to acknowledge the women in my family, especially the grandchildren of my sisters. Knowing that this book has the potential to shape their understanding of themselves as Choctaw women gave me the determination to keep working on this manuscript through difficult times. To them I say, *"Chahta ohoyo chia kvt ish-ikhaiyana bilia chike!"*

Introduction

Early on the morning of September 22, 1830, seven elder Choctaw women seated themselves in the center of a circle of about sixty Choctaw councilmen and two U.S. commissioners, their secretary, and other white observers. The Choctaw council, as well as hundreds of Choctaw spectators that encircled them, prepared to listen to the treaty details that would call for their removal from their beloved land and the beloved bones of their ancestors (Halbert 1902b, 374–75, 381–82). These women were an important part of the council. Yet just a few months earlier, Greenwood Leflore, chief of the Upper Towns, had tried to make himself chief of the whole Choctaw Nation, which would have eliminated not only the leadership of the other two districts but possibly the involvement of women in decision-making. In fact, just two days earlier Leflore had tried to gain support for a committee of twenty persons to represent the Choctaw in the immediate proceedings. After the council decided not to sell their lands, many of the Choctaw left the treaty grounds and returned home, satisfied with the council's decision. Imagine the indignation of those elder women when a few days later, on September 27, a small party of Choctaw who had remained behind signed away their land in the Treaty of Dancing Rabbit Creek (Foreman 1932, 26–27; Debo 1934, 54–55; Halbert 1902b, 381–87, 390, 394).

That fateful moment in history is the last documented time that the voices of Choctaw women were heard in a council meeting until the twentieth century. In fact, little evidence exists to suggest that they participated in councils prior to the Treaty of Dancing Rabbit Creek. Yet the actions of Middleton Mackey, the government interpreter, indicate that an accepted protocol for acknowledging women's presence in council existed. He rose and addressed the women, telling them that he would faithfully interpret to them everything said by the commissioners. He recognized the women's power when he ended his address by saying, "and if I tell a lie, you may cut my neck off" (Halbert 1902b, 382). These women, no doubt, were treated in accordance with the Southeastern native custom of recognizing honored or beloved people, those who are held in high esteem.

Although those and other Choctaw women participated in influential ways in all parts of society, including councils, memories about an ideal or office of beloved women are all but nonexistent. The paucity of accounts about Choctaw beloved women is even more intriguing because of ample evidence of the existence of beloved women among their close neighbors, the Cherokee, Creek, and Chickasaw, to name a few.[1] Although the title "beloved" could be applied to any person who had distinguished herself in any one of a number of ways, the most common descriptions of women are those who participated in councils or became peace leaders. The earliest documented account of an influential native woman in the Southeast is the Lady of Cofitachequi, a powerful leader that Hernando de Soto encountered during his 1539–42 expedition through the Southeast. Other important female personages include those of the Natchez known as female suns, and Nancy Ward, the Cherokee war woman who became a Supreme Beloved Woman (Bourne 1904, 64–65; Bossu 1962, 41; Woods 1980, 25–26; Parker 1991, 122–25). If Europeans noted the presence of beloved native women such as these, one is faced with the question of why they took so little note of important women among the Choctaw.

Patricia Galloway, an anthropologist, gives us some insight into the lack of information about Choctaw women. She points out that when one tallies the times when the French visited the Choctaw, these visits never took place during ceremonial times (1986, 16). Of course, ceremonial time would have been an ideal occasion for publicly recognizing women's contributions formally and informally. In addition, she writes that we must consider the intentionalities and observational blind spots of those European individuals who met with native women (1986, 19). Documentary evidence about eighteenth-century native people, as many scholars have noted, comes from European males, who brought their notions of women's places in society into their observations and writings. Those men also were not able to observe women in women's spaces and often were not interested in what women were doing (Perdue 1998, 4). Galloway cautions us not to forget "that they can be looking straight at it and not see it," or that there were instances of intentional censorship by observers and by those writing reports often third-, fourth-, and fifth-hand, or that some simply made errors (1986, 20).

Such limitations might lead one to assume that a viable study of Choctaw women in the eighteenth century is not feasible. Although contemporary accounts of Choctaw women in the eighteenth century are limited to the reports of Europeans, primarily the French in the first half of the century, those documents can be studied in the context of Choctaw cultural narratives, archaeological evidence, and cultural patterns in the greater Southeast and from later periods in order to reimagine Choctaw women's lives. The use of cultural patterns from later periods or from other native nations in the Southeast may give some scholars pause, those who would question the reliability of such an approach. However, to depend solely on documentation specific to Choctaw women's lives written during the eighteenth century effectively relegates Choctaw women to the realm of the unknown or perpetuates the continued misinformation about them. European documents cannot be ignored, and in fact are quite helpful. However, we must take note that "nothing substantive—and very little of an anecdotal nature . . . describes Indian societies in the Southeast from a woman's point of view" (Galloway 1986, 19). A viable reconstruction must be one that questions the objectivity of European male descriptions and draws on broader cultural patterns in order to more fully uncover Choctaw women's roles.

In order to address a much-ignored aspect of Southeastern history, we must look to innovative ways to theorize about women's roles. In this book I will construct a profile of Choctaw women in the first half of the eighteenth century by drawing on European documents, Choctaw oral history, archaeological records, linguistic and anthropological studies, histories, and the experiences of native people throughout the Lower Mississippi Valley in order to determine if Choctaw women were involved in tasks typically valued by Choctaw people and that ideally could lead to recognition as beloved. However, rather than trying to prove the existence of Choctaw beloved women, we will focus our attentions on reconstructing Choctaw women's lives by taking a regional approach to the study of native women in the Lower Mississippi Valley. The intention of this reconstruction is to explain the various ways in which Choctaw women exercised influence in their communities, and how in a relatively short period of time conditions changed so drastically in the Southeast that Choctaw women had to withdraw from many activities that at one time had given them the kind of status that among many nations in the Southeast would have been associated with beloved people. A regional approach is used because although we must not assume that similar languages, environments, cultural attributes, and proximity indicate similar lifestyles, we also should not ignore cultural patterns that characterize regions.

Beginning with the first French explorers in 1682 until the French ceded Louisiana Territory to the Spanish in 1762, the Choctaw witnessed tremendous changes in the entire Southeast due to the presence of Europeans, and those changes impacted women's roles in significant ways. To suggest that changes due to colonization could happen so quickly and completely that the memory of Choctaw women's participation in many aspects of Choctaw society was lost is not only reasonable but also probable. In her study of Huron and Montagnais people in the early seventeenth century, Karen Anderson traces how the relationship between women and men changed in not more than three decades after the arrival of the first French (1991, 4–5). She explains how the change in social relations in their matrilineal societies radically altered their economic and political systems, leading to the dependence and subjugation of Huron and Montagnais women.

Although changes in the political lives of the Choctaw are important to understanding the loss of status among Choctaw women, this study takes a broader approach. Attention is given to the participation of women in councils and other political aspects of Choctaw life as one way in which women would have gained status; however, I do not want to reify the notion that only political leaders could gain status as beloved. Nor is it my intent to suggest that Choctaw women held political power or influence over others, including men, primarily because such approaches are so thoroughly informed by Western concepts of gender relations and political systems. To suggest that one gender held power over the other because of their political authority belies the ideals of communal cooperation and leadership that were recognized but not enforced by threat of law or religion. The balance and boundaries between genders were more fluid than has often been depicted, and there was more than one way for women to earn status.

Gendered division of labor provides another approach for studying changes in the kinds of power or influence a woman might have in Choctaw society. The responsibility, some may even argue ownership, of the produce of fields and orchards and of the home provided Choctaw women leverage in determining community actions and becoming involved in all aspects of society, since social, religious, and political events revolved around the gift of food. Through economic contributions Choctaw women had many opportunities to gain status and many ways of losing those opportunities as economic patterns changed. The purpose of this book, however, is not solely a study of women's economic contributions. Many excellent studies have been written on the intersection between economic and gender roles and the impact of Western influence on both that led to the subordination of women in the public spheres of native life. Theda Perdue, in her study of gender and culture change in *Cherokee Women* (1998), examines the effects of trade and the incorporation of a centralized government on the roles of women that previously had been largely determined by clan affiliation and matrilineal descent. In his study on Choctaw women (1999), James Taylor Carson examines how women adapted to the introduction of a market economy in ways that allowed for the continuation of women doing women's things.

In contradistinction to most studies about native gender relations that draw on agricultural societies, Henry S. Sharp argues that among the Chipewyan, who had a 90 percent hunting subsistence economy, women used weakness to assert power. According to Sharp (1995), men needed women to process meat in order to gain prestige. If a man asserted the incompetence of a woman, he in essence called himself incompetent because he was dependent upon the woman's competence for prestige and thus was also responsible for her incompetence.

Another way to analyze changes in Choctaw women's roles is to examine the complementary and interrelated contributions of women and men and to trace the ways in which European colonization altered that relationship. However, many studies have also been written on the construction or process of complementary gender relations, including Perdue's and Carson's work. A number of excellent studies on various native nations appear in *Women and Power in Native North America*, edited by Laura F. Klein and Lillian A. Ackerman. In "Beyond Domesticity: Choctaw Women Negotiating the Tension between Choctaw Culture and Protestantism" (1999), I offer a model of gender relations based on multiple complementary constituents rather than the typical farmer/hunter, private/public dichotomies. While the change in the relationships between Choctaw women and men is an important part of this study, it also is not the only focus of this book.

Rather, the intent of this study is to reconstruct Choctaw women's lives in the early 1700s and then to examine the pressures or tensions that created changes in their early contact roles. By examining the various ways in which Europeans, primarily French males, affected the entire landscape of the Lower Mississippi Valley during the French colonial period, this study will provide multiple, interrelated explanations for changes in women's roles that curtailed their involvement in many aspects of Choctaw society, which in turn altered perceptions toward Choctaw women. For the purposes of this study, the Lower Mississippi Valley includes what is now known as Louisiana and Mississippi, but also reaches west into parts of Arkansas and Texas and as far north as St. Louis and east into Alabama.

The first chapter, "In Search of Beloved Women," draws on cultural narratives, archaeology, and history to provide background on the Choctaw and to reconstruct Choctaw women's roles at the time of first French contact in the Lower Mississippi Valley. This chapter demonstrates the multiple ways in which Choctaw women contributed in influential ways to society. The second chapter, "A Violent Landscape," focuses on how increasing violence and changes in indigenous concepts of captivity and torture because of French and British interests restricted women's participation in the more public aspects of Choctaw life. The third chapter, "The Novel World of the Jesuits," looks at how missionary actions were inextricably tied to French political and civil concerns and how missionary work altered relations between Choctaw women and men, leading to ideological changes about women's behavior. Chapter Four, "Struggle for Survival," examines how the French civilian struggle to survive in the harsh gulf and riverine environment of the Lower Mississippi Valley meant the displacement and dehumanization of native people as women, in particular, were coerced into concubinage and slavery. Chapter Five, "When the Dancing Stopped," uses the Green Corn Ceremony as a lens for understanding how the interdependence between ceremony and Choctaw women's status contributed to the rapid decline of both. These five chapters pull together the multiple and interdependent ways in which changing women's roles led to a decline in women's involvement in the more public aspects of Choctaw society.

The last two chapters emphasize the ways in which women continued to carry out certain valued responsibilities in Choctaw society, roles that were not equally valued or recognized in Western society. Chapter Six, "Restoring Balance to the World," argues that the story of culture contact is not only one of loss, but also one of adaptation and continuity. Through the medium of funeral ceremonies this chapter demonstrates one way in which women continued to carry out honored functions in Choctaw society up to the nineteenth century. The conclusion, "The Legacy of Corn Woman," reexamines the ideal of beloved among Southeastern cultures and explains how Choctaw women continued to embody many of the values of early eighteenth-century Choctaw culture albeit through new structures and without formal recognition.

Although this book is a study of the experiences of Choctaw women in the French colonial period (1699–1763), it is important to note that French influence in the Southeast continued long after France ceded Louisiana Territory to Spain. However, this study is limited to the time of European recognition of French control of the territory because this was a pivotal period of intense change for Choctaw women that has gone unrecognized for too long. Also, French colonization did not take place in isolation but involved a complex dynamic among the French, English, and Spanish. However, as the majority of the Choctaw remained allies of the French during most of this period, a study of the French impact on Choctaw society is crucial to understanding the changes that women underwent during the time of French colonization. The Choctaw also did not live in isolation, but had ongoing relations with numerous native nations in the region. I identify particular native nations when possible; however, when referring to native people in general in the Lower Mississippi Valley I use a variety of terms such as indigenous people, native people, Southeastern native people, or Indians.[2]

This book is the culmination of my efforts to understand culture change and the roles of women among the Choctaw of Oklahoma. I grew up in a family of Methodist Choctaws and in a community of Choctaw, Creek, and

Cherokee Methodists and Baptists in a predominately white town in northeastern Oklahoma. As a young person I became painfully aware of the extent of loss of ceremony among the Choctaw in comparison to our Cherokee and Creek neighbors. I initially began studying Choctaw history by examining the retention of Choctaw culture and identity in Choctaw Protestant churches, which led to my later analysis of the construction of gender roles among the Choctaw (1994; 1999). I became aware not only of the absence of women from many of the histories on Choctaw people, but also of the way in which observers and scholars have depicted the Choctaw in ways that denied the existence of their ceremonies and cultural ideologies. I have also spoken to Choctaw women who are much interested in the leadership roles of Choctaw women in earlier periods. This book is an effort to rectify both omissions by contributing to our understanding of Choctaw women's roles in society and of the way in which change and continuity occur in simultaneous and multifaceted ways in a relatively short period of time.

1

In Search of Beloved Women

In the eighteenth century the Choctaw occupied a rich area marked by floodplains and multiple ecological zones that supported farming, hunting, fishing, and gathering of wild plant foods. Much of the sustenance of the Choctaw came from the labor of women, who worked the fields and gathered a wide variety of fruits, nuts, and wild plants. From spring until fall Choctaw women could be seen in their fields caring for the squash, beans, and corn that they grew in abundance. Elder women guarded the fields from marauding birds and animals while the younger women tilled the soil. Men could be seen helping out the women during planting and harvesting time. Later, in the fall, the women hiked to their favorite groves of fruit and nut trees and berry stands to gather wild foods. As the women walked through the woods or worked in their fields, they were always accompanied by young children, boys and girls, and elders. The women also regularly traveled with the men on hunting and fishing expeditions, and they would take care of the camps and clean the game and fish brought in by the men (MPA:FD 1984, 4:234; Galloway 1985a, 94; Galloway 1991, 72).

At home the women processed deerskins, prepared meals, sewed clothing, and cared for the small children and the sick. Older women skilled in midwifery tended to pregnant women (Swanton 1931, 118). They might also be diviners. Women as well as men had herbal and ritual knowledge. They treated the sick with emetics, cathartics, sweats, cold baths, scarification, cupping, and sucking. Like the men the women might be appointed as "medicine givers" prior to becoming *alikchi*, or healers. Medicine givers had responsibility for administering certain medicines to patients. In the case of female patients, a female medicine giver had to be present when women took medicine, and a male medicine giver had to be present when men did (Swanton 1931, 118, 226, 235–36; Cushman 1899, 307).

The matrilocal, matrilineal Choctaw society provided women with a strong support system before and after marriage. Typically, a married couple lived in the woman's house. If the wife died, her property went to her children and not her husband. If the couple died without having had children, her house as well as any other property that belonged to her generally went to her relatives. In fact, upon her death her relatives' right to care for the children superseded that of the father. In matters concerning the children, the family consulted the oldest maternal uncle or nearest male relative on the maternal side. The support of male relatives on her maternal side as well as that of her children meant that women did not suffer undue economic loss as a result of separation or death of a spouse (Swanton 1931, 103–4, 125). In fact, Choctaw people depended upon a system of relationships that involved the contributions of women and men and ensured a broad support system.

Although the Choctaw were a matrilocal, matrilineal society and women controlled the fields and homes—responsibilities that afforded them influence in all aspects of Choctaw life—we know surprisingly little about their contributions beyond field and home. Our lack of knowledge can be attributed in large part to scholars who have tended to present Choctaw history and ethnography from the perspective of male experience with only passing reference to women. In addition to a cursory treatment of women, Choctaw society, in general, has been little studied, primarily because of its lack of exceptional characteristics in the eyes of Europeans, and later Americans. Such an assessment was clearly expressed by John R. Swanton, the notable ethnographer of Choctaw culture. He wrote of the Choctaw that "there were few customs observable among them sufficiently striking to attract the attention of European travelers." His often quoted explanation for the lack of attraction was that "there were no complicated religious ceremonials to arrest the attention of the foreigner." Swanton judged the Choctaw "poor subjects for ethnological study" because their lack of pronounced native institutions led to their rapid assimilation of European and American ways (Swanton 1931, 2).

Daniel H. Usner Jr., an historian, argues that historians largely ignored the entire region of the Lower Mississippi Valley because the earlier period of French colonization was overshadowed by an obsession with the antebellum period and because the region had been dismissed as relatively unimportant to American development. He notes that the area was not completely neglected by all historians, but that "the focus on geopolitical affairs has long obscured the ordinary people" (1992, 2–5). Although historians are now beginning to seriously study the Lower Mississippi Valley, their studies of the French colonial period continue to focus on the activities of men, particularly in the economic and political realms of society.

The lack of interest in the unexceptional characteristics of Choctaw society and inattention to women's roles in the Lower Mississippi Valley have resulted in superficial or uninformed statements about Choctaw women up to the present time. Because so much of our contemporary knowledge about Choctaw women comes from the twentieth-century works of Swanton, it is important to determine what changes took place in Choctaw society prior to the twentieth century if we are to understand women's roles. The best place to begin is with French exploration along the Mississippi River in 1682. It is within the French colonial period that we will get the earliest possible documented descriptions of Choctaw society. By reconstructing changes that took place in Choctaw women's roles during the period of French control of Louisiana Territory (from a European perspective), we can gain a better understanding of the loss of status Choctaw women experienced, particularly in those areas considered the domain of men in the twentieth century.

This chapter will undertake this reconstruction first by situating the Choctaw in the Lower Mississippi Valley and second by identifying the ways in which Choctaw women participated in society, based upon an examination of Choctaw cultural narratives and their earliest recorded history, which in this case is the French colonial period. Although a few references by Europeans indicate that certain Choctaw women were recognized as honored or beloved women, the record is too limited to determine if such appellations were commonly recognized. However, we can identify the ways in which Choctaw women gained influence or status in their communities. We will do this through careful interpretation of European documents and archaeological, anthropological, and cultural narratives and by drawing on the experiences of late seventeenth- and early eighteenth-century indigenous cultures in the Lower Mississippi Valley. Native women, in general, had similar experiences with European men or were aware of the treatment of other native women at the hands of Europeans. This approach will allow for a fuller analysis of changes in Choctaw society than might otherwise be possible, and more specifically, of women's roles as a result of nearly one hundred years of French colonial contact.

Our task of reimagining Choctaw women's roles in the seventeenth century is complicated by several major factors influencing change among the Choctaw. First, according to historical evidence the Choctaw as a distinct group came into existence sometime between the 1560s and 1670s and thus were in the early stages of formation, a state of intense adaptation, at the time of contact with Europeans (Galloway 1995, 166, 170). Second, the Choctaw were coming into existence as a distinct group at a time when the entire region of the Southeast was experiencing pressures on their societies because of contact with the Spanish, British, and French. Disease, warfare, and economic changes contributed to changing populations in the form of displacement and depopulation (Galloway 1995, 138–43). Third, the only written documentation of observations of early Choctaw society occurs after contact with the Spanish, French, and British around the beginning of the eighteenth century (Galloway 1995, 183, 193).[1] Fourth, oral history can provide us with contemporary Choctaw memories about women's roles, but as Kim Anderson notes in *A Recognition of Being: Reconstructing Native Womanhood*, we have to be careful about our assumptions about memories because many of the traditions native people now know have been influenced by centuries of Western hegemonic patriarchy (2000, 36).

Thus, when the French first encountered the Choctaw they were observing a population that was experiencing change on two fronts: internal reorganization and external pressures from European activities. It is likely that early French reports reflected changes in women's roles as a result of Choctaw society's undergoing adaptations. However, French reports also reflected the diversity among French colonialists and their imaginations. The French, as well as the English and Spanish, who encountered the Choctaw and other Lower Mississippi Valley societies brought with them a wide range of experiences by which to interpret what they saw and heard. As these chroniclers recorded their experiences in journals and reports, they necessarily invoked what Mikhail Bakhtin refers to as "professional stratification of language." In other words, the language they used and the decisions they made on what to record manifested their interests and intentions that were "permeated with concrete value judgements." Their words expressed, as Bakhtin argues, "points of view peculiar to particular professions" (1981, 289). Those professions can be understood as culture, class, gender, religion, or position. Their reports reflected their attention to particular aspects of native culture that they considered relevant to their own concerns. Military personnel would be interested in gathering intelligence on Indian military capabilities. Traders, however, would be more interested in goods produced by native people.

Not only must we take into consideration the concerns of chroniclers as we study their reports, but also, as Patricia Galloway states, we must note when reporters change. The early French explorer chronicles were replaced by military, missionary, and trader reports.[2] Each group brought to the written page their experiences and understandings of the world as well as their judgments in the context of language meant for a particular purpose. Often this purpose was to elicit support, whether in the form of supplies, money, labor, or authority, from European monarchs or ruling parties that determined what they chose to report about native people. Thus each group's interests must be taken into consideration as their reports are gleaned for information about Choctaw women. To decipher the intentional dimensions of language is challenging but possible. In her examination of Spanish representations of native towns, Galloway argues that the Spanish described those native towns in terms consistent with sixteenth-century Spanish city-states. She argues that the Spanish assumed that an indigenous town bore the same name as its chief, similar to the practice of referring to a nobleman by the name of his estate. She also points out that Hernando de Soto and his men were seeking population concentrations such as seen in a city-state society that would support their *encomienda* system. She offers examples that contradict Spanish descriptions and assumptions (1995, 111). In the same manner we must be motivated by intentions to separate French (and later, English and American) assumptions from Choctaw conceptions.

This professional stratification of language in the form of European interpretations of Choctaw society undoubtedly imposed change upon those societies just as the contact experience did. As Europeans and Choctaw dialogued with each other, each brought into the conversation their own understandings. The Choctaw act of understanding European efforts at communication, and vice versa, required assimilation of the word to be understood into their own conceptual systems, which was "indissolubly merged with the response." In other words, the Choctaw and the Europeans influenced and reacted to exchanges of information whether verbal or visual. Thus, in Bakhtinian fashion, their understanding and responses were "dialectically merged" and were mutually conditioned by each other (Bakhtin 1981, 282).

We can see the effects of such conditioning in the way in which conceptions of particular ideas changed over time as a result of contact. For example, James Adair, a trader among the Cherokee, Chickasaw, and Choctaw in the eighteenth century, whose influential book has served as an important resource for scholars of Southeastern native traditions, tried to understand the Southeastern idea of beloved in a Christian way. He was convinced that native people in North America were descended from the Israelites. In order to convince others of his theory, he provided twenty-three detailed arguments in which he argued for similarities between native people and Israelites. When he encountered contradictions in his comparison, he dismissed the difference by attributing it to the failure of native people to maintain tradition. He wrote that the Indians like the Jews believed "that God chose them out of all the rest of mankind, as his peculiar and beloved people" (Adair 1775, 36). Adair's use of "beloved" had a specific meaning within a Christian context. When he translated the Chickasaw or Choctaw word *hatak holitopa* into the English phrase "the beloved people," he ascribed a particular meaning to it. He understood beloved people as having a covenant with God. Thus he found the idea of God's choosing the Indians as beloved people bothersome. He judged that Indians "flatter themselves with the name *hottuk oretoopah*" (Adair 1775, 35–36).[3]

Although we may never fully comprehend the precontact Southeastern native sense of beloved, we can look at how the term has been used in postcontact documentation. From these usages we can tease out what is decidedly Christian or Jewish to make some sense of the Indian usage of "beloved." For example, Adair related how a Chickasaw "*Loáche*," or "prophet," recalled how his people once knew the beloved speech that brought down the rains. The Chickasaw spoke of a time among his ancestors when people with "extraordinary divine power" could foretell the future and could control nature (84, 97–98). Here we see "beloved" signifying something powerful, beyond the ordinary, an aspect dismissed by Adair, who referred to rainmakers or prophets as charlatans.

At the same time, as we move further and further into the postcontact period, we have to recognize that Indian meanings of "beloved" became influenced by the European understanding. Adair noted that the Indians saw themselves as separate from whites, whom they referred to as "nothings" or "*hottuk ookproose*," "the accursed people." In other words, whites were perceived as those who were not good, who "possess the dark regions of the west," the malevolent (34–35, 38). Yet later, Adair recorded an instance in which a Chickasaw described a French Catholic exercise wherein the beloved French brought rain during a dry season. The Chickasaw was surprised that the French had gained the beloved speech that the Chickasaw had lost (98). At this point the Chickasaw conception of the French and of beloved had to be reconceptualized. As the French and Chickasaw continued to interact with each other, both had to reconceptualize their own and the other's idea of "beloved." European influence can also be seen in the way the word *holitopa* has been translated by Cyrus Byington, who compiled the Choctaw dictionary. The idea of power is missing from the definition. However, along with words such as *beloved*, *dear*, and *sacred*, we find *holy*, *sainted*, *consecrated*, and *venerated*, all Christian ideas (Byington 1915, 164).

The processual nature of conceptualizing ideas suggests that any reconstruction of events or images must take into account the multiple and diverse interpretations taking place among Europeans and native people in the French colonial period as well as among those of us who endeavor to understand the events of the past. As we undertake the reconstruction of Choctaw women's experiences in the French colonial period, we recognize that this is but one of many possible interpretations and permutations of Choctaw women's experience, but one that will broaden our understanding of the changes that impacted their roles in society both conceptually and physically. As we gain insight into the nature of those changes, we can also interpret those changes in relation to the changing status of Choctaw women.

Intertribal Relations in the Lower Mississippi Valley

Since Choctaw society was only beginning to distinguish itself as separate and distinct from other indigenous societies in the Mississippi area at the time of white contact, one can with reasonable certainty assume that the Choctaw people were at one time part of one or many of the other groups existing in the area.[4] See figure 1 for distribution of tribal groups in 1700. For example, Galloway notes that the Mobilian, Naniaba, and Tohomé of the Mobile delta east of the Choctaw Mississippi homeland were considered in some sense Choctaw.[5] She also states that the Chickasaw, Choctaw, Chakchiuma, and Alabama were clearly "related somehow in prehistory—they all belonged to the Western Muskogean language family and spoke closely related languages, they all lived in the Mississippi-Alabama area, and they supported intertribal alliances."[6] Galloway adds that the core of what became the Choctaw perhaps provided connections between the Moundville chiefdom of the Black Warrior river valley and the Natchezan people (1995, 311; 1991, 58, 61).

In his study of frontier exchange in the Lower Mississippi Valley, Usner notes that "frontiers were more regional in scope, networks of cross-cultural interaction through which native and colonial groups circulated goods and services" (1992, 6). Although it is important not to ignore the cultural diversity among Indian nations, it would be shortsighted to not recognize the "fluidity that characterized social and economic relations between all groups of people" (Usner 1992, 8). The similarity of environments, trails that connected different communities, language similarities, trade items, practices, and a trade language indicate that the Choctaw were not only aware of other communities and their practices and beliefs, but also that they most likely shared or had similar social structures and practices.

For example, the Alabama, Apalachi, Biloxi, Pacama, Pascagoula, Taensa, and Tunica all spoke a Choctaw or Choctaw-like language referred to as the Mobilian or Chickasaw trade language (York 1982, 139–40). Other Muskhogean peoples had Choctaw names indicating linguistic similarity or familiarity by the Choctaw. Some of those tribes include the Bayogoula, from the Choctaw words *báyuk-ókla* ("bayou people"); the Pascagoula, meaning "bread people" in Choctaw; the Acolapissa, translated from the Choctaw as "those who listen and see"; and the Alabama or Alibamu, believed to be from the Choctaw *alba ayamule* ("I open or clear the thicket") (Hodge 1907, 1:9, 43, 137; Hodge 1907, 2:205; McWilliams 1981, 126).[7] Lusser recognized Tohomé as "Choctaws settled on the Mobile River." They were a Muskhogean group of the Gulf Coast that spoke a dialect of Choctaw (Hodge 1907, 2:771; MPA:FD 1927, 1:117). T. Dale Nicklas points out that the Choctaw language

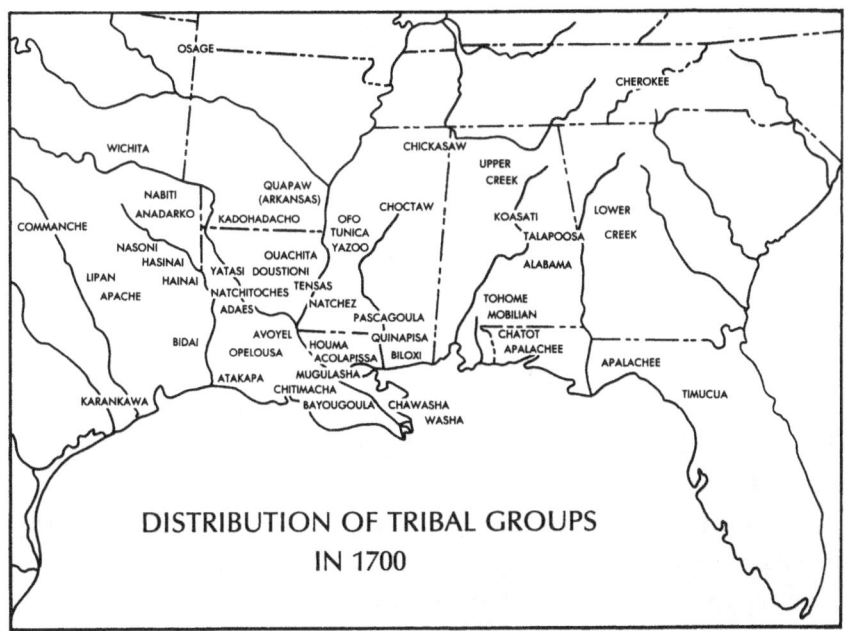

Fig. 1. Reprinted by permission of Louisiana State University Press from Fred B. Kniffen, Hiram F. Gregory, and George A. Stokes, *The Historic Indian Tribes of Louisiana: From 1542 to the Present.* ©1987 by Louisiana State University Press.

has two traits that indicate an influence from the Lower Mississippi Valley. The changes in the Choctaw fricative *s* appear to be the same changes that took place in Natchez and Atakapa. He also notes that there are several noteworthy examples of the Choctaw language's being influenced by Northern Tier groups from the Cherokee westward (1994, 10).

In his study of ceramics, Kenneth H. Carleton indicates that some similarities exist between eighteenth-century Choctaw pottery and that of various Mississippian populations of the late sixteenth and/or seventeenth centuries. For example, the temper used in Choctaw pottery referred to as Addis-like paste is very similar to that found among the Pearl River Mounds occupied from AD 1200 to 1600 located in what is now Lawrence County, Mississippi. The Pearl River Mounds pottery type was influenced by the Mississippian cultures to the north and east and the Plaquemine cultures of the Lower

Mississippi Valley. Carleton notes that the Addis-like paste used by the Choctaw is also similar to that used by Natchezan culture in the Lower Mississippi Valley (1994, 86–87, 91). He also found some similarities in the various motifs found on Choctaw pottery with those of the Natchezan cultures, the Doctor Lake Complex in the lower Tombigbee and upper Mobile region, and Pensacola series ceramics in southwestern Alabama (83, 91). Carleton suggests that this mixing of pottery elements from various regions indicates a "fusion of shared motifs, and hence beliefs and identity . . . well past initial confederation" (93).

Reports by French explorers confirm exchanges of information passed between nations. The explorers quickly learned that Indian villages all along their routes were aware of their every movement. According to Henri Joutel, one of Robert Cavelier de La Salle's chroniclers, when La Salle encountered some Indians (unidentified) while trying to cross Texas in 1687, he learned that their allies had already apprised them of the French presence and they were expecting him to pass through their country (French 1846, 135). La Salle also found that whenever he stopped at a village, delegations from other villages would arrive throughout his stay to greet him and his men. Joutel wrote, "no day passed without seeing some of the natives, who sometimes spent the whole day with us, and said they were of several nations" (French 1846, 136). Pierre Le Moyne d'Iberville, who made his first expedition in the Mississippi region in 1699, had a similar experience. He encountered members of different communities traveling together who knew of the whereabouts and activities of others in the region. For example, on February 25, as he traveled towards the Bayogoula, whom he had arranged to meet, he encountered two men and two women (community not identified), who informed him that the Bayogoula had returned home (McWilliams 1981, 49). The French often gained strategic information about the Choctaw from other indigenous communities.

Clearly there was significant interaction between the various nations, sometimes in the form of alliances, other times as enemies. French documents provide evidence of similarities in habits or language among the many different groups. Although distinctions most certainly existed between groups, the homogenizing pressures as a result of interaction, as well as similarities in environment, language, and experiences, support the strategy of studying Choctaw society by drawing on supplemental information gained from various indigenous groups in the Lower Mississippi Valley. For example, from French documents we learn that women and men in the Southeast regularly traveled together. On several occasions in 1699 Iberville encountered small parties comprised of women and men, sometimes on foot, sometimes traveling by canoe. In March Iberville chanced upon some Ouacha,[8] five men and two women, on their way home by canoe, and four Bayogoula including one woman (McWilliams 1981, 58).

Men and women also went on hunting and fishing expeditions together (MPA:FD 1927, 1:186). In 1738 two French brothers encountered a Choctaw couple who were out hunting for settlers on the Pascagoula. The brothers, who had agreed to transport the couple to Mobile, later murdered the couple (Galloway 1991, 72; Galloway 1985a, 95). In 1745 M. de Louboey, king's lieutenant at Mobile, learned that fourteen or fifteen Choctaw men and women from Boucfouca had been captured by enemies while they were in their hunting camp (MPA:FD 1984, 4:324). Although we find only a few documented references to Choctaw women traveling with hunting expeditions, the widespread practice in the Lower Mississippi Valley indicates Choctaw women participated more often than European documents suggest. Galloway makes the observation that the "usual division of labor between the sexes among the Choctaw would make such a team a convenient one" (1985a, 94).

Choctaw Cultural Narratives

The Choctaw explain their arrival in the Mississippi region, their relationship to other nations in the area, and the significance of women's agricultural responsibilities through their migration and emergence stories. These stories are in many ways in agreement with archaeological evidence. Although the area seemed suitable for habitation, archaeological studies indicate the land area occupied by the Choctaw did not support any significant population prior to the sixteenth century.[9] However, numerous groups in various stages of evolution and devolution populated the areas surrounding the Choctaw homeland. These groups may have emerged as a confederacy following a period of decline in multilevel chiefdoms and of epidemic disease left by Spanish explorers.[10] Galloway argues convincingly that the Choctaw most likely had antecedents from neighboring groups, most likely the "prairie" peoples of the upper Pearl and western tributaries of the Tombigbee and the

"Burial Urn" peoples from the Mobile delta (Galloway 1994, 399; Galloway 1995, 28, 142, 267; Penman 1977, 304).

Choctaw creation stories tell of a migration from the west or southwest of Nanih Waiya, their central sacred mound located on the west side of Nanih Waiya Creek in what is now Winston County in Mississippi. Galloway locates the prairie peoples around and northeast of Nanih Waiya and on the Upper Pearl, which is southwest of the mound. The Burial Urn sites are located primarily southeast of Nanih Waiya, although one site is located northwest of Nanih Waiya and several are located in a northeasterly direction (Galloway 1995, 65, 267). While most of these locations are not consistent with a west to east migration as described in Choctaw cultural narratives, the northeast and southeast locations are significant in that they coincide with the homelands of the Chickasaw and Creek, who are linguistically related to the Choctaw.

Some Choctaw versions say that the Creek, Chickasaw, and Choctaw migrated together, moving to the east following a pole they placed in the ground each night. The next morning it would be leaning to the east and they would walk in that direction until night came again. Some stories refer to oppression by a more powerful people, of an exhausted land due to overpopulation, or of a message from Aba, the sacred one above, that motivated them to journey eastward. One story tells of a great sickness that forced the people to move. This version is consistent with archaeological evidence of a westward movement of the Burial Urn people possibly to escape devastating diseases left by Soto's expedition (Swanton 1931, 27–33; Carson 1999, 11).

In one account, after the Choctaw had traveled a great distance they needed to resupply their group with food. As the warm season was upon them, they camped long enough to plant and harvest corn for the remainder of their journey. After the sojourners resumed their trip they became divided during stormy weather; one group, which became known as the Chickasaw, went in a northerly direction, the Creek in a southerly direction, and the Choctaw remained in the area or in some versions continued farther east until the pole stayed upright. This would place the Chickasaw north-northeast of Nanih Waiya and the Creek southeast of the mound.

In this migration account we see that the Choctaw were once part of a larger group, but later became separate and distinct upon arrival at Nanih Waiya. Many of the versions tell of how they traveled across marshy areas and waterways, which are descriptive of the Mississippi region. These stories could also indicate an easterly or northerly route, as the area towards the southwest is marshy with many waterways. In one story the group stopped to plant corn. This pause may have taken place in the Mississippi region before or after they separated from the Chickasaw and Creek. The remainder of their trip may have been the inevitable relocations that took place as a large group of people broke into smaller groups and formed separate towns.

Further elaborations are given in the more common versions of the later migration or emergence story, where as each group of people left or emerged from Nanih Waiya they proceeded in different directions, becoming the Creek, Chickasaw, and Choctaw.[11] Swanton noted that there is a considerable cave located within a mile of Nanih Waiya and suggested that the Choctaw may have stayed in the cave for a period of time before emerging to establish themselves near Nanih Waiya (1931, 7). In an account related by John F. Schermerhorn, the areas around the banks of streams were marshy and probably impassable. This is reiterated by Peter Folsom, a Choctaw, who said his father told him that when the Choctaw and Chickasaw arrived at the creek near Nanih Waiya "a great rain fell, and it rained several days. In consequence of this all the low lands were inundated and Nanih Waiya Creek and other tributaries of Pearl River were rendered impassable" (Swanton 1931, 33).

The emergence may have been metaphorical in that the Choctaw emerged from the wet and marshy lowlands to occupy the higher ground of Nanih Waiya. From Antoine S. Le Page Du Pratz and Bernard Romans, we learn that the Choctaw seemed to suddenly appear in the area in great numbers, surprising their neighbors. Again we have a metaphor for emergence (Swanton 1931, 5). While variations in their cultural narratives and incongruities with linear time and place give us pause as to the reliability of the stories collected long after European contact, we know from these stories that the Choctaw knew that they did not exist in their present place from time immemorial, but believed that they had been led to this particular place by the One Above through their prophets.[12] The stories of migrations from the southwest and northwest, and possibly east, are consistent with a destination or emergence from the Upper Pearl (Galloway 1995, 337). Also, the migrations of different groups who later came together as the Choctaw account for the different versions of the migration story. The accounts of migrations from the east, northwest, and southwest may have coalesced into one account of a western migration. Their stories also provide their explanations for the locations of the Chickasaw and Creek homelands, areas identified by Galloway as burial urn sites (1995, 66, 336–37, 359).

When the Choctaw reached Nanih Waiya they faced the daunting task of establishing a relationship with the land and with their neighbors. The land provided game, wild nuts, tubers, fruits, honey, and fish. However, food was not always plentiful enough to support the people, especially as their populations began to grow. In one such instance, as is told in their stories, two hunters went out in search of game for their hungry village. After searching all day they managed to catch only a single black hawk. Just as they began to partake of their meager meal they heard a soft and melancholy sound reminiscent of a dove. They jumped up and looked for the source of the sound, when in the direction opposite of the moon

> they discovered standing upon the summit of a grassy mound, the form of a beautiful woman. They hastened to her side, when she told them that she was very hungry, whereupon they ran after their roasted hawk, and gave it all into the hands of the strange woman. She barely tasted the proffered food, but told the hunters that their kindness had preserved her from death, and that she would not forget them when she returned to the happy grounds of her father, who was Hosh-tal-li, or Great Spirit of the Choctaws. She had one request to make, and this was, that when the next moon of midsummer should arrive, they should visit the spot where she then stood. (Swanton 1931, 208–10)

A year later the hunters returned to find a corn plant, a food source that would become a mainstay of their diet and ceremonial life.[13]

The gift of corn was a tremendous and appropriate event in the life of the Choctaw because hunting and gathering strategies already had been maximally diversified because of population pressure (Galloway 1995, 33; Swanton 1931, 33). Again, although the story is not consistent with Western concerns with linear conceptions of time and place, the Choctaw story says they stopped and planted corn. Corn allowed them an alternative means of subsistence in the floodplains of the Mississippi region. John T. Penman, an archaeologist, speculates that the area in northeast Mississippi may not have been suitable for corn production prior to the Mississippian period (approximately AD

1100–1600), but that the development of hardier strains allowed for farming among Later Mississippian Period groups (1977, 304). Such a development would also indicate a migration. Thus we see the Choctaw undergoing change not only through relocation to a new place, but also through increased subsistence options, both of which most likely led to changing patterns of social, ceremonial, and political relationships.

With these creation stories we begin to see the importance of the feminine in the Choctaw sacred world. The ancestors of the Choctaw emerged from disease, oppression, and hunger at Nanih Waiya, often referred to as Iholitopa Ishki, or Beloved Mother (Swanton 1931, 30).[14] As their population began to grow, creating stresses on the land's ability to provide sufficient wild foods and game, they received the gift of a domestic plant that they could grow in abundance from The Unknown Woman, Ohoyo Osh Chisba, or Corn Woman herself.[15] Thus women have provided for and nurtured the Choctaw since the beginning of their existence, a fact that was reiterated in their ceremonies and in their daily experience of the land.

Beloved People

The importance of the feminine in the oral traditions of the Choctaw indicates that women as mothers and providers were held in high esteem, as they were in other Southeastern cultures. In the Southeast those indigenous peoples who embody the ideal attributes of society are beloved. "Beloved" encompasses all that is vital and sacred to the Choctaw—beloved lands, beloved towns, beloved leaders, and beloved speech. To be called "beloved" is to be highly honored. A beloved person is not only someone dear to the community, one who is respected, revered, and venerated, but also one who is sacred.[16] A beloved person is distinguished from others by any of a number of attributes including expertise in ceremonial practice. Beloved people who are called upon to perform sacred tasks must never have caused even small injuries to others. Before engaging in sacred rituals they must be "clean of every stain of blood" (Swanton 1928b, 423). Thus postmenopausal Cherokee women who had become powerful through their child-bearing years could become beloved women responsible for handling medicines, retrieving the first fruits of the new harvest, and performing other duties that required a high degree of purity.

Adair, in his *History of the American Indians*, suggests that Choctaw women of child-bearing age were considered beloved when he wrote that there were "women set apart" who were referred to as "*Hoollo*," which he translated as meaning those who sanctify themselves to Ishtohoollo, or God (1775, 48). The "women set apart" were those who spent time in menstrual houses during their menses or during childbirth. Women were expected to separate themselves from areas where men carried on their regular activities. Obviously this was considered a sacred time because the women went to the menstrual houses for ritual purification during menstruation and after childbirth. Their seclusion would have proclaimed their continuing fertility, a central concern of agricultural people (Galloway 1998, 203–4, 206). The same practice was carried out by men after returning from war or a hunt where they had spilled blood (Swanton 1931, 231). The value placed on women's seclusion during this sacred time is evident in the respect they garnered when they carried out ritual seclusion even in the face of danger. Among the Chickasaw those women who isolated themselves in the face of attacks were recognized as valorous because they helped preserve the men's virility (Galloway 1998, 204; Bossu 1962, 171).

Another ritual related to the loss of blood is the loss of relatives. The Choctaw revered the bones of their ancestors and took great care of them. When someone was near death the women ritually prepared the person for the journey to the other world by washing his body, painting him, daubing his face, and dressing him in his finest clothes. Later, several months after the person had died, an honored woman, whom an anonymous French man called the *femme de valleur*, cleaned and prepared the bones for placement in a charnel house (Swanton 1931, 170–71). The entire funeral ceremony was long and involved, indicating the importance placed upon people who carried out the necessary rituals to ensure that the deceased had a safe journey to the afterlife.

Beloved people might also be those who had distinguished themselves during times of war or as leaders.[17] Among the Cherokee beloved women might also be War Women, those who had shown valor in wartime or had participated in war dances and eagle dances, both associated with battle (Perdue 1998, 38–39; Reid 1970, 187). Perhaps the best-known beloved woman in the Southeast is Nancy Ward, a nineteenth-century Cherokee woman who led her people in battle against the Creeks. She later became a Ghighau, or Supreme Beloved Woman, a leader and chief justice of the

Overhill Cherokee from 1755 until 1817 (Parker 1991, 37). Choctaw women also could, under certain conditions, become leaders. According to a letter dated January 15, 1714, by Father Le Maire, a priest who spent seven years in Louisiana, "Power is handed down from father to son. There are tribes, like that of the Choctaw, among whom the power, for lack of male children, is transmitted to the girls" (1985, 145). The limited visibility of Choctaw women as well as the European's male-centered political world may have prevented observers of Choctaw culture from recognizing the existence of influential Choctaw women.

Outsiders also might not have known that particular Southeastern women were beloved because a woman honored for bravery did not necessarily carry the title. Albert S. Gatschet, who studied the Creek in the nineteenth century, told of a Hitchiti[18] case in which a "woman's brave deed was recompensed by conferring a war title upon her son" (Swanton 1928b, 421). The Creek, however, accorded warrior rank and title upon women for their brave deeds. The rarity of reports about women leaders no doubt is also a product of European conceptions of male-centered, institutionalized leadership.[19] They may not have been aware of the influence of women in political affairs because they did not recognize forms of leadership that were not consistent with their experiences.

We can better envision Choctaw women's political activities, however, if we reconstruct native women's involvement in political affairs throughout the Lower Mississippi Valley. One of the earliest accounts we have of Indian women's involvement in international affairs comes from Tonty's report dated March 22, 1682. According to him La Salle and his men had stopped along the Mississippi opposite the village of the Taensa,[20] and he had sent Tonty to inform them of their arrival. The next day the chief arrived with some of his people accompanied by the sound of drums and singing by the women (French 1846, 62). In another account by Henri Joutel, historian for La Salle's expedition, in July 1687, shortly after La Salle's murder, his men sought an Indian escort to the next village on their route. Their escort consisted of "at least twenty persons, as well women as men" (French 1846, 178). They were seeking safe passage and introductions to other villages. While Abbé Jean Cavelier, La Salle's surviving brother, and his men were resting on a bank of a river in July 1687, a Cahayrohoua[21] appeared who signaled them to follow him to his village. They were taken to the chief's house where they were fed and then "a throng of women came to see us [them]" (French 1846, 170). Later that evening, a group of elders, and young men and women carrying a calumet, arrived at his cabin to sing. The singing was followed by a ritual washing of Cavelier's face. Next they held a pipe ceremony to establish a peaceful alliance between the French and the Cahayrohoua, a ceremony that included singing by men and women (French 1846, 171).

On February 15, 1699, when Iberville met with a group of Biloxi and Pascagoula, three men and two women sang the calumet of peace to him and offered him "a little plank of whitened wood," and feasted him and his men with a meal of corn (McWilliams 1981, 44).[22] Diron D'Artaguette noted a similar procedure in his journal entry for October 10, 1722. On that day twenty Tunica, including men and women, led by their head chief, "sang the calumet to M. Bienville" (Mereness 1916, 29–30).[23] It was common among the indigenous peoples of the Southeast to establish peaceful relations by displaying a white object such as a staff, string of beads, wing, or banner followed by the smoking of a pipe. From these examples we see that women participated in various forms of diplomatic exchanges that took place near their villages.

Some French accounts indicate that women also traveled long distances as part of political delegations. During Iberville's second expedition to the Mississippi in 1700, a Colapissa chief, his wife, and twelve of his men traveled from their main village to Fort Maurepas on Biloxi Bay to meet with Iberville (McWilliams 1981, 142).[24] Two years later, in late winter of 1702, Tonty, a party of ten Frenchmen, two Mobilian, two Tohomé, and a Choctaw chief traveled to the Chickasaw to urge them to accompany them to Mobile to negotiate a peace with the Choctaw and French. The Chickasaw delegation that accompanied Tonty included three women. Since Tonty did not mention the women doing the household work of the travelers, Galloway argues that this absence suggests that the women may have played a part in the delegation's political decisions (1982, 149, 162–63). An earlier incident seems to suggest the same thing. On March 29, 1690, a woman visited Tonty who, he said, "governed this nation," along with the principal persons of the Cadadoquis village (French 1846, 73).[25] Father Jacques Gravier also made references to female chiefs among the Natchez and Houma, although European interpretations indicate that this title referred to the wife of a chief (JR 65:143, 147). The wife and children of Natchez leaders received the same treatment as the chief; however it is not clear how much authority or power the female chief had. When the Talapoosa negotiated a peace meeting between the Choctaw and Chickasaw in December 1745, the Chickasaw sent a Choctaw woman, whom they had captured from the village of the Cushtusha, and the nephew of their great chief to the Choctaw to tell them that they wished to live in peace with the Choctaw (MPA:FD 1984, 4:260).

What is clear is that certain women who accompanied delegations received or at least expected the same deference as men. In one case, on May 17, 1699, the commandant of Fort Maurepas at Biloxi Bay, Sauvole, saw smoke to the west of the fort. He sent his men out to check on it, and they returned with the chief of the Bayogoula and three men. Sauvole presented gifts of shirts to each of the men and paid homage to them with a feast. The next day he was informed by the Bayogoula that their wives were on the opposite shore and that the chief's wife should receive the same homage as he had (Higginbotham 1969, 22–23). Apparently, among at least some of the nations in the Mississippi region, women participated in diplomatic missions and they were accorded the same consideration as men.

Among Southeastern native people, food served as a primary means of sealing relationships and expressing thanks through ceremony. Thus it was customary among native towns to offer food or trade food to the French as a gesture of friendship, but also as an offering to reestablish relations after conflict. Since women controlled the cultivation of corn and other crops, they played a major role in the preparation and distribution of food. However it was not unusual for a large group, or even an entire village, to deliver food in the manner of gifts. During Iberville's visit to the Ouma, a Choctaw people located above the Red River on the east bank of the Mississippi River, in 1699, food was used in a number of ways to cement relations or to emphasize a point. When Iberville and his men first went ashore at the Ouma's landing, they fired a gun announcing their arrival. The Ouma arrived singing songs and offering the calumet of peace. Once they arrived at the village, the Ouma honored the French with dances followed by a feast. The next morning Iberville returned to his boat, and a little later the chief of the Ouma along with more than 150 men, women, and children showed up with corn and pounded meal for him and his men. The morning after that, they brought the Frenchmen three more barrels of corn (McWilliams 1981, 67–70).

After an exploratory trip farther up the river with six Ouma and one Taensa, Iberville returned to the Ouma landing to join his men and begin the journey back downriver. However, he had difficulty getting his guides, the Bayogoula who were still at the Ouma's village, to return to the boats. Thinking that Iberville was angry that his men did not return immediately, the chief of the Ouma along with eight of his men and women delivered corn, pumpkins, and fowls to him the next day. In response to this gesture of pacification, Iberville gave them some glass beads, awls, knives, and needles (McWilliams 1981, 78). In this one situation, women participated in several diplomatic endeavors through the exchange of food.

Women also used food as a way of expressing displeasure. In March 1699 Sauvole had been sent by Iberville to sound the middle channel of the Mississippi but had to quit because he had run low on food. He was unable to get any supplies from the Bayogoula because a Récollet Father had accused the Bayogoula of stealing his breviary. Angered by the accusation, the women took away the bread they had earlier given to Sauvole's men (McWilliams 1981, 86). The protocol of men and women extending aid to allies through food still existed thirty years later. Lusser, who traveled to the important Choctaw town of the Yowani with goods for presents, camped outside their village on the evening of January 18, 1730.[26] According to his report, "At about eight o'clock two men and a woman came to bring food," which they greatly needed because they had traveled all day under poor conditions without eating dinner (MPA:FD 1927, 1:84). Thus we see that women participated in diplomatic exchanges, and that men and women distributed food together. And, as we saw in the case of Sauvole's men, women also withheld or removed food as a punitive measure.

Native women's participation in political affairs, however, went beyond diplomatic missions. They played a significant role in times of war primarily through dances and torture of captives. Early descriptions of war dances indicate women participated in them and that they were much more than a gathering for social purposes.[27] For example, when Iberville, escorted by the Bayogoula, arrived among the Ouma on March 20, 1699, the whole village assembled in the center of the town, where they held a dance for him. Twenty men and fifteen women danced for him for three hours. Later that night men, women, and girls sang war dances until about midnight (McWilliams 1981, 68–69). Earlier, in February, Iberville had met with the Bayogoula, who smoked the pipe with him. They indicated to him that he was now the ally of several nations including the Ouma (McWilliams 1981, 47–48).[28] Thirty years later, in 1730, Joseph Christophe De Lusser, captain of the infantry garrisoned at Mobile, described Choctaw women from Caffetalaya, Cushtusha, and Boucfouca "armed and daubed with paint, with bonnets of eagle feathers" dancing after the feast celebrating a successful attack on the Yazoo.[29] Later, following an attack on the Natchez, the Choctaw warriors returned with the head of one of their own who had been killed. The men assembled around the head and wailed for a few minutes. The head was then taken to the women, who wailed in the same manner. Bernard Romans also mentioned Choctaw women dancing around scalps until they were tired (MPA:FD 1927, 1:102, 104, 107; Romans 1775, 50).

Although women did not as a matter of course engage in battle, they did provide assistance to returning warriors, particularly the wounded. On occasion this assistance included seeking out the wounded or dead following a battle. In one documented case in March 1730, Captain Lusser encountered about twenty women from Chickasawhay,[30] a former Choctaw town, between the bayous of Nitabouc and Nacchoubananya. They were on their way to meet their husbands, who had a wounded man with them (MPA:FD 1927, 1:108). M. Étienne Périer, governor of Louisiana, later wrote in April that the wife of Patlaco, head chief of the Chickasawhay village who had been wounded during the battle with the Natchez and was treated at New Orleans, heard that her husband was dead and had come to retrieve his body (MPA:FD 1984, 4:33, 35 n. 6). In addition to aiding the wounded after battle, women sometimes accompanied war parties. This placed women in danger of being captured by any number of enemies including the French and the British. For example, in 1706 aide-major Pierre Dugue de Boisbriant and Gabriel Phillippe de Saint-Lambert with about fifty Canadians encountered a party of Alabama on their way to attack a Choctaw village. During a brief skirmish the French killed two warriors and took a woman captive who was later sold as a slave to a family in Mobile (Higginbotham 1977, 243).

The responsibility of the women was to sing war songs for their warriors before or during battle. The women's songs were intended to excite the courage of their men who were going to war, but apparently their songs could also incite fear in the enemy. In one instance Jean Baptiste le Moyne Sieur de Bienville reported in September 1734 that approximately one thousand to twelve hundred Choctaw set out to attack the Chickasaw. However, as they approached the enemy they heard the war songs of the women and could tell by their different cries that the enemy was quite excited. This discovery discouraged the Choctaw and they abandoned their mission (MPA:FD 1927, 1:241–42). Embarrassed by their failed mission, six hundred Choctaw marched to Chatelaw village to attack the Chickasaw. Lying in ambush, as D'Artaguette described the ensuing battle, they sent fifteen men to fire upon the Chickasaw to entice them to come out of their two forts. "Fifty of them came out as well as a woman who encouraged them by war songs . . . The woman was captured still alive, having received a gun-shot wound, but as she was of an advanced age the Choctaws dispatched her" (MPA:FD 1927, 1:245). In 1740, according to the journal of Father Pierre Vitry, during Bienville's attack on three forts occupied by the Chickasaw, an Indian woman had positioned herself on top of a hut within one of the forts and "from this vantage point this heroine was urging her people to deeds of valor" (Vitry 1985, 53). Especially during times of surprise attacks the songs of the women were important to bolstering the courage of the men and urging them to fight. Thus, in the event a party of Indians, for example a hunting camp, was attacked, it was common "for the women to sing the enlivening war song in the time of an attack" (Adair 1775, 343).

Choctaw women were also known to take up arms in support of their communities. Romans, writing of his travels among the Choctaw in 1770 and 1771, said he was informed by a woman who traded provisions for ammunition "that she kept a gun to defend herself as well as her husband did." He also wrote that several times he had "seen armed women in motion with the parties going in pursuit of the invading enemy" (Romans 1775, 50). In another account, published in 1768 by Jean-Bernard Bossu, a French naval officer, some Choctaw women accompanied their husbands to war. He described women carrying quivers of arrows for the men while encouraging them not to fear their enemies (1962, 164).

From these examples, we can see that Choctaw women participated in the military life of the Choctaw. Recognition of their contributions to military efforts is perhaps best illustrated by an event described by Andre Pénicaut.[31] According to Pénicaut's narrative, in January 1699, while Iberville's men were building Fort Biloxi, the chiefs of the Pascagoula, Moctoby, Biloxi, Chickasaw, and Pensacola arrived at the fort to present the calumet of peace. On the third day of the ceremony, the Indians sank a stake into the ground after which the men and women took turns striking the stake as they related their noble deeds in war (1953, 5–7).[32] Interestingly, seventeen years earlier Minet reported a similar ritual among the Arkansas. However he does not mention women participating in the relating of war deeds (1682, 47). Evidently, the Choctaw recognized the war efforts of women. However, any titles women might have earned remain largely unknown to us.

A major incentive for going to war was to obtain captives. Responsibility for the fate of captives typically lay with the women. They determined whether male or female captives were tortured or adopted into a Choctaw family. Because anyone could become a captive, everyone had to prepare for such an event. According to Pénicaut, the Mobilian, Tohomé, and Naniaba held a festival at the beginning of September at which time everyone in the village including boys and girls and men and women were scratched until they bled.[33] Afterward they danced all night while the chiefs and the elder men encouraged them by telling them they were scratched "to teach them to be good warriors that would never cry out or shed tears even in the middle of the fire" (1953, 64–65). In other words, they encouraged everyone, including women and girls, to be brave even when being tortured by burning.

Male captives, as the ones who engaged in the actual killing of enemies, were almost always tortured. Since warriors documented their war successes with tattoos on their breasts and arms, the more tattoos the captive had, or the older the captive, the more likely he had killed Choctaws and their deaths must be avenged. Women also had tattoos, but no documentation exists as to whether any of those tattoos signified the killing of an enemy or bravery in battle. However, we do know women were also tortured, indicating that they, too, were held liable for loss of life and that as prisoners of war their lives held value. Joutel told of an instance where Cenis women tortured two female captives.[34] In another case where the Tunica wanted to demonstrate their alliance to the French who had been attacked by the Natchez, they took a Natchez female captive to New Orleans. They then proceeded to torture her until she died (Swanton 1928a, 686; Adair 1775, 417; Bossu 1962, 166; French 1853, 5:96; French 1846, 1:160). Women ritually beat captives with dry canes followed by burning with torches, all the while singing war songs, as did the prisoner. In fact, the Natchez woman who was tortured by the Tunica derided their unskillfulness at torturing her, "insulting them, and threatening that her death would soon be avenged by her tribe" (French 1853, 5:96). The scalps of the slain captives were attached to twigs of green-leaved pine and placed on top of the circular winter houses of their deceased relations. This act avenged the deaths of those killed by the enemy and enabled their spirits to travel to the land of the dead. Avenging a slain relative was of utmost concern to the Choctaw. In fact, the knowledge that relatives would avenge the deaths of their loved ones often encouraged caution over rashness in initiating internal conflicts. Thus women were vested with the responsibility to avenge a death by enemies, an act that was accompanied by songs of triumph and that provided support for the spirits of the killed relatives, who would then enjoy the afterworld (Adair 1775, 417–18, 425–26). Enemies or captives might also be tortured immediately following a battle or chance encounter. The records do not indicate in those cases whether men or women did the torturing, but these actions suggest that women might be traveling with warriors expecting battle.

Change in Women's Roles

There were many ways in which Choctaw women earned respect or honors, whether through handling medicines, bearing children, providing plant foods, distinguishing themselves during times of war or as political leaders, or caring for deceased relatives. All of these activities earned women recognition as beloved people in other Southeastern nations. Although we find few references to indicate that Choctaw women held the title of beloved, we know they carried out functions associated with such titles among other nations. We also know that women as mothers were highly esteemed, as is indicated in their stories about Ohoyo Osh Chisba or by the way they addressed the place of the birth of their people as Beloved Mother. Their ritual acts of seclusion during menstruation and after childbirth as well as their participation in caring for the body of the deceased reflect the attention given to their association with fertility and life as well as with death.

When we look at the ways in which Choctaw women held tremendous responsibility for the existence of community, we begin to see the many ways in which they were influential and valued members of their society. They ensured the continuation of families and clans through childbirth and through their decisions regarding adoption of captives. They ensured the well-being of society by helping to continually restore balance to society.

Through torture they avenged their dead and, just as important, released the spirits of the dead. Their decisions decided how balance was restored after the spilling of blood, and they enabled the spirits of their dead relatives to complete their journeys to the afterworld, thus maintaining a proper relationship with the spirit world. As valued members of their communities Choctaw women could, through their own torture by enemy nations, make the ultimate sacrifice because honor and revenge could lie in their very lives.

Choctaw women's participation in many aspects of Choctaw society, however, began to decline during the time of French colonization. Women ceased to participate in some aspects of society, or in some cases their roles changed over time, becoming less visible or less relevant to those who observed Choctaw people in the first half of the eighteenth century. As contact experiences increased with the French and other Europeans, fewer and fewer references to women in the Southeast appear in written documents except in reference to domestic activities. In order to understand the changes in Choctaw women's roles and the concurrent decline in observations about them, we examine the impact of French colonization on Choctaw society. The next chapter looks specifically at the changing political landscape in the Southeast to ascertain the impact of French colonization on Choctaw women's presence in Choctaw society.

2

A Violent Landscape

When the first French explorers wrote about their encounters with indigenous people in the southern Mississippi region in the late 1690s, they noted the presence of native women in a number of diplomatic and military contexts including peace delegations, war parties, torture of captives, and war dances. However, by the time of Régis du Roullet's travels among the Choctaw in 1729 fewer observations were being recorded about native women's involvement in diplomatic and military affairs.[1] This change in recorded observations reflects a declining interest in the activities of women by the French military, the withdrawal of women from public spaces as a result of increasing dangers, and changes in the conventions of warfare. Women's participation in political activities not only went unrecognized by the French, but also, as violence toward Indian women increased and the concerns of warfare changed, women's diplomatic and war-related activities declined rapidly. By studying historic events coincident with decreases in observations of women, we can ascertain how French military and political interactions with the indigenous peoples throughout the Lower Mississippi Valley contributed to a decline in the influence of Choctaw women.

Although the arrival of the French marked a period of intense and sustained conflict in the Lower Mississippi Valley, it is important to note that Southeastern native people had already experienced conflict with Spanish and

British colonists, both of whom presented a threat to Indian women. Hernando de Soto's expedition in 1540–43 was the first Spanish group to penetrate the interior of the Southeast. All along his route Soto and his men left behind carnage. They demanded food, bearers or carriers, and women from villagers. The Spanish chained the bearers and forced them to carry their baggage. Since Spanish chroniclers distinguished between bearers and women, it is likely that the women were forced to prepare their meals and work around the camps while the men were forced to carry the Spaniards' supplies. Soto's men also raped the women they seized (Galloway 1995, 108). The available evidence, however, indicates that Soto encountered few proto-Choctaw people, most likely because news of his actions and whereabouts preceded him as he crossed the Alabama-Mississippi region. Enough similarity existed between language and culture of autonomous villages that native people were able to forewarn others of the approaching Spanish so that they could evacuate their towns (Galloway 1995, 118–19). The proto-Choctaw, no doubt, learned of Spanish depredations that included the capture and rape of women. Although Soto and his men caused considerable injury to native people, his expedition was of short enough duration that little in the way of acculturative adaptations or changes took place in women's roles. None of the Spanish expeditions that followed Soto's penetrated as deep into the Southeast and thus they had little impact on the people who later became known as the Choctaw (Galloway 1995, 131, 136).

Nearly one hundred years passed before the British arrived and began organizing slave-raiding of Choctaw villages and other nations by their neighbors. By the middle of the seventeenth century Virginians were sending Westo to capture slaves among the Indians of the interior of the Southeast. Beginning in 1698 English traders in Carolina territory encouraged Chickasaw, Tunica, and Yamasee and later Cherokee and Creek to raid villages for captives. When the French Récollet missionary Father Antoine Davion settled among the Tunica in 1699, he learned that a British slave-trader had been resident among them for several years (Martin 1994, 308–9, 312; Galloway 1994, 406; Galloway 1995, 312). According to Iberville an Englishman, probably the same one that Father Davion referred to, had "been among the Chicachas [Chickasaw], where he does a business in Indian slaves, putting himself at the head of Chicacha war parties to make raids on their enemies and friends and forcing them to take prisoners, whom he buys and sends to the islands to be sold" (McWilliams 1981, 110). Most of the Indians enslaved by the English and their allied tribes were women. For example, in 1709, a party of Alibamon, allegedly influenced by Carolinians, destroyed a Mobilian village and took thirty women and children captive (Usner 1992, 20).

With the arrival of the French the Choctaw began to have direct and sustained contact with Europeans that had a lasting impact on women's roles. Although the Spanish reported hearing about the powerful Chacta as early as the 1660s and the French first met two Choctaw in 1700, it was not until 1701 when Henri de Tonti traveled to Choctaw territory that Europeans visited Choctaw villages (Galloway 1995, 166, 170, 193). As the Spanish, British, and French began to struggle for alliances and control of territory, the Lower Mississippi Valley became a more dangerous place for everyone concerned. Indian women across the Southeast, in particular, faced the threat of capture and enslavement from British- and Spanish-allied Indians. The Chickasaw to the north of the Choctaw, the Creek and later the Cherokee to the east, and the Natchez to the west staged raids in search of captives. In addition, as slavery began to replace indigenous treatment of captive enemies, Indian women lost an important function in their societies. Choctaw women, like all Indian women in the region, experienced a decline in their contributions to their communities' military and political affairs.

Invisible Women

As the three European groups vied for control of the Lower Mississippi Valley, their attentions were drawn more toward military concerns than observations about the daily activities of native people, particularly those of women, whom they considered unimportant in matters of state. French interests in the habits of native people quickly gave way to strategizing about lines of defense and developing alliances because they had entered a region already fraught with conflict. By the time of the founding of the French colony at Old Biloxi in 1699, the culture of warfare in the Southeast had been affected by Spanish and British influence for at least twenty years. In a speech to the Chickasaw and the Choctaw in 1702, Iberville pointed out that the two had been attacking each other at the instigation of the English for the last eight to ten years (McWilliams 1981, 171–72).

Remains of fortified villages indicate that conflict had been a concern in the Southeast for some time. Among the Choctaw, their large villages were built on second terraces or ridge tops that provided good defensive positions. However, it is not clear whether these defensive measures developed in response to conflicts with the Spanish- or English-allied Indian nations or whether the different native nations were fighting one another for prime farmland before contact (Penman 1977, 90, 306; Larson 1972, 389). In any case, before 1699 the effects of Spanish and English contact had forced some villages to relocate and integrate with other villages for safety purposes. When Soto and his men approached some towns, they found the women and children had already fled to safety. In some cases entire towns fled European aggressions. For example, in 1680 three villages fled Cherokee country to escape persecution by English traders and Chuchumeco warriors. They became part of the Alabama nation and by 1681 they had allied themselves with four smaller villages speaking a Choctaw dialect (Higginbotham 1977, 117–18).

The arrival of the French introduced a new element of tension into the Lower Mississippi Valley that quickly changed their approach to native people. At first the French were primarily concerned with obtaining food, transportation, and intelligence on Indian people. They took note of their encounters with women and men as they tried to quickly establish alliances that would lead to supplies of food, canoes, and guides. However, the French quickly found themselves in a position of competition with English traders and somewhat tangentially with Spanish colonialists. They had to contend not only with other Europeans but also with native people who staged attacks and raids on behalf of the English and Spanish. The French and English, in particular, were forced to deal with each other as well as with native peoples' shifting alliances. Both sides encouraged warfare among Indian nations and imposed European rules of conduct as they tried to gain the advantage in the struggle for control of the Lower Mississippi Valley.

It is this attention to warfare, to protection of territory, that coincided with the decline in observations of women in French journals. Unlike the earlier explorers who were interested in learning about the region and its inhabitants, French officers and their informants were more concerned with military strategy, with the number of warriors available among allies and potential allies. As conflict increased in the region, the French sent reports to France filled with the number of warriors wounded and killed, the location of battles, and the successes or failures of military expeditions.[2] For the most part, French officers simply were not interested in Indian life beyond native military capabilities. Since women typically were not soldiers or warriors, the French considered their numbers or activities of little benefit for military strategizing. By the time Tonti visited Choctaw towns in 1701, Iberville was already focused on developing alliances with large inland nations, particularly the Choctaw, who had the largest population in the Lower Mississippi Valley and who were suitably located to provide a barrier against English incursions from the east. The Choctaw themselves were fortifying their towns and moving them closer to each other in order to protect themselves from enemy raids (Galloway 1995, 193). Thus, before the French actually observed Choctaw communities they were already focusing their attentions on military strengths of Indian nations. From 1682 to 1701 French chroniclers did not mention Choctaw women because they had not yet met any, and after 1701 they tended to report on military affairs that they assumed did not concern women.

Imminent Warfare

While attention to military strength might account for the relative absence of women in French documents, increasing violence and the threat of warfare had a greater impact on the presence of native women in international affairs. As the political landscape of the Lower Mississippi Valley became more violent and complex, the movements of Indian women correspondingly became more constricted. The French and English and their allied Indians destroyed villages and killed the men, but they often took women captive and sold them as slaves. Destroyed villages meant loss of homes and cornfields, the domain of women. The threat of captivity forced the withdrawal of women, children, and elders from potentially dangerous situations. Women had to withdraw from public and unprotected spaces such as council grounds, and sometimes they had to evacuate from towns and cornfields in order to limit the possibility of their capture. Not only did women have to withdraw from public spaces where influential decisions were made, but they also faced the loss of the produce of their labors.

By examining French and Choctaw interests in the Lower Mississippi Valley, we can see how conflict and competition between them and English colonists created a climate of danger that prevented native women from participating in some aspects of village and national concerns. When the French began their explorations down the Mississippi River, they were motivated by desires to find a water route between their northern and projected southern settlements and to tap the natural resources of the Mississippi Valley. They were also in a race with Spain and England for colonization of the Gulf Coast. While the English Crown initially did not seem disturbed by French occupation of the area, English merchants were quite alarmed. They were the ones advancing into the Mississippi Valley and competing with the French for control of the deerskin trade (Stubbs 1982, 41; Coker 1982, 129, 132–33). The French worked to block English expansion toward the west in order to control the resources of the region. Both groups turned to Indian people to provide military support for their interests, which led to widespread conflict.

The Choctaw, who had seen some of their people—particularly women—sold into slavery by South Carolinians for a number of years, were easily persuaded to ally themselves with the French, who could provide them with firearms to use against the English and their allied Indians (Mereness 1916, 259; Galloway 1994, 406). They were already in conflict with the Chickasaw to the north and the Cherokee to the east, both of whom had been supplied with guns and metal knives by the English (Higgenbotham 1977, 54; Reid 1970, 201). Thus both the French and the Choctaw found it beneficial to ally with each other. However, the superiority of the weapons meant greater casualties for those facing enemies armed by Europeans and it often meant abandoning homes and fields to escape further injury. When the Chickasawhay, formerly known as the Choctaw of the prairie, and the Concha,[3] an important Choctaw town, who had only bows and arrows, were attacked by former allies armed by the English, they lost more than two thousand warriors. They had to flee their villages and seek the protection of Bienville, the commandant at Mobile (MPA:FD 1984, 5:14; MPA:FD 1927, 1:156–57).

Weapons alone, however, did not account for the increased cruelty in war. The intent to destroy the enemy completely seemed to gain precedence over the indigenous philosophy of warfare as a means to exact reparation for lives lost or to gain captives. Imbedded in the indigenous concept of warfare was the idea that order or balance of an injured nation could be restored by the victims' nation taking as many lives as it lost. This philosophy was demonstrated in 1725 when some Chickasaw messengers told the Cherokee that they planned to "kill as many Choctaws as the Choctaws had killed Chickasaws some while earlier" (Reid 1970, 168; Mereness 1916, 122). Whether or not total destruction of villages occurred before European contact is not known, but it was part of their modus operandi after contact. During the Soto expedition native people destroyed their own villages in order to leave the intruding Spanish unprotected. As the Spanish crossed the interior of the Southeast they left destroyed and burned villages behind them (Galloway 1995, 118–19). The French and British often demanded that the Choctaw or other indigenous peoples initiate or assist in the total destruction of nonallied towns. In 1751 Vaudreüil wrote to Antoine Louis Rouillé that he would "not neglect anything to keep urging the Choctaws to make such frequent incursions upon the Chickasaws that in the end we shall be able to succeed in exterminating them" (MPA:FD 1984, 5:108). Although the Choctaw rarely met French demands for total destruction of nonallied towns, aggressive actions on the part of the Choctaw opened them up to counterattacks and the possible capture and enslavement of their women.

As the Choctaw and other nations were drawn more and more into a relationship with the French or British, the customary rules and justification for warfare changed. Earlier, indigenous attacks most likely occurred in order to defend territory or to carry out acts of restitution for loss of lives due to war. With the entrance of European interests Indian nations began attacking Indian nations not because of some assumed wrong that required restitution or because they were protecting agricultural territory, but because of the association one had with the French or English. For example, in 1705 the chiefs of Alabama, Coweta, Kasihta, Okmulgee,[4] and several other villages signed a proclamation drawn up by three Carolina Indian agents that all natives allied with the French were to be attacked and annihilated. That fall, three thousand natives attacked the villages of the Choctaw, who fortunately had been warned and had abandoned their homes (Higgenbotham 1977, 219).

The possibility of attack became a constant part of life for Choctaw towns as alliances shifted between indigenous nations. The uncertainty of alliances meant that in the case of Choctaw women they always had to be concerned about their safety in their cornfields or menstrual houses, and in unprotected towns. The Choctaw never knew when a previous ally or neutral nation might become their enemy. When one tribe acted on behalf of the French or British or themselves, they could potentially draw their allies into a conflict or find themselves at odds with former allies. Declaration of war meant that a previously neutral nation could find itself suddenly drawn into battle because of its alliances. For example, in 1751, while attacking the Chickasaw, the Choctaw were forced back into the hunting grounds of the Abihka,[5] which resulted in confrontations with them. The situation could have escalated if the Abihka had decided to call upon their allies, the Alabama, Tallapoosa,[6] and Kasihta, to join the conflict. As luck would have it, however, the Alabama, Tallapoosa, and Kasihta had their sights on the Cherokee (MPA:FD 1984, 5:73–74). However, the Shawnee[7] considered joining the Abihka against the Choctaw because of attacks waged against them by the nations along the Wabash River. The Shawnee mistakenly believed the French and their allies had influenced the Wabash nations to attack them. Since the Choctaw were allies of the French, the Shawnee held them liable for the attack and thus determined to capture Choctaw as restitution for the loss of Shawnee lives (MPA:FD 1984, 5:75, 78).

When the Choctaw engaged in battles they left their towns open to retaliation. In 1702 Iberville's brother, Bienville, found several abandoned villages on the islands located not far from Massacre Island.[8] The people had fled the attacks of the Choctaw and Alabama. In another instance, in 1725, news spread that the English were encouraging some of the Choctaw to kill the French by cutting their throats and enslaving all the small Indian nations that were their neighbors. These threats so frightened the smaller nations that the Apalachee, Chatot, and Tawasa[9] left their towns and resettled on the east side of Mobile Bay. The Pascagoula, the Biloxi, and the rest of the Indians of the Pearl River sought safety on the south side of Lake Pontchartrain, where they remained until the defeat of the English who were inciting the Choctaw to attack the French (MPA:FD 1984, 4:20).

No one was exempt from the violence of the times. The French drew numerous nations into their wars. When Bienville took action against the Natchez in 1723 in what is sometimes called the second war of the Natchez, he called upon the Tunica, Yazoo, and a party of Choctaw to accompany his army (French 1853, 51). When Tonty brought a delegation of five Chickasaw men, three women, and two warriors to Mobile for the purpose of negotiating an alliance, Iberville reminded the Chickasaw that over the last eight or ten years the English had been responsible for the deaths of over eighteen hundred Choctaw and eight hundred Chickasaw. Iberville warned the

Chickasaw that if they continued to ally themselves with the English he would arm all the Choctaw, Tohomé, and Mobilian along with the Natchez and their other allies, and he would incite the Illinois to make war on them (Higgenbotham 1977, 77). The French determined that they had to either create an alliance between the Chickasaw and the Choctaw, thus squeezing out the British and neutralizing the Cherokee threat, or urge hostilities between the Choctaw and Chickasaw that would serve to concentrate Chickasaw attention on defense rather than solicitation of Choctaw trade on behalf of the English. A Choctaw alliance would also provide a buffer against possible British-directed Creek incursions from the south and east of the Choctaw.

Even during times of peaceful trips Choctaw people risked their lives. While several Choctaw families were visiting Chickasaw villages, some Chickasaw warriors at the urging of the British seized several Choctaw families. The Chickasaw leaders, realizing the implications of their warriors' attack against the Choctaw, took an entourage of seventy Chickasaw, including women and children, to Fort Louis to mend relations with the French. Bienville was angry but he decided to provide the Chickasaw safe escort back to their country in hopes of reestablishing a Choctaw-Chickasaw-French alliance. As the group passed through Choctaw country, however, the Choctaw retaliated against the Chickasaw, killing nearly all of their men (Higginbotham 1977, 212). In 1748 after the English-allied Choctaw attacked a German settlement, a detachment of French soldiers and militiamen mistook a peaceful Choctaw hunting camp near Lake Pontchartrain as the attackers and opened fire on them (Usner 1992, 93; MPA:FD 1984, 4:318–21).

The violence was not limited to nation against nation either. In the case of the Choctaw, when members of the western division decided to entertain negotiations with English traders because they seemed better able to provide European-made supplies that they had become dependent upon, they planted the seeds for a civil war that lasted four years. When the western division's efforts were foiled by Choctaw loyal to the French, they retaliated by attacking the French. The French, in turn, demanded that the Eastern Choctaw demonstrate their loyalty to them by punishing their western relatives. They threatened to cease providing arms or to allow traders in the Choctaw nation unless they gave them satisfaction for the French lives. The French warned the Choctaw that without French weapons they would become targets of their enemies and they would die of hunger and destitution (Mereness 1916, 266, 274).

Although the French treated the Choctaw as one nation, in actuality each town had its own leaders and individuals were free to choose whom to follow. To be forced suddenly to attack their own people for exercising what had always been a right did not sit well with the French-aligned Choctaw. Moreover, the Choctaw saw the benefits of having a trade relationship with both the French and English. They reasoned that when either the French or the English were not able to supply desired merchandise, they would have recourse to the other. They also pointed out to the French that they would still have the loyalty of a majority of Choctaw towns. Fearing such an arrangement would provide English access to French settlements, Vaudreüil dismissed their arguments, insisting that the eastern Choctaw "make war on their rebellious colleagues and to keep the English from bringing them any assistance." He was convinced that as long as the Choctaw were engaged in civil war, the English would not risk entering Choctaw territory with a great deal of merchandise with which to bribe the Choctaw into entering a trade association with them (MPA:FD 1984, 5:23, 218).

French tactics also included manipulating alliances and conflicts in order to safeguard their interests (MPA:FD 1984, 5:52, 75). When the Abihka and Tallapoosa seemed to be getting too close to the English, Vaudreüil worried that the English might use them as emissaries to make inroads with the Choctaw. To prevent such a possibility, he strategically ignored hostilities between the Abihka and Tallapoosa and the Choctaw. He knew if he could maintain hostile relations between the Choctaw and the other two nations the tension would prevent them from acting as ambassadors for the English. Just a few years later, however, Louis Billouart de Kerlérec, who succeeded Vaudreüil as governor, expressed concern that if the Choctaw declared war on the Abihka, the Abihka's allies, the Alabama, Tallapoosa, and Coweta, would come to the aid of the Abihka. The combined forces of the Abihka and their allies would put such a strain on Choctaw resources that they might find it necessary to negotiate peace with the Chickasaw. Kerlérec also wrote to De Machault d'Arnouville that it was essential that the Chickasaw continue to occupy the Choctaw. He said if the Choctaw succeeded in completely destroying the Chickasaw, then it would "be necessary to raise up some new objectives that may detain and occupy them." In 1756 he wrote Arnouville that he was going to tell the Alabama and Choctaw that he would not try to stop the civil war that seemed to be imminent among them, which he believed was stirred up by the English, but that in reality he intended "to do all within my [his] power to succeed in doing so (MPA:FD 1984, 5:113, 154, 158, 170).

The French also made use of intelligence about indigenous customs and beliefs to maintain distrust between the Choctaw and the English. They quickly learned that among the Choctaw, medicine people, or *alikchi*, used formulas in songs and prayers as well as ritual paraphernalia to help their people succeed in war and in hunting. In the case of war they used medicine to determine whether their warriors would be successful and thus whether they should go forth to battle. They also had formulas for giving their warriors strength, speed, and courage in battle. They might also use medicine against their enemies to cause them to feel weak and to fear their enemies (Swanton 1931, 166, 228). Alikchi used poison to sicken or kill Choctaw enemies. They might poison a stream or the meat of their enemies (Swanton 1931, 169). The French benefited from this knowledge by helping spread rumors of the English using medicine to sicken Indian enemies.

On January 24, 1731, Roullet received a visit from a Choctaw of the Yellow Canes, who told him that many of the people in his nation were sick and dead. Roullet told him that the sickness came from the medicine that the English put into their *limbourg* cloth that was used for trading purposes. Several days later, on February 6, Tichou Mingo, a spy Roullet sent among the Indians, reported that a detachment of warriors from the Choctaw village of Concha was planning to attack the Chickasaw because their English allies were "compounding a medicine in order to cause their death" (MPA:FD 1927, 1:184). He described how Toupaoulastabé, honored man of Concha village, stated publicly "that the sickness which was current in the nation came from a medicine that the English made with cane sugar and put in the *limbourg* that they had sent to trade by way of the Chickasaws for the purpose of making all the Choctaws die . . . " (MPA:FD 1984, 4:58–59). His brother Alibamon Mingo expressed the same belief. In another case that took place in 1754, the chief of the Coweta, who had been ill for six months, believed that the English were slowly poisoning him. Kerlérec reported to Arnouville that he and his men did "not fail to second him in that idea" (MPA:FD 1984, 5:157). The French encouraged such beliefs in order to ensure continued animosity between the Choctaw and English-allied Indians.

During the French colonial period warfare remained a constant reality in the Southeast. The ever-present danger of attack meant that people had to be more careful about traveling alone to hunt or fish, or even leaving the safety of their villages for water or firewood. Although French reports indicate that Indian women traveled away from home as part of peacetime activities, they curtailed their activities during times of violence. As early as the sixteenth century Cabeza de Vaca mentioned that no women were seen among two different groups of Indians that the Panfilo de Narvaez expedition encountered along the Gulf Coast in 1528. Galloway suggests that the women in the village of the first group may have hidden in anticipation of trouble as others did during the later Soto expedition (1995, 85). Similarly, during the years of warfare in the French colonial period, women avoided leaving villages without the protection of the men. As danger became more imminent from the English and other indigenous nations, the Choctaw took steps to protect women from danger. The fear of attack was so great that in one case, as Lusser wrote in March 1730, when he and his men approached the villages of Okeoulou[10] and Boucfouca the women fled, fearing they were Englishmen (MPA:FD 1927, 1:96).

Choctaw women, however, also had reason to fear their French allies. They knew that French soldiers or militia took Indian women as slaves for labor and sex. When Roullet visited the Choctaw in January 1730 to solicit their aid against the Natchez who had slaughtered the French garrison there, the "Great Chief" reportedly sneered at the request, stating that French warriors carried away Natchez women by force (MPA:FD 1927, 1:176). French officials were not above colluding with their English antagonists to obtain slaves. For example, in 1716 one of Bienville's nephews was killed while buying Indian slaves from some Carolinians. He had planned to transport them to the Caribbean (Wiegers 1988, 192). The danger for women from their allies and enemies forced the Choctaw to rethink the participation of women on trips away from their villages and at home. The unspoken law of safe conduct for peace emissaries in the Southeast, perhaps not always honored, became less certain in the French colonial period (Reid 1970, 204; Mooney 1891, 485). Women could be captured while on peaceful missions or even taken from their homes, resulting in a significant curtailment of their contributions to society.

Captivity and the Ethic of Restitution

A major change that Choctaw women faced as a result of the introduction of slavery was a decline in the practice of women deciding the fate of captives.

The decline occurred on two levels. One, the marketing of captives as slaves began to replace the indigenous practice of killing or adopting captives, in which case women no longer needed to decide if a captive lived or died. Two, men typically went to war and captured people whom they then traded or sold to Europeans as slaves. Since the world of commerce had become primarily the domain of men, women no longer played a significant role in the disposition of captives. The loss of this responsibility had a significant impact on women's influence in Choctaw society because the fate of captives determined how balance would be restored to a family or clan that had lost someone through warfare. The lives of captives could be used to restore balance in two ways. They could restore balance to the living relatives or to the spirit of the one who was killed. In either case, captives restored order and wholeness to a family or clan that had lost a relative. Thus, if a non-Choctaw caused the death of a person through an act of war, the town or nation of the killer was held responsible for reparations for that life. Captives restored balance to the survivors of the deceased by replacing the deceased relative, male or female.

The clan members of the deceased were obligated by what has been misleadingly characterized as "blood revenge" to restore balance to their world by avenging the death of kinspersons.[11] This obligation to seek restitution for a life served an important societal function. It worked to foster consideration before undertaking warfare. The custom of restitution also helped to circumscribe the occasion of warfare because any act of violence resulting in death could lead to prolonged fighting between families, clans, or nations (Swanton 1931, 104–6; Reid 1970, 92). The people understood that such a death required a life in order to restore the community to a whole state. However, they also understood that once that life was given the matter was settled. Thus, by determining the fate of captives, Choctaw women participated in crucial decisions about the restoration of balance in their communities and indirectly helped to foster careful consideration of war.

The idea of restoration also applied intra-tribally. Thus, if a member of the community caused the death of someone else, that person was obligated to give his or her life in exchange. However, the family or clan of the deceased could choose to restore balance to the community by adopting the responsible person. That person then became a member of the deceased's family with all the rights and obligations that were once those of the deceased. In other words, the person now had an entire new set of kinship responsibilities that would be his or hers for life. The family or clan could also choose to take the life of the person who did the killing rather than adopt the person. In the case of the Choctaw, there are several nineteenth-century cases in which the one who caused the death was given time, maybe a day or even a year, to put his or her affairs in order before submitting to execution. Although unheard of among the Choctaw, if the killer failed to show up at the appointed time for giving up his or her life, a member of that person's family or clan could offer his or her life instead (Swanton 1931, 104–10; Reid 1970, 83). The family members would do that in order to restore balance to the affected family, to avoid possible feuds that could go on indefinitely, and to maintain status and respect within the community.

This ethic of restitution also applied to casualties of war. If one nation or town attacked another and caused the deaths of their enemies, the attacked community would initiate a counterattack. During these counterattacks the attackers would try to obtain captives to take back to their villages. Some nations left behind small pieces of wood with their tribal markings on them so that their enemies would know exactly who had exacted restitution (Swanton 1928a, 686). In the same manner as restitution within a community, women could choose to adopt war captives to replace those who were lost in battle. Initially those captives were kept under constant supervision while they were forced to work to prevent them from running away. Later, when they adjusted to their new community, sometimes through marriage, they could gain all the rights and privileges of a member of the family and community, and in some cases, even become leaders. However, the women could also choose to torture captives until they died to offset the death of their relatives and to return balance to their world. In other words, both the attacked and the attacker lost equal numbers of relatives. Once that balance was achieved, ideally the attacks would end. However, any unavenged deaths could mean continued warfare (Reid 1970, 196; Jacobs 1954, 52; Perdue 1979, 11).

Captives could also restore balance by having their lives sacrificed in order to release the spirits of those killed by violence rather than old age (Cushman 1899, 206; Swanton 1931, 220). For the Choctaw, as with other Southeastern indigenous people, care of the ancestors who had passed on was a sacred duty. If they failed to care for the bones, the spirits of the dead would be offended and punish the living with sickness, bad luck, or death. In their creation stories the Choctaw tell of how some of their ancestors carried all the bones of their deceased relatives during the long migration to Nanih Waiya. They had so many bones to carry that they could only carry half of them, which they did for half a day, returning to their last campsite to pick up the remainder of the bones to carry to the next camping place. They would have preferred to die rather than leave the bones behind. For those who were killed in war, the living had to provide everything the deceased needed for the journey to the land of the spirits, or risk the lost spirit's coming back and frightening or harming people (Swanton 1931, 12, 14, 217).

With the introduction of the European system of slavery, captivity began to lose its function among Southeastern native people. The indigenous people continued to respect their rules of captivity, but those rules were not congruent with French and English notions of slavery. If Indian people captured an enemy, then the rules usually applied. An example of this practice occurred in 1730 when Lusser learned of a French woman captive held by the Chakchiuma.[12] He told the chief of the Cushtusha "that it was not right that they should regard the French woman, whom they had with them, as a slave." The chief replied that he did not regard her as such. The woman herself told Lusser that the Chakchiuma had shown "all sort of kindness" (MPA:FD 1927, 1:100). Lusser considered the French woman a slave, whereas the Chakchiuma treated her as an adopted captive, a relative. In a similar case Mary Hughes, who was taken captive by the Cherokee around 1760, told Lieutenant Henry Timberlake that the Cherokee initially had treated her harshly and had not allowed her sufficient clothing. However, after she married the Cherokee who killed her husband her situation apparently changed because she refused to leave her Cherokee husband even after the English ransomed her (Perdue 1979, 11).

The intersection of the indigenous ethic of restitution with the European system of slavery undermined women's ability to help restore balance to their communities. In response to French demands or interests, captives might be turned over to them rather than adopted or sacrificed for the deceased (MPA:FD 1984, 5:174). The French and British encouraged expeditions solely for the purpose of obtaining captives. These captives did not replace killed family members, but rather became slaves without the rights and freedom of kinship. Instead of integrating captives into the capturing nation, captives became a commodity to be bought and sold. La Salle quickly realized that trafficking in slaves was a lucrative practice. By buying

Indian captives and then selling them back to their own people he could obtain much-needed trade items as well as the goodwill of the indigenous nations involved (Surrey 1916, 226).

The indigenous people quickly learned to use captives as a commodity to bargain with the French and English. As the Choctaw became more dependent upon European items, especially arms, they began to attack other people for the purpose of obtaining scalps that could be exchanged for rifles (Higgenbotham 1977, 219). Or they would take the captives to New Orleans or Mobile to exchange for gifts or at least the promise of future gifts (MPA:FD 1984, 5:16). Whereas captives obtained through war once represented a means for restitution, through adoption or torture, now Indians also viewed captives as a trade item. They also began to use captives as pawns in their negotiations with the French and other Indian groups. For example, when Bienville sent some men to negotiate peace with the Chickasaw in 1740, the Chickasaw assumed he was sending his entire army and decided they ought to establish peace. After meeting with French representatives Lieutenant de St. Laurent and Captain Sieur de Celeron, a deputation of Chickasaw accompanied the French back to the camp of the army. They immediately sued for peace and as a demonstration of their sincerity, they gave Bienville two English captives they held and swore their allegiance to the French from thenceforward (French 1853, 117). They used the English captives as a way to avoid conflict with the French or at least to delay retaliation for having encouraged English trading among their people.

The goal of restitution began to give way to the practice of retaliation only as the French and the British put pressure on the Choctaw and other indigenous peoples to attack each other, not for the loss of clan relatives, but to further French or British interests (MPA:FD 1984, 5:15, 19, 47). The act of retaliation became more important than the obligation to restore order and balance to the offended community and to release the spirits of the deceased. As the principle of retaliation gained primacy as justification for war, attacks might be directed at anyone associated with the offending party. When some Tohomé, a Choctaw-related group, killed an Alabama, some Alabama in turn killed two Choctaw instead of a Tohomé. Since the Choctaw were allies of the French, Vaudreüil felt it imperative that he order the Alabama to make restitution to the Choctaw for having killed two men innocent of the murder of the Alabama (MPA:FD 1984, 5:15). Ironically, the French forced the Alabama to adhere to their own restitution policy.

The Choctaw were never one unified nation, and as various towns or groups negotiated with the British or French to their best advantage, divisiveness arose between those towns dealing with British traders and those towns allied with the French. Those Choctaw who wanted to maintain their alliance with the French found themselves caught between French demands for punishment of Choctaw partisan to the English and their own ethic of restitution. In November 1748 British-supplied Choctaw attacked nine French colonists near Mobile and a settlement of Germans living in French-controlled territory.[13] Although the French defeated the Choctaw party, they demanded that loyal Choctaw attack the English-allied Choctaw to demonstrate their continued goodwill. On December 23, leaders and warriors of the French-allied eastern faction of the Choctaw attacked and destroyed the villages of three of the principal chiefs with ties to the English. They delivered more than a hundred Choctaw scalps to Vaudreüil. They told Vaudreüil that the reason it had taken them so long to fulfill the demands of the French was that they had to consider that doing so meant they had to "renounce their own blood and decide to destroy their kinsmen, their friends, and in general all those of their nation, who, having let themselves be seduced by the malicious speeches of the English, had risen against the French." They hoped in return for such a large sacrifice to receive a double present that year, plus three times the price for the scalps that they had paid for Chickasaw scalps, "since they had done themselves much more violence in killing their own brothers than in killing strangers" (MPA:FD 1984, 5:13, 16, 31).

When the Choctaw asked for double presents that year, their request and Vaudreüil's response were informed by differing ideologies. For the Choctaw, gift-giving embodied the idea of reciprocity, of giving something of like value for that received. The value of Chickasaw or British scalps had long ago been established. However, when the Choctaw asked for double the gifts they were considering the value of their own relatives versus the lives of their enemies. They had forfeited many more lives than the English-allied Choctaw had taken. What they had done by killing their own people had exposed their people to dangers far more significant than those threatened by enemies. They risked a continuous cycle of attacks, of family against family, of parent against child, attacks that affected the spirits of the deceased and those yet unborn.

In addition to putting their own people at risk of civil war, they had to face their own people and convince them of the propriety and necessity of their actions. Part of that negotiated process involved gift-giving. They needed more gifts to maintain their leadership status and to recompense people for the death of clan members in other villages. Without alternative restitution the Choctaw faced continuing internal acts of violence. Vaudreüil, on the other hand, short on supplies and wanting to make the best deal possible, hoped to give the Choctaw only the usual number of presents that year. He understood the Choctaw system of restitution, diplomacy, and recognition for distinguished action, yet he made inquiries to determine if he could give the usual number of presents to the Choctaw and still retain their loyalty (MPA:FD 1984, 5:17).

Vaudreüil also manipulated the indigenous system of restitution to benefit the French. When the British-supplied Choctaw responsible for attacks on French-allied towns sought peace with the French and their eastern kin, Vaudreüil demanded, "First, that every Choctaw chief, honored man, or warrior who shall dip his hand in the blood of a Frenchman shall be killed without mercy, and that if the kinsmen of the aggressor oppose this justice, the entire nation shall take up arms against them and shall subject them to the same fate as the guilty ones." In other words, he forced the Choctaw to abide by their own system of restitution. Vaudreüil continued, "Second, that every Choctaw chief or warrior who introduces the English into his village shall be punished by death together with the Englishmen, and no one whoever of the nation shall be permitted to take vengeance for it. . . . Fourth, that the villages hitherto in revolt shall disband their forces as soon as possible and that both sides shall return the prisoners and the slaves taken during the war" (MPA:FD 1984, 5:58, 60–61). In essence, Vaudreüil undermined women's roles by demanding that the Choctaw give up their ethic of restitution for slain relatives in exchange for peace with the French.

In spite of French and English efforts to end what they deemed barbaric blood revenge, the Choctaw and other indigenous peoples did not completely abandon their customs regarding captivity and clan responsibility. In June 1753 Alibamon Mingo and several other chiefs, along with warriors and honored men of different villages of the Choctaw nation, arrived at Mobile for their annual gifts and to present a complaint to Kerlérec and other French officers about the imprisonment of seven deserters. Two years earlier they had delivered seven deserting soldiers to the French on the condition that they receive mercy. At that time Alibamon Mingo had told the French that when the two moieties, Inoulactas and Imongoulachas, "go so far as to ask for the life of a man it is never refused them, even though the man should already be fastened to the frame." He also said that he asked for their pardons on behalf of his entire village (MPA:FD 1984, 5:89–90, 125). His statement suggests that women were also consulted about Choctaw intervention on behalf of the French deserters.

One of the chiefs accompanying Alibamon Mingo in 1751, Red Chief of the Chichatalaya, added that if the deserters were killed then he would charge himself with having killed them inasmuch as he was the one who had them arrested. He told the French, "I have served the French too well to be able to think that they wish to cause me to die of sorrow and regret, which would happen to me as surely as I tell you this." In accordance with Choctaw beliefs, the two chiefs believed that having granted life to the deserters, they had to ensure their safety no matter where the deserters resided. The imprisonment of the deserters meant that the Choctaw chiefs had broken their own laws. Thus, two years later Alibamon Mingo warned Kerlérec that they would no longer feel compelled to oppose the passage of any soldiers through their country who might be deserting and in fact said they would provide guides for them. Kerlérec knew that if the Choctaw demands were not met, more of his men were likely to desert. He therefore granted the pardon (MPA:FD 1984, 5:91, 125–26).

In a similar case that took place in June 1756, Guedelonguay, a Quapaw chief, and Toubamingo of the Ofogoula[14] arrived in New Orleans with the honored men of their nations to claim pardon for three French deserters and the soldier Jean Baptiste Bernard. Guedelonguay told Kerlérec that he regarded the deserters as his own children, "and that if they were put to death it would be to him as though it were his own children." To strengthen his argument for pardon he said that his nation was at war with the Chickasaw "as a mark of affection for the French" and that his son was killed there and his daughter wounded. He felt that the loss of his son and the spilled blood of his daughter were ample payment for the pardon he asked. He also told Kerlérec that "any man, guilty of whatever crime, who finds a way to take refuge in their sacred cabin where they practice their religion, is regarded as washed clean of his crime, and that it is customary among them that the man who is chief of the said cabin would sooner lose his life than allow the refugee to suffer the penalty for his crime." In other words, he was telling

Kerlérec that if pardon were denied these men who had sought refuge, then "he would not answer for the dangerous attacks and the rebellions that the chief of the sacred cabin could bring about and that would not fail to take place" (MPA:FD 1984, 5:173–75).

In these examples, we see that although the French and English were affecting the system of restitution in the Southeast, the practice continued, at least into the nineteenth century; however, women were becoming less involved in the decision-making. Since Choctaw men were the ones who traveled to French towns to receive or exchange goods, they also negotiated the fate of the French deserters. And since the French soldiers who visited the Choctaw typically met with the men, it makes sense that Choctaw men would express the decisions of their villages to the French. Thus the decline in the practice of restitution as well as the increasing responsibility of men to deliver those decisions involving French captives meant that Choctaw women were losing an influential role in their communities. Furthermore, with losses such as the Choctaw incurred in 1748 when they attacked their own people, women would not have been able, even with full decision-making power, to restore balance to their communities. The losses were too great to overcome with child-bearing or adoption of captives, a system that no longer worked as it once did.

Disappearance of Women

Although anyone, male or female, could be captured and sold or traded as a slave, the French and British typically desired female Indian slaves. European interest in female slaves created a region-wide climate of apprehension that all native women experienced. Native people were aware that the French often sold captives to French or Canadian families who needed laborers or shipped them overseas where they were never seen again. In one case when Boisbriant and Saint-Lambert, with some fifty Canadians, encountered an Alabama war party, they seized two Alabama men whom they bludgeoned to death and took one woman prisoner. Boisbriant later turned the woman prisoner over to Bienville, who sold her to one of the colony's families, where she remained for many years (Surrey 1916, 226; Higgenbotham 1977, 243). The French also shipped Indian captives to Cape Francois in Santo Domingo, "where they were sold as slaves for the benefit of the company"

(French 1853, 102). They sent Indian captives to the American islands in order to exchange them for West African slaves because Indian slaves often escaped and blended into other Indian communities or found their way back to their own communities, thus causing loss of an "investment" and a source of labor for the French (MPA:FD 1929, 2:23, 45).

Enemies of the Choctaw often sold Choctaw captives to the English. When English traders obtained Indian slaves, they bound them with cords and held them in some sort of barracoon-like holding area until enough slaves had been accumulated to ship off to Carolina. The purchasers in Charleston would then sell Indian captives, primarily women and children, as slaves to the English seaboard colonies (New England and New York) or overseas to the West Indies. Although male Indian slaves were usually sold overseas, it is likely that some women were too. Some of the Indian captives were kept in the South where they worked alongside black slaves in rice and other crop fields (Galloway 1982, 159–60; Perdue 1979, 28; Wright 1981, 148).

Although the French most likely did not enslave Choctaw women because it would have jeopardized their alliance with the Choctaw, the English did. The number of Choctaw women enslaved is not known. However, Iberville noted in his log that he reminded the Chickasaw about the number of lives it had cost them to capture five hundred Choctaw who were sold into slavery. Galloway estimates that British allies probably enslaved several hundred Choctaw before the coming of the French in 1699 and only a few hundred after that date (1995, 196, 203). Knowing the exact number of Choctaw women enslaved is less important than understanding the impact of living in a region where Indian women slaves were constantly sought. J. Leitch Wright Jr., a scholar of Southeastern history, estimates that "between the sixteenth and eighteenth centuries tens of thousands of southern Indians" were enslaved (1981, 148). The fear of capture and enslavement affected all native women.

Although the Choctaw could reconcile the deaths of their men in accordance with their ideas of restitution, they could not account for the enslavement and disappearance of women according to their traditions. Holding captives in conditions similar to those for holding convicts and selling them as slaves were antithetical to the meaning attached to indigenous ways of dealing with captives. The captives were neither treated as relatives, in other words, with kindness and affection, nor were they given opportunity to demonstrate valor and courage through torture. Their lives were not even used to release the beloved spirits of their enemies' relatives. In other words, detention in holding areas and slavery had no meaning within a Southeastern native context. Thus the captives, mainly women and children, became nonentities. They were unable to demonstrate courage and honor through torture and their lives were not valued as replacements for those who had died at the hands of their people. While women were usually treated as property to be bought and sold, the men as warriors were typically killed.[15] So, although the death of a male Indian meant the death of an enemy or elimination of a potential threat to the French or English, for native people the death still fit into their system of restitution. The Choctaw could reconcile the deaths of their men as restitution for the killing of European men or Indian allies of Europeans. They could reason that the French and British had killed the men in response to some perceived wrong. In the Southeastern indigenous world those men died according to the rules of warfare; women, however, simply disappeared.

The French enslaved women but they typically killed male Indians because they perceived them as threatening. They assumed men went to war and women did not. Since the French and the British did not tend to view women as threats, they became highly valued as slaves and served as a medium of exchange. The value placed on women slaves can be seen in the risks some of Bienville's men took when they marched on White Apple Village in 1723 to attack the Natchez. Bienville garnered volunteers by promising the men they could keep as slaves any women that they caught. Upon discovering some men and women in a cabin near the village, a recent settler at Fort Rosalie probably in great need of laborers, "wishing to profit by the commandant's promise, that whoever took a squaw might keep her as a slave, in hopes of carrying off one of those he had seen, and without observing the risk he ran, left the main body and ran up to the cabin door." He was shot ripping open the door of dry canes and when he fell another settler entered the cabin and managed to grab the man who had shot the first settler. The men in the cabin were killed, the women taken as slaves (French 1853, 51–53).

Native people were drawn into this world of slavery, which not only increased the danger of enslavement for women but also took away women's responsibility for the disposition of captives. If men were killed by the enemy, or were away from villages, the women had less protection from enemies seeking slaves. In 1702 the Chickasaw who had taken a young Choctaw captive told

Tonty that the Englishman in their country "made them kill every day in order to get slaves" (Galloway 1982, 169). When the French entered the country they and the English began using captives as a way of controlling the political landscape. For example, in February 1705, the English convinced some Chickasaw warriors to seize several Choctaw families who were visiting the Chickasaw villages. The English then took the Choctaw captives to Carolina, hoping to cause a breach in the French-negotiated alliance between the Choctaw and Chickasaw. The result was a retaliatory act by the Choctaw that cost numerous Chickasaw lives. A year later, Bienville felt he had successfully reestablished an alliance between the Chickasaw and Choctaw, only to learn two months later that the Chickasaw had attacked a Choctaw village, taking one hundred and fifty captives that they sold to the English as slaves (Higgenbotham 1977, 209–10, 242). More than likely, many of those slaves were women.

Breakdown of Choctaw Societal Structures

The increasingly dangerous landscape in the Lower Mississippi Valley contributed to the lack of information about Choctaw women's lives as well as to changes in their roles in Choctaw society. The threat of captivity, rape, and slavery meant that Indian women throughout the Lower Mississippi Valley had to curtail, change, or eliminate those activities that required leaving the safety of villages or that took place in the presence of outsiders such as the French. In the case of the Choctaw, as women withdrew from public spaces, the French had fewer occasions to observe the women and to document their activities. As the Choctaw began to interact more and more with French militia or civilian officers, reports about Choctaw women declined because the interests of those French men were directed elsewhere. The French were more concerned about Choctaw military strength and they did not perceive women as an important factor in Choctaw military activities. The Choctaw also took actions to safeguard women, which meant they were less visible to French visitors. Thus fewer observations about women's roles appeared in the pages of French documents. However, limited documentation does not mean Choctaw women did not participate in political activities. The fact is we do not know the extent of Choctaw women's participation in political activities. However, we do know that as late as 1830 Choctaw women elders participated in the council at the Treaty of Dancing Rabbit Creek.

Just as critical for those women who escaped captivity and slavery was the undermining of the system of restoring order and wholeness to a community that had suffered losses due to violence. In early contact history women had responsibility for the adoption or torture of captives. This made sense in the matrilineal world of the Choctaw because women determined one's clan membership and status in the community, whether by giving birth or by declaration. Women also fulfilled clan responsibilities to the spirits of the deceased by deciding the fate of captives. When Vaudreüil demanded that the Choctaw not seek restitution for the lives of pro-British Choctaw who were killed by French loyalists, and that the Choctaw return all captives taken during the Choctaw conflict, he was undermining the matrilineal system of the Choctaw. Through the matrilineal system Choctaw women determined family membership. In their role as the determiners of the fate of captives they also impacted their communities' well-being by deciding whether or not a captive took over the responsibilities of a valued contributor to the community who had been killed. The decision to trade captives for European goods or for the goodwill of the French or other Indian nations undermined women's ability to influence the conditions of their community. The breakdown of the system of restitution meant the breakdown of women's responsibility for family and ancestors, and in turn, a breakdown in their means for contributing to the economic and political life of their communities.

The French and later Spanish pressure to desist in torturing captives eventually led to the cessation of the practice. In 1779, according to historian Charles Gayarré, after an army of Spanish, free African Americans, and 160 Indians forced the surrender of the English at the fort of Baton Rouge, the Indians for the first time, "abstained from doing the slightest injury to the fugitives whome they captured" (1885, 3:132). After Great Britain, France, and Spain signed treaties of peace in 1783, the Spanish held a congress with the Chickasaw, Alabama, Choctaw, and other smaller nations on May 22, 1784, to sign treaties of alliance and commerce. The sixth article read:

> In conformity with the humanity and the generous sentiments cherished by the Spanish nation, we (the Indians) renounce for ever the custom of raising scalps, and of making slaves of our white captives; and, in case of our taking any prisoners . . . we bind ourselves to treat those prisoners with the kindness to which they are entitled,

> in imitation of the usages of civilized nations, reserving to ourselves the privilege of exchanging them against an equal number of Indians, or of receiving for them the quantity of goods which may be previously agreed upon, without making the slightest attempt against the lives of those captives. (Gayarré 1885, 3:161)

In other words the Choctaw agreed not to torture or adopt captives, but rather to exchange them for Choctaw captives or to trade them for goods, effectively eliminating women's roles in determining the fate of captives. Women could no longer help restore balance to a family or clan that had lost someone to an unnatural death. In essence they lost an important role that had given them status in their villages.

Choctaw women were also affected by the slave practices of Europeans that affected everyone throughout the Southeast. The English and French, who preferred women slaves, often sent slaves to Carolina, where they were confined in pens until they were sold. These women did not replace people who were killed nor did they give their lives in order to release the spirits of the deceased. In other words, they could not, as prisoners or slaves, reconcile their fate according to Southeastern native beliefs. They did not have rituals or teachings that prepared them for such a possibility. Among the Tohomé and Naniaba, two Choctaw-related nations, there was a scratching ritual that took place during the time of the harvest festival that prepared everyone for the possibility of being captured and tortured (Pénicaut 1953, 65). They did not have one that addressed bravery during enslavement. In fact, by not adopting a woman or taking her life, the French and British devalued her life. Her captivity served no purpose within the understanding of warfare and restitution among Choctaw people. She not only disappeared physically from the landscape, she also disappeared ideologically. She could not justify her enslavement according to her understanding of the world.

3

The Novel World of the Jesuits

French explorers, military personnel, and colonial officers were not the only French people to affect the lives of Choctaw women in the French colonial period. The missionaries who were sent to Louisiana Territory to work among the native people inevitably had an impact upon women. Their story is well known. Missionaries wanted to replace indigenous customs and beliefs with Christian morals and habits. In the case of native women, the missionaries wanted to teach them to be subservient to their husbands, to restrict sexual relations, and to dress more modestly. This familiar story, however, has received little notice in the case of French missionaries in the Lower Mississippi Valley primarily because many scholars have assumed French Catholics had a minimal effect upon the Choctaw and because little documentation exists on the French missionary experience. Such assumptions have left us with a picture of late eighteenth-century Choctaw women that does not adequately take into account the effects of missionary contact upon those women during the French colonial period.

In order to understand the extent of missionary influence on Choctaw women's roles, we cannot approach this study as if missionaries operated in a vacuum. The influence of the missionaries spread beyond the communities they encountered, as native people shared stories with one another. The missionaries also did not function solely as messengers of Catholicism. Their actions were inextricably tied to French political and civil concerns. Thus this study of missionary impact on Choctaw women's roles will draw upon the experiences of native people throughout the Mississippi Valley and will examine missionary work within the context of the French colonial experience.

In many ways the impact of French military and civil affairs upon Choctaw women's lives is easier to discern than that arising from missionary work. French officers, military and provincial, of necessity had to report their encounters with indigenous people, particularly since they needed to support requests for military-related and civil-related activities. The complicated system of constantly shifting alliances between and among various Indian nations and the French and British required continuous negotiation, gift-giving, and military presence on the part of the French. Adroit strategizing required that military intelligence be gathered from native people, traders, colonists, military personnel, and especially missionaries. Officers, historians or recorders, soldiers, and missionaries recorded French encounters with indigenous people, thus providing multiple impressions from which to reconstruct military and political events and their impact upon women. The same cannot be said for religious matters. The paucity of written narratives by or about the French Catholic missionaries makes it difficult, but not impossible, to ascertain their impact on native people in general and more specifically on Choctaw women.

Documentation about French missionary activities in Louisiana Territory is not as rich as that for the missionaries in Canada for a number of reasons. One reason is that on February 10, 1673, Clement X prohibited the publication of books without written permission from the Cardinals of Propaganda. In obedience to the pope, the Society of Jesus stopped publishing the *Jesuit Relations*, although they continued to send annual reports to their superiors and to correspond with friends and officials in Louisiana and the Home Government in Paris (Delanglez 1935, 375–78). Another reason for the scarcity of material is that in addition to the disincentive to publish the *Jesuit Relations*, the later collection of *The Jesuit Relations and Allied Documents* included little from the Louisiana mission. According to Reuben Gold Thwaites, who wrote the introduction to the 1925 compilation of selected reports from the *Jesuit Relations*, "the Louisiana mission, an offshoot of that of New France did faithful work here, but the documentary result was neither as interesting nor as prolific and necessarily occupies but a small space in the present series" (Kenton 1925, xxvii–xxviii).

The study of French Catholic missionization in Louisiana Territory also suffers from lack of scholarly attention. Although French missionaries were in the Lower Mississippi Valley for seventy years, many historians as well as French colonial officials of the time argue that French Catholics had a negligible impact among indigenous peoples.[1] Their ineffectiveness has been attributed to lack of funds, poor organization, too few missionaries, and a constant state of warfare (Baudier 1939, 22; Delanglez 1935, 477; Bekkers 1902, 357). Because of the generally accepted view that the French Catholic missionaries were ineffective, many accounts of the Choctaw missionary experience gloss over the French colonial period and begin their story with the 1817 Choctaw request to the American Board of Commissioners for Foreign Missions that missionaries be sent to them, thus leaving out an important component of the process of colonization of the Choctaw.[2]

For church historians and scholars of the colonial Southeast, negligible impact is determined by the failure of foreign mission work to become fully established in the Lower Mississippi Valley. They point out that the foreign mission was never adequately organized and too few missionaries were sent to work among native people. Those missionaries who established missions seemed to make little progress in converting Indians. In the case of the Choctaw, John Gilmary Shea characterized missionary work among them as "unproductive," although the Jesuit Father Michel Baudoüin labored among them for twenty years (1855, 450). Jean Delanglez attributed Baudoüin's ineffectiveness to the constant state of war among the Choctaw as well as to the limitations of having one missionary cover such a large nation (1935, 477). Some Choctaw people also may have felt that Baudoüin was ineffective. According to Romans, the Choctaw he encountered told him of a missionary they called "a woman" and whom they frequently asked to "undo his ceremony of baptism" (1775, 52).[3] The missionaries' impact is also considered minimal because little of Catholicism remained after they left Louisiana in 1763. What edifices and religious paraphernalia that the French Catholics left behind did not survive long nor were they replaced. In the case of the Choctaw the chapel Baudoüin had built for them was destroyed; however, a cross constructed of yellow pine was still standing as late as 1771 (Romans 1775, 52). Scholars also cite the few records that exist of Indian baptisms or Christian marriages as further proof of the missionaries' ineffectiveness among the native people. Those records that exist indicate that the missionaries often had a difficult time making converts to Catholicism (Shea 1855, 441).

The missionaries realized their service was viewed as ineffective because they failed to gain converts or to baptize large numbers of Indian people. One Jesuit made known his awareness of the charges leveled against them when he wrote, "If our missions are not so flourishing as others on account of the great number of conversions, they are at least precious and beneficial *to us*" (Delanglez 1935, 380; JR 66:255). However, lack of conversions and baptisms does not of itself constitute negligible impact. To begin with we do not know how many baptisms took place. The absence of records of baptisms can be attributed in part to limited information about the Louisiana Territory missions in the *Jesuit Relations* and the unlikeliness of missionaries regularly traveling long distances through difficult and dangerous territory to record baptisms in parish registers (Delanglez 1935, 477 n. 52; Higginbotham 1977, 303).

More important, conversions and baptisms are not the only indicators of missionary effectiveness. If we limit our analysis of missionary influence in the Lower Mississippi Valley to number of converts to Catholicism, then we ignore the numerous ways in which missionaries insinuated French and Catholic thought among indigenous people directly and indirectly. For example, although French militia or traders preferred to negotiate with men, they also wanted the company of women. Missionaries, however, not only excluded women from many of their activities, they avoided being alone with them. Their conspicuous roles as religious leaders meant native people noticed their actions and talked about them. No doubt, stories about the behavior of individual missionaries were told and retold throughout the territory, including among the Choctaw, through a complex network of kinship, alliance, and trade networks.

Missionary responsibility to civil, military, and religious authorities meant that numerous interests influenced their actions. The French government wanted missionaries among the Indians to "counteract the influence of the English, or to have among them permanent ambassadors on whom they could rely" (Delanglez 1935, 412). In November 1702 Iberville wrote letters to Louis-Marc Bergier, vicar-general of the bishop of Quebec and missionary to the Tamaroa; Father Albert Davion at the Tunica; Father Nicolas Foucault at the Arkansas; and Father Jean-François Buisson de Saint-Cosme at the Natchez, asking them to relay information to various Indian nations and to persuade them to join the French alliance (Higgenbotham 1977, 79). The Commissaires in Paris informed the Council of Louisiana in 1721 that "nothing is more advantageous than to attach these nations to France by means of religion" (Delanglez 1935, 412–13). To support their efforts, colonial officers in New Orleans constantly requested missionaries who would not only Christianize Indians, but also make allies of them. When Sieur de Lusser, Captain of Infantry, traveled to various Choctaw towns to question the Choctaw about their allegiance to the French following the Natchez attack, Father Baudoüin accompanied him. Father Baudoüin also helped Monsieur de Beauchamps, major of Mobile, to convince Quikanabé Mingo, a Concha, to sever his ties to Ymatahatchitou[4] and the English who were enemies of the French (Delanglez 1935, 457; Mereness 1916, 275; MPA 1927, 95). Such alliances fostered a climate of violence that forced women to circumscribe their activities in numerous ways.

The French particularly desired missionary aid in fostering alliances with the Choctaw, who represented the largest and most strategically placed group between the French and the English. In December 1758 Kerlérec described how Father Baudoüin, who had been residing in Chickasawhay, one of the largest villages of the Choctaw Nation, had "always maintained the Choctaws of this part in the most marked attachment to us" (MPA:FD 1984, 5:213). Father François Philibut Watrin suggested the same when he said that the Jesuits in Louisiana kept the Indians "in alliance and friendship with the French . . . especially in the Chactas nation" (Biever 1924, 54). When the French were unable to provide the requisite gifts to the Choctaw in exchange for their alliance, Father Baudoüin was the one to convince the Choctaw that the presents would be forthcoming. He also accompanied the Choctaw to Mobile where they assembled for the distribution of gifts. Since he spent time visiting each of the Choctaw villages, he could inform the governor as to who was the most friendly and most important among the Choctaw delegates (JR 70:239–41). Although the missionaries were concerned with converting Indians to Catholicism and resocializing them according to French culture, they also were invested in providing military intelligence to colonial officials. Often the only French occupant in Indian villages who also traveled through dangerous country, the missionaries required military protection. They also depended upon French commissaries for food and supplies. The Jesuits knew that they had to appeal to the pecuniary and material interests of the Directors of the Company of the Indies and the French government in order to convince them to provide more missionaries and supplies. Once missionaries settled in Indian villages they became intermediaries providing intelligence to French leaders and relaying French considerations to the Indians (Delanglez 1935, 414; Higgenbotham 1977, 79; Peyser 1992, 148). Their missions became centers for teaching Christianity as well as for negotiating military and political strategies. Missionary homes served as gathering places for males to consult about national affairs to the exclusion of women. In the case of the Choctaw, the importance of Baudoüin's mission to French/Choctaw relations meant Baudoüin had many opportunities to insinuate French Catholic ideas about women into the consciousness of Choctaw people.

Indian Mission Fields

In order to appreciate the extent to which missionaries entered the consciousness of Choctaw people, we have to take a look at their entire mission field in Louisiana Territory. Native people traveled throughout the Lower Mississippi Valley and had interactions with each other. Thus, whether Choctaw parties encountered other native people on their hunting and gathering trips, or visited other tribes, or were visited by them, they had many opportunities to hear about the missionaries and their efforts. Most likely the Choctaw heard about the French in 1682 when La Salle began his exploration of the Mississippi River, accompanied by the Récollet Zénobe Membré as chaplain.[5] La Salle, while not a Jesuit, as a youth had been part of the order, and his brother, Jean Cavelier, was a Sulpitian priest (Fortier 1904, 14). La Salle thus had an interest in supporting missionary efforts in the Lower Mississippi Valley. Although the Choctaw did not meet Membré, they undoubtedly heard of him through their neighbors the Arkansas,[6] Chickasaw, Taensa, Natchez, Coroa,[7] Ouma, and Quinipissa,[8] who had encountered La Salle's expedition (Fortier 1904, 23–24; Galloway 1982, 148–49; Minet 1682, 45, 47, 50–51, 53). Native people would have shared stories about observing strangers disembarking from their boats to rest or hunt for food, and beloved men who carried out rituals they later learned were called masses.

More certain is that native people came upon the crosses and signs that the early missionaries left behind. Wherever the missionaries and explorers went, they marked their passing with crosses and by carving the name Jesus upon trees. When La Salle's expedition reached the mouth of the Mississippi, they erected a column painted with the arms of France and a cross. As they erected the column and cross, they sang *Te Deum*, the *Exaudiat, Domine, salvam fac Regem*, and *Vexilla* (Biever 1924, 11, 17; Fortier 1904, 24–25). The missionaries also left behind by design and by accident other artifacts that made their way into Indian villages. For example, a prayer book, probably left by Tonty's 1685 expedition, was found among the Choctaw-related Mongoulacha[9] by Iberville in 1699 (Baudier 1939, 25). All of these artifacts left some kind of imprint on the cognitive world of the indigenous people, and they became part of the stories told about the strangers.[10]

French missionaries quickly settled among the native people in Louisiana Territory to begin mission work. Although their tenure was often short, nonetheless they changed the lives of native people. Fathers François de Montigny, Davion, and Saint-Cosme set up the first missions in 1699. Father de Montigny settled for a short time among the Natchez and the Taensa in northeast Louisiana and Father Saint-Cosme stayed with the Arkansas and Tamaroa[11] for a little while before traveling farther south to work among the Natchez for six years. Father Davion remained the longest of the three, working with the Tunica and other Indian people for twenty-two years. The following year Father Anastase Douay, a Récollet, arrived and spent a short time among the Mongoulacha, and Father Jacques Gravier, superior at Michillimackinac and vicar-general of the bishop for the Illinois country, visited the Natchez and Tamarois. That same year Bergier, vicar-general of the bishop of Saint-Vallier of Quebec for the missions in the Mississippi Valley, and his helper Michel Buisson de Saint-Cosme, succeeded the older Saint-Cosme at the Tamarois mission. Other missionaries who spent time among native people included Alexandre Huvé, who was assigned to the Apalachee immigrants from Talimali and Chacato villages; Father Joseph de Limoges, a Jesuit from Canada, who began to preach among the Houma; and Father Paul Du Ru,[12] a Jesuit who took up residency at Biloxi and visited the neighboring nations. The following year, in April 1701, Abbé Nicholas Foucault arrived among the Tamaroa to assist Bergier. However, he soon left the Tamaroa to work among the Arkansas, Yazoo, and Tunica (Baudier 1939, 19–27; McWilliams 1981, 109; DCB 1966–, vols. 1 and 2; MPA:FD 1929, 2:13 n. 3; Higgenbotham 1977, 97, 293; JR 65:265 n. 13).

After four years most of the missionaries had left the mission fields in Louisiana and Mississippi. Father Davion was the only missionary among those who had been assigned to the Indian mission to remain, although he no longer lived among the Tunica. Sometime after 1716 he moved to New Orleans, where he remained until his death in 1727. One other missionary, a Carmelite, Father Charles de St. Alexis, arrived as *curé* in Old Biloxi in 1721. He later was assigned to work among the Catholic Apalachee, who had relocated near Mobile after their missions and villages had been destroyed in 1704 (Baudier 1939, 32–33, 50–51; Shea 1855, 444–45 n.; Hann 1988, 305, 306, 310). In 1722 the Capuchins, Carmelites, and Jesuits were assigned mission territory in Louisiana; however, the only nation to have a resident missionary was the Apalachee, who were served by the Récollet Father Victorin (Baudier 1939, 75). In February 1726, the Company of the Indies and Bishop de St. Vallier determined that the Capuchins were not as suited for Indian mission work as the Jesuits. Thus the coadjutor of Quebec turned over the care of all Indians in Louisiana territory to the Jesuits, and the following year the mission among the Arkansas was restored (Baudier 1939, 67, 119).

Although missions were not established among the main body of Choctaw until 1727, Choctaw delegates traveled to and from the indigenous nations along the Mississippi as well as the French settlements at Biloxi, Mobile, and New Orleans, where they encountered missionaries or native people familiar with Christianity.[13] Father Mathurin Le Petit established the first mission among the Choctaw in 1727 (MPA:FD 1929, 2:594; MPA:FD 1984, 4:35 n. 6).[14] However, the most influential missionary among the Choctaw was Reverend Father Michael Baudoüin, a Jesuit who knew the language and lived among them from 1729 to 1748.[15] According to Baudoüin he traveled through a majority of the Choctaw villages and he resided in Chickasawhay, whose chief had authority over the Six Towns. Although the Chickasawhay chief was never the most influential in the Choctaw nation, the town's southern location meant it was frequented by the chiefs of the nation who passed through it continually either to go get their presents at Mobile or to trade at the Yowani where they had a storehouse (MPA:FD 1927, 1:156; Galloway 1985b, 126, 133). Thus the Jesuit mission was located in an area where the missionary had opportunity to interact with a great number of Choctaw directly and indirectly.

Father Nicolas Le Febvre arrived in Louisiana in 1748 as a successor for Baudoüin. He wrote to Father Pierre Potier that missionary efforts would be concentrated on the Choctaw. However, both missionaries were forced to return to New Orleans that year because of the civil war that had broken out among the Choctaw. Father Le Febvre returned to Choctaw country after the war, probably in 1750. There are no records to indicate how long he remained among the Choctaw although he left New Orleans in 1764. One other Jesuit, Father Morand, went to the Choctaw mission in 1734 after he was forced to leave the Alibamon mission. He probably did not stay long before returning to New Orleans (Delanglez 1935, 474, 476 n. 45, 485, 527; JR 71:176).

Mission work among the Choctaw and other native people in Louisiana Territory ended in 1763. During the previous year, on August 6, following a period of struggle between the Jesuits and the government of France over the ecclesiastical-state relationship, the Parlement of Paris announced that the Jesuits were to be barred from France. Although the king did not agree with the Parlement's actions he suppressed the Jesuits, but allowed them to remain in the country (Bangert 1972, 377–78; JR 70:213). The Superior Council of Louisiana followed suit and on July 9, 1763, decreed that the Jesuits were "hostile to royal authority, to the rights of Bishops and to public peace and safety." Like the Parlement of Paris, the committee also charged that "the Jesuits established in the colony *had not taken any care of their missions, that they had thought only of making their estates valuable and that they were usurpers of the vicariate-general of New Orleans*" (JR 70:221). The Superior Council declared that "the vows pronounced by the Society of Jesus were null and void." They forbade the Jesuits to take the name of Jesuit or to wear the habit of the Order. From then on they were to wear the garb of secular priests and they were ordered to return to France. Everyone left except Father Baudoüin and Father Mourin, both of whom retired to New Orleans. Their expulsion effectively ended seventy years of French Jesuit work in the Lower Mississippi Valley (Baudier 1939, 162–63, 166–67; Shea 1855, 451; JR 70:219).

Although the missionary program in Louisiana was never stable, it was not completely ineffective. The missionaries left their mark on the material and cognitive world of the indigenous people. To appreciate the impact of French Catholics on Choctaw people, we have to consider their influence within a larger context. The lack of established missions among the Choctaw prior to 1727 does not mean Catholic missionaries did not have an effect on the Choctaw. The Choctaw regularly interacted with other native people throughout the Lower Mississippi Valley and the missionaries frequently made trips between French posts and Indian missions. The missionaries and the Choctaw had many opportunities to learn about each other directly and indirectly, and such interactions had the potential to impact Choctaw women's lives.

We also cannot assume that the impact of French Catholic missionaries was limited to their tenure among the Choctaw or other native people. Just as relevant to our concern about missionary influence on the immediate lives of Choctaw women is the lasting influence of seventy years of French Catholic influence on women's roles long after the expulsion of the Jesuits. Some elements are immediately apparent. The Choctaw handed down stories about white holy men for many generations. In 1822 one elderly Choctaw, Chahta immatahah, told Gideon Lincecum that when he was a young boy an elderly man related the history of the Choctaw to him. He told of how the Nahullo (white people) dishonored their women, and in particular, a "large fat man, with long black dress, and the golden cross" who "often succeeded, to decoy their young women into his presence" (Lincecum 1861, 48–49, 78, 82–83, 85). Although the Choctaw elder obviously confused Spanish and French events, nonetheless, memories of mistreatment of Choctaw women were being passed down from generation to generation.[16] However, less evident to us is how the experiences of those Choctaw women might have shaped later impressions about Choctaw women in general.

Those impressions, over time, however seemingly imperceptible to our much-distanced gaze, continued to order and reorder themselves in Choctaw consciousness. By taking a *longue durée* perspective, we should be able to discern changes that took place in Choctaw society or women's roles between 1698 and 1763 by making "full use of evidence, images, and landscapes dating from other periods, earlier and later and even from the present day" (Braudel 1972, 23). We can expand our thinking about the study of French Catholic influence in two ways. First, we can look beyond the "history of brief, rapid nervous fluctuations" of a single period "as it was felt, described, and lived by contemporaries whose lives were as short and as short-sighted as ours" (Braudel 1972, 21). We can search for ways in which the influences of a single period affected the longer history not only through concrete, easily discernible ways, but also through more subtle changes in consciousness. The impact of the missionaries was not limited only to the epoch within which they lived but flowed onward, perhaps in diminishing forms, into subsequent periods. Mikhail M. Bakhtin, a social thinker and philosopher of language, wrote that "trying to understand and explain a work solely in terms of the conditions of its epoch alone, solely in terms of the conditions of the most immediate time . . . makes it impossible to understand the work's future life in subsequent centuries" (1986, x, xiv, 3–4). The fullness of the work "is revealed only in *great time*," in its continuation of the past and its shaping of the future (1986, 5). Although Bakhtin is referring to the creation of literary works, to the way in which literature draws on the past and affects the future, the same could be said of history. The present grows out of the past and influences the future.

The stories the Choctaw told of missionaries cannot be separated from the entire French colonial experience nor can they be understood only in terms of the epoch in which they were created. Although the missionary experience seemed unproductive in its epoch from a Western, French Catholic perspective, the stories the Choctaw told about the missionaries and the French continued to have an impact long after the stories ceased to be told. I suggest, for example, that the Choctaw's "ardent desire" for a mission school in 1817 may have reflected their memories of black robes or holy men's willingness to live among them and to educate them. Their eagerness "for education, not Christian salvation" may also be an indication of their memories about French Catholic ideas that did not suit them (Kidwell 1995b, 27–28).

In addition to recognizing the "great time" nature of the early missionary experience, we also must be aware that the nature of contact is acquisition of knowledge and new understandings. In his reading of Bakhtin's dialogism, Andreas Kriefall suggests that each individual involved in a dialogical relation recognizes the "other" and becomes through that recognition more than one was. In other words, the individual acquires new understanding (1998, 180). When Indian people recognized the "other," in this case French missionaries, that new understanding they acquired had to be integrated into their cognitive world. This dialogical relation took place through language as well as material culture. Thus questions arise as to what meanings the Indian people assigned to religious ideas and paraphernalia of the missionaries and how they integrated those symbols into their cognitive world. More pertinent to this study, we need to ask how the integration of new symbols impacted Choctaw women and their daughters and granddaughters.

Resocializing Choctaw People

The French Catholics assigned to Louisiana Territory to work among the indigenous people had decades of Jesuit experience among the Indians of New France to prepare them for what lay ahead. They no doubt had studied the Jesuit accounts of missionary encounters with Algonquian, Montagnais, and Huron people. The stories of native people running around practically naked, unrestrained in their sexual activity, must have convinced them of the urgency to bring Christianity into Indians' lives. The Jesuits, in particular, were prepared to go among native people and learn their languages quickly and to study their cultures so they could communicate Catholic ideas to them through native concepts. The Jesuit order demanded that missionaries working among native people have the ability to learn their language. Otherwise, they were "useless laborers" (Delanglez 1935, 384). The missionaries also utilized "religious pictures in an effort to make them understand something about God." They urged native people to build churches and crosses. One of the most impressive works involved the Houma. With Du Ru's urging they built a fifty-foot-long chapel and a cross that was thirty-five or forty feet high in the center of the public gathering place in the village (Baudier 1939, 26; JR 65:149). Catholic mission work included resocializing native people to French customs.

Missionary goals and French habits often intersected with indigenous customs in ways that facilitated the resocialization process. For example, part of the adaptation to French culture included giving Indian people French names. And Indian customs included naming a child after a beloved person to demonstrate respect and, hopefully, to reinforce the desirable traits of the beloved one in the child. So it is not surprising that when Saint-Cosme, who began to missionize among the Natchez in 1700, apparently gained the favor of the female chief, she was "so attached to the Black-gown that she conferred his name on one of her sons" (Shea 1855, 441). The female chief was following Natchez custom, but in doing so, she participated in a resocialization process that kept the missionary alive in their consciousness at least as long as the child carried his name.

Although not enough evidence is available from the French Catholic missionary period to indicate whether Choctaw commonly adopted French names, we know that it was common among other missionized native people. A few Choctaw people had names that reflected their experience with the French. For example, the western chief from West Yazoo, who came to be known as the English chief, went by the name Franchimastabé, which translates as "Kills a French Man." John R. Swanton translates his name as "He-took-a-Frenchman-and-killed-him" (1931, 122). The chief of the Sixtowns in the Southern Division was known as Chatenoqué. Unfortunately, the origin of his name is not known. Whether a missionary or a Choctaw conferred a French name on a Choctaw person, the outcome was the same. The name became a symbol, a reminder, of the French Catholic presence. Through the simple act of naming, French Catholic culture entered the cognitive world of the Choctaw. The act of naming connected the one named to another family or community, in this case the French. Intermarriage also contributed to the presence of French names among the Choctaw. At the very least Choctaw matrilineal conventions met French Catholic patriarchal practices that necessitated recognition and integration into their cognitive world.

The missionaries understood that customs and ideologies reinforce each other. They believed if they could change the habits of native people, they could also change their ideologies. Paul Le Jeune, who worked among the Huron and Montagnai-Naskapi in Canada, wrote that he wanted to make the Indians "so accustomed to our food and our clothes, that they will have a horror of the savages and their filth" (JR 9:107). Le Jeune believed if he could convince native people that their customs reflected ignorance and savageness, then it would be only a matter of time before they would desire to be like the French, which also meant being Catholic. The missionaries serving in Louisiana, many of whom trained in Quebec, adhered to the same methods and goals as the Jesuits in Canada. Thus by 1716 the Tunica chief had adopted European clothing and had acquired some facility in the French language (Shea 1855, 444). Reportedly, a Tohomé leader who had converted to Christianity refused to see his relatives. According to Beauchamp the Tohomé chief had said "that being Christian he no longer thought about the red men, and thought himself lucky to have left them" (MPA:FD 1984, 4:273; Mereness 1961, 267). The adoption of French names, mode of dress, or food was just the beginning of efforts to resocialize the indigenous people.

The missionaries were particularly concerned with the dress and sexual habits of native women. Since they were often the only French people living in Indian towns, the missionaries worried about their own exposure to what they considered to be licentious behavior on the part of women. Jesuit theologians in the seventeenth century taught young scholars that those who fall into sin did so because girls had looked at them. In fact, Father J. J. Surin, a seventeenth-century Jesuit, instructed students in Jesuit colleges that in order not to be debauched they should avoid having conversations with women (Anderson 1991, 71). The missionaries' fears about their own weaknesses and their abhorrence of native women's sexual behavior worked in concert with the changing political landscape to estrange women from diplomatic and military activities.

The rapidity with which native people adopted some French expressions gives us an indication of how quickly missionary influence could infiltrate Choctaw society. A case in point is the diplomatic ritual among native people in the Lower Mississippi Valley that included the presentation of a white staff or feather by an entourage of men and women followed by a ceremonial caressing of each other. For example, in February 1699, a group of Biloxi and Pascagoula signaled their peaceful intentions to Iberville by presenting him a plank of whitened wood. Two days later when Iberville reached the village of the Bayogoula the chief of the village passed his hands over Iberville and his guides, the Annocchy. He caressed their faces and breasts, and then passed his hands over their hands, after which he raised his hands to the sky rubbing them together. Iberville then caressed the chief in a similar manner. A short time later, all of the Bayogoula then embraced all of Iberville's men (McWilliams 1981, 44–46). Caressing another person or object signaled a welcoming as well as indicated that the person or object was beloved. Caressing could also indicate an extending of power or blessings to a loved person. For example, among the Taensa, mothers extended their hands toward the sun and then transferred the blessings of the sun to their children by rubbing their hands on their children's bodies. People also wiped their hands in the dirt where important people had stepped and then rubbed their bodies (Swanton 1911, 263).

Native people recognized that the missionaries and French explorers treated the cross with great respect and they responded to the cross accordingly. When La Salle and Father Membré planted a cross in the Arkansas region together with the royal arms, a curious crowd of Indians watched. Afterward, the Indians rubbed their hands over their bodies, then over the cross. Later they erected a palisade around the cross (Galloway 1987b, 47; Ogg 1904, 107–8). In another example, after Iberville's men planted a cross at the village of the Houma in March 1699 and distributed some presents, the chiefs of the Houma, "each holding a wooden cross in his hand, made a circuit processionally of the cross ... throwing tobacco upon and around it, and singing after their manner" (Swanton 1911, 287). In both cases native people quickly acknowledged the importance of the cross to the French by showing respect for it and by appropriating the symbol. This example also demonstrates how quickly Indian people could adopt foreign ways.

Thus, when the Biloxi and Pascagoula presented a white plank of wood to Iberville and his men, and then caressed the French men's bodies, they were signaling their peaceful intentions and respect for the French. The French explorers in turn indicated their peaceful intentions by presenting crosses to the native people. The native people recognized the sacredness of the cross to the French and immediately treated it appropriately according to their customs by sometimes running their hands over the cross or by protecting it with palisades. Interestingly, just one year after La Salle's visit, in March 1700, the chief and two distinguished men of the Ouma greeted Iberville with white crosses in their hands (McWilliams 1981, 68). The Ouma knew that the French explorers and the missionaries who accompanied them planted white crosses along the Mississippi River. They most likely did not understand that the French were proclaiming the land as French territory but they did understand that the cross was sacred to the French. More importantly, the Ouma added the symbol of Christianity to their own emblems such as the calumet as an international symbol of diplomatic intentions.[17] From this example we can see how quickly some Christian symbols were adopted by native people.

Of particular importance to this study is the presence of men only among the French explorers. French men were the ones who presented crosses to native people. Native people noticed the absence of women among the French expeditions they encountered, especially since women were present in their own excursions away from home.[18] For example, according to Father Le Petit, whenever an Indian nation approached the Natchez seeking peace, the delegation ordinarily consisted of thirty men and six women (JR 68:157–58). Certainly the Biloxi, Pascagoula, and Ouma as well as other Lower Mississippi Valley native peoples recognized that the beloved people of the French who carried the crosses were always men. If Indian people wanted to demonstrate respect for the diplomatic acts of French explorers, it is possible they would in like manner have only their men present white crosses to French expeditions. Later, this practice may have become more institutionalized as women withdrew from diplomatic encounters because of the increasing dangers of warfare and slavery.

Concurrent with the normalizing of men only as ambassadors of peace is the missionary concern with the sinfulness of the human body and sexual impropriety. It is very likely that Indian people also caressed the missionaries as part of their diplomatic rituals and the missionaries probably did not approve of such exchanges. During the same 1699 expedition, after Father Anatase Douay, a Récollet, said mass before the Indians and blessed the cross that Iberville had planted, the Mongoulacha, in turn, held "elaborate ceremonies for the French visitors, which included the rubbing of their stomachs," to which Father Douay reportedly "submitted reluctantly" (Baudier 1939, 25).[19] Father Douay no doubt would have thought twice about submitting to caressing by Indian women because the Jesuits of the time perceived women as threats to their chastity. Father Le Maire, who spent some time among the Apalachee, wrote of Indian women as "weak and impudent" and warned that missionaries must be strong because "occasions are always present" that would challenge their call to be chaste (1985, 154).

Missionaries were particularly concerned with the immodesty of women's dress. Indian women in Lower Louisiana Territory tended to wear covering only on the lower half of their bodies, sometimes with tassels, which made their bodies "appear sinuous" whenever they moved (McWilliams 1981, 44–45 n. 55). Choctaw women wore skirts made of bison wool and plant fibers. Their upper bodies were covered with elaborate tattoos made up of whorls and lines (Swanton 1946, 450; Romans 1775, 54, 56). The Jesuits viewed women's manner of dress and sexual activities as evidence that they were temptresses.[20] Fear of their own susceptibility would have caused the missionaries to cringe at the thought of women greeting them with ritual caressing. Although embracing was common among the French, the missionaries probably avoided the more intimate caressing with women that would have caused native people to wonder about their behavior. In addition to their own celibacy, the missionaries also encouraged native women to clothe more of their bodies and to limit sexual relations to the marriage bed for purposes of procreation. Thus, not only did missionaries contribute to changes in women's appearance and intimate relationships, but through their proprietorship of crosses and their reluctance to participate in ritual greetings with women, combined with increased violence in the Lower Mississippi Valley, they also played a pivotal role in the withdrawal of women from many diplomatic encounters.

Missionary concern with fidelity and marriage also affected relations between Choctaw men and women, and, in turn, community customs. The Jesuits taught Indian people that their sexual relations and their customs of polygamy and divorce were sinful. A study of *The Jesuit Relations* reveals a distinct and strongly motivated desire on the part of the Jesuits to change the roles of Indian women in their societies as well as rules governing marriage and divorce. In speaking of native people in New France, Le Jeune wrote, "the inconstancy of marriages and the facility with which they divorce each other, are a great obstacle to the Faith of Jesus Christ" (JR 22:229). The Jesuits paid extraordinary attention to the conduct of women, which they commented on regularly. A typical response was repeated by Father Gravier, who described the Natchez as "polygamous, thievish and Very depraved—the girls and women being even more so than the men and boys, among whom a great reformation must be effected before anything can be expected from them" (JR 65:135). As far as the missionaries were concerned, responsibility for licentious behavior fell to the women.

The missionaries also had cause for concern about native women's sexuality because French soldiers and civilians engaged in sexual relations with them. Some of the French men had wives back in France and others seemed content not to marry. Although the church initially frowned on marriages between Christian French citizens and "heathen" Indians, some of the missionaries soon found themselves encouraging marriage rather than having French men living in sin. The missionaries also felt that marriage to French men would serve to instill proper Christian behavior in Indian women. Saint-Cosme reported in 1698 that "We saw Indian women married to Frenchmen, and they edified us by their modesty" (Schlarman 1929, 147). Father Marest wrote of the Kaskaskia on November 9, 1712, "they are very different . . . from what they were formerly. Christianity, as I have already said, has softened their fierce habits, and they are now distinguished for certain gentle and polite manners that have led the Frenchmen to take their daughters in marriage. Moreover, we find in them docility and ardor in the practice of Christian virtues" (Schlarman 1929, 157).

Although marriage between French men and Indian women alleviated Christian concerns of sinful sexual relations, it complicated relationships within native communities. In some ways it alienated Indian men from Indian women as women grappled with their split loyalties to their French husbands and their native communities. One telling case involved the Natchez, who were told by the commandant at Fort Rosalie to abandon one of their principal villages because he wanted to build his plantation there (Bossu 1962, 37–38; Fortier 1904, 111). The Natchez, incensed at the arrogance of the commandant, decided to attack Fort Rosalie. As they strategized on how to carry out the attack, the elder men decided not to tell the women about their plans. They took every precaution to ensure that none of the women, including the Sun-Woman (mother of the Great Sun), got wind of their plans to attack the French (Bossu 1962, 38–41; Schlarman 1929, 250–51).

The mother of the Great Sun, Tattoed Arm,[21] became suspicious when she realized that each time a delegation of Natchez returned from a visit with the French, all the men got together in secret. Their secrecy raised her suspicions because such meetings were usually public. Tattoed Arm arranged to talk to her son in private and reportedly asked him, "Are the *Soleils* not brothers? Is their interest not a common interest? Yet, all the *Soleils* keep a secret from me, as though I could not hold my tongue. Am I a woman who speaks in her sleep? I am heartbroken to see myself thus scorned by my brothers and even by thee." After her shamed son told her of their plans she tried to warn the wives of French men as well as the commandant at Fort Rosalie (Schlarman 1929, 253–56; Bossu 1962, 44).

Not only did marriage to French men lead to the exclusion of women from decisions about war that affected everyone in the community, it led to distrust between men and women. The men's greatest fear that certain women might foil their plans because of their attachment to the French came about. Tattoed Arm not only tried to warn the French, she also removed a few sticks from the bundle of sticks the men had put together to mark the number of days until the day of attack (Bossu 1962, 45). In order to coordinate their attack plans with their allies, which reportedly included the Choctaw, the Natchez had sent out similar bundles of sticks to other villages. Each village removed one stick each day until there were none, indicating that that day was the day of attack (Schlarman 1929, 251). By removing a few sticks from the Natchez's bundle, Tattoed Arm ensured that the Natchez attacked the French alone.[22]

The Natchez expected the Choctaw to attack the French in New Orleans. However, whether it was sabotage that caused the Natchez to attack before the planned date or whether the Choctaw changed their minds, the Choctaw did not carry out the attack. In fact, they later attacked the Natchez on behalf of the French. According to Dumont, during their first visit following the attack, the Choctaw forbade the Natchez to put to death any of the captive women and children (French 1853, 83). The Choctaw were aware that the French had enslaved Natchez women and that had been a mitigating factor in the Natchez's decision to attack Fort Rosalie (MPA:FD 1927, 1:176). According to their system of restitution, the Natchez could kill as many captives as people they had lost to the French through death, which ideologically may have included the enslaved women. Nevertheless, the Choctaw chose to prevent the killing of the captives. Their position may have reflected loyalty to the French, which meant the captive women were like their relatives. The Choctaw had been moving toward a system of retaliation rather than restitution because the French and British influenced them to attack their enemies, not to restore balance but to further European interests (MPA:FD 1984, 5:15, 19). The Choctaw response reflected a confluence of French, Christian, and Choctaw ideas that altered a pattern that once reinforced women's central place in determining captives' fates.

As we can see from the two examples above, missionary concern about women's sexuality contributed to women's exclusion from two important political activities: diplomatic ceremonies and war councils. However, control of women's bodies was not the only aspect of mission work that contributed to the exclusion of Indian women from community decision-making. Missionaries introduced ideas of forgiveness and sin to Indian people that challenged their ideas about human nature and the spirit world. The new ideas affected their system of restitution and balance whereby the death of a person obligated the family or community of the deceased to restore balance by taking the life of the one who had done the killing. Rather than take a life for a life, the people involved now had to consider the implications of taking the life of a Christian, of committing a sin by violating the commandment not to kill, and even the possibility that the spirits of the deceased might not all go to the same place.

In one case that took place in April 1723, a French man, Perrillaut, killed another French man, Morin, for speaking impertinently to him. In such a situation local native custom would require that Perrillaut give up his life, through death or adoption, in exchange for the deceased person's life.

However, on April 29, 1723, the day Perrillaut was to be executed for his crime, three Kaskaskia chiefs with thirty of their people arrived at Fort de Chartres to ask that their friend, Perrillaut, be released. One of the chiefs, Kiraoueria, reportedly pleaded with M. de Boisbriant, "'I now come to beg thee not to redden thyself with his blood. . . . Let us conceal thy blood that was shed in this earth, for the love of us, do not spill any more . . . I am of the Prayer, that is how I know that the Great Spirit, the Spirit Creator, God, forbids us, my father, to kill our children. . . . He forgives; pardon as He does, my fathers and for the love of Him . . . it is in the name of all my nation that I ask thee to spare the life of one of thy own children, of one who acted the madman only once. We are here to blot out his fault and to hide it from thee for ever'" (Schlarman 1929, 226–27).

What Kiraoueria was saying was that the Kaskaskia and French were Christians, and as Christians, the French should not execute someone as punishment, but rather they should "cover the body of him who was killed" by which he meant either take the life of an enemy of the Kaskaskia and French such as a Fox or Chickasaw, or rectify the wrongs and sorrows suffered by the kin of the victim by calming them with gifts such as slaves, calumets, or merchandise. Bossu noted a similar practice of calming the victim's family among the Choctaw. According to him the leader of a returning war party distributed part of the booty to the relatives of those killed in battle in order "to dry their tears" (1962, 164). In the case of the Kaskaskia, they were no longer willing to kill their own or other Christians to restore balance, but they were willing to take the lives of enemies in order to fulfill their obligations to the deceased. It may be that the Kaskaskia recognized a difference between Christians and heathens, and heathens as enemies of Christians and God could be killed to satisfy their obligation of restitution.

The Kaskaskia were willing to forgive the crime rather than replace a life with a life, not because human beings had the freedom to forgive, but because a higher power, God, required them as Christians to forgive. They could also restore peace or balance through symbolic or material means. In other words, the French could offer the family of the deceased the calumet of peace and hope that the family would forgive the killer, or they could offer merchandise to demonstrate that they valued the life of the deceased and hope that the family would accept merchandise in lieu of a life. In either case, the role of women to decide the fate of those who have killed someone was being affected. The idea of restoring balance now included forgiveness in the name of God, or the taking of an enemy's life, or accepting gifts in exchange for the deceased's life. It may be that native people in Louisiana territory, including the Choctaw, accepted gifts in lieu of a life prior to Catholic intervention, but the reason for accepting the gift had clearly changed. Instead of replacing the missing family member or releasing the spirit of the deceased, the family of the deceased could choose to forgive the killer or they could accept gifts as symbols of the value of the life lost. In this particular instance men negotiated with the French on the issue of restitution without the presence of women. Changing attitudes toward restitution is one more way in which women's responsibility for the welfare of the family and community, including the spirits of the deceased, was being eroded.

Native people, however, did not respond in consistent or uniform ways to missionary efforts, making it difficult to ascertain the extent of missionary impact on women. Some native people, for example, thought little of the missionaries. In 1704 the Superior of the Foreign Missions sent a request to Jerome Phelypeaux de Pontchartrain, Minister of the Colonies, that two soldiers or Canadians be sent to the Indian villages to assist the missionaries in "assembling the Indians in order to make large villages of them and to protect the missionaries from the insults of the most brutal ones" (MPA:FD 1932, 3:17). Even those Indians who treated the missionaries with respect often resisted Catholic ritual. Father Davion lamented the fact that "notwithstanding the profound respect that these savages showed him, only with the greatest difficulty could he succeed in baptizing a few children at the point of death" (Baudier 1939, 21). When Father Davion could not get the Tunica to accept Christianity, he broke the figurines in their temple, including a figure of a woman who is believed to have represented the sun, put out their sacred fire, and destroyed the temple, which the Tunica never rebuilt. The angry Tunica drove him out of their village for a short period. In spite of Davion's tenuous efforts, he was able, as D'Artaguette noted, to infuse a "smattering of Christianity" among some of the Tunica before he was forced to leave (Kniffen et al. 1987, 252; Baudier 1939, 21–22; Shea 1855, 443–44; Mereness 1916, 44).

Even when missionaries convinced native people to submit to baptism, the rite did not necessarily have the same meaning for them as it did for the missionaries. In one telling case, a Choctaw man, who attributed his poor hunting season to his recent baptism, asked Father LeFévre to take away his worthless medicine. To avoid the hunter's resentment, Father LeFévre "debaptized" him (Bossu 1962, 168–69). Romans also noted that the Choctaw at Chickasawhay frequently asked Baudoüin to undo his baptisms. Apparently, shifting loyalties between the French and the English also determined Choctaw attitudes toward the French. According to Romans, whenever the English would arrive the Choctaw would ridicule the Jesuit by mimicking him and telling the English they were not foolish enough to listen to him (1775, 52).

However, Catholic baptisms or conversions are not the best indicators of missionary impact on women's roles, but rather their actions or attitudes toward women-centered activities. For example, when a Taensa chief died, the medicine person called for some men and women to prepare to sacrifice themselves in accordance with their religious customs. The Taensa procedure for sacrificing oneself may have been similar to the practice of the Natchez, who are related to the Taensa. Among the Natchez, when a leading figure died, spouses, officers, and volunteers swallowed pills of tobacco that brought on unconsciousness. Their relatives then executed them. Their role was to accompany the beloved person to the spirit world where they would continue to serve that person as they had in this world (Mereness 1916, 47; Kniffen et al. 1987, 245). Father de Montigney intervened and prevented the Taensa men and women from killing themselves. However, after lightening struck the main temple of the village, the medicine person determined that the spirit was angry because no one had accompanied their beloved chief to the other world. He called for women to bring their children to sacrifice to the spirit, which five of them did (JR 65:132; Baudier 1939, 27).

Following the sacrifice of the children the women were led "ceremoniously to the hut of the Indian who was to be made chief of the nation." Then "they were caressed and highly praised by the old men; and each of them was clothed in a white robe made from mulberry bark, and a big white feather was put on the head of each. All day they showed themselves at the door of the chief's hut, seated on cane mats, where many brought presents to them." Later, the women were purified in a lake after which they sang throughout each night for a week. Apparently, other women would have offered their children as sacrifices to accompany the spirit of the deceased chief except that some French men had stopped them (Baudier 1939, 27; McWilliams 1981, 129–31).

According to Iberville "the act of those women was considered by the Indians as one of the noblest that could be performed." In fact, many of the Taensa told Iberville that the men or women who accompanied deceased beloveds into the other world considered their acts an honor. Iberville, however, expressed strong doubts about their attitudes toward sacrifice (McWilliams 1981, 129). It is difficult to determine how the Taensa felt about sacrificing themselves or what sacrifice meant to them.[23] D'Artaguette reported that the Natchez "die of their own accord in order that (so they say) they may go to serve their great chief in the other world" (Mereness 1916, 47). According to Le Page du Pratz, who lived among the Natchez, they believed that those who sacrificed themselves would be eternally happy (1774, 314). Fred B. Kniffen, Hiram Gregory, and George Stokes, authors of *The Historic Indian Tribes of Louisiana*, suggested that Natchez and Taensa beliefs about death may help to explain their participation in this practice. They point out that tribal religions did not have concepts of eternal punishment and sin. Rather, death released spirits to a place like home, only better (1987, 255–56). Thus relatives and friends accompanied the beloved to a better place.

Many studies have been written about sacrifice among different cultures, and they constitute an important area of study. However, the concern of this book is not so much about the institution of sacrifice as it is about how the community treated mothers who sacrificed their children. Sacrificing oneself or one's children was considered an act of honor. Among the Natchez the relatives who performed the executions also gained recognition by being raised in rank (Kniffen et al. 1987, 245). While Father de Montigney and the French men's actions are understandable, their intervention nonetheless had a direct impact on the women. Women, as well as men, lost a means of gaining honor that was not replaced within the structure of the Catholic Church. Women could not gain honor in the Catholic Church by becoming priests or handling the sacraments. The missionaries also singled out women who sacrificed their children as particularly heinous. In Father Gravier's account of the event, he referred to the mothers as "unnatural" and "cruel," a sentiment that the Taensa surely noticed (JR 65:137). Not only were the women being faulted for what was a culturally sanctioned act, they were also being characterized as evil. As mothers responsible for the sacrificing of children, they, as well as medicine people, could not carry out the customs associated with the death of an honored member of the community. They no longer could fulfill their responsibilities to the dead or the living.

Redefining Choctaw Women's Nature

The intersection between Catholic religious ideas and French colonization constituted a tremendous force for change throughout the Lower Mississippi Valley. The concerns of the missionaries reinforced the actions of French explorers and military personnel whose actions, in turn, were informed by a culture of Catholicism. Thus Catholic mission work in Louisiana Territory cannot be understood as an isolated factor, but can only be fully imagined in the context of the entire French colonial experience. For example, the Natchez reportedly contacted the Choctaw about their plans to attack Fort Rosalie in 1729 in order to prevent the commandant from taking one of their principal villages. After the attack on Fort Rosalie the Choctaw visited the Natchez and found them and their horses adorned with chasubles and drapery of the altars, some wore gorgets they had made out of patens around their necks, and some used chalices and ciboria to drink brandy.[24] Later, when the Choctaw, at the behest of the French, attacked the Natchez and the Yazoo, they took these articles and adorned themselves in the same manner that the Natchez had. During the dance they held, probably a victory dance, one Choctaw man hung a paten around his neck, another wrapped a maniple around his arm, and others wore the clothes of the French who had been killed. Father Baudoüin later recovered the sacred items by trading with the Choctaw for them (JR 68:195; MPA:FD 1927, 1:102). We do not know what this act meant to the Natchez or the Choctaw. The appropriation of religious paraphernalia could have represented the desecration of what was beloved to the French missionaries, or it could have been the appropriation of beloved Catholic symbols or the power of the sacred into their own system of beloved. The point is that these Catholic artifacts, like Catholic ideas about women's nature, became part of the Choctaw world and had to be accounted for in their understanding of the world.

No doubt the Jesuits among the Choctaw tried to encourage them to conform to French Catholic ideas about social relationships. They believed that in order to save the world from evil forces all heathens had to be christianized as quickly as possible, which meant everyone had to adhere to the same rules of conduct. In the case of women this meant curtailing their exercise of free will, particularly in the area of sexual relations, and limiting their attentions to concerns of the home and family (Anderson 1991, 21). The missionaries, like the French military, may have failed to report the presence of women at diplomatic and war-related activities. However, Jesuit ideas of women's place in society, along with the dangers of the French colonial period, most certainly contributed to the curtailment of women's presence during times thought of by the French as male concerns.

Jesuit missionaries lived and worked among the Choctaw for approximately twenty-three years beginning with Father Le Petit in 1727 and ending with Father Le Febvre in 1750. In addition to the three resident missionaries, the Choctaw had occasion to interact directly and indirectly with possibly twenty missionaries who served among indigenous nations as well as numerous missionaries who were assigned to French posts in New Orleans, Mobile, and Natchitoches. The Choctaw wanted to maintain good relations with missionaries as is indicated by their repeated visits to Father Le Petit in 1730. While in New Orleans they visited Father Le Petit, who had left the Choctaw over a year earlier and had become superior of the whole mission (Delanglez 1935, 455; JR 68:195–96). Father Le Petit wrote Father d'Avaugour that the Choctaw asked him when he was going to return to them, saying, "our hearts and those of our children weep since we shall not see you more; you were beginning to have the same spirit with us, you listened to us, and we listened to you, you loved us and we loved you; why have you left us?" (JR 68:197).

The Choctaw apparently felt a growing affinity between the two. Although Father Le Petit believed that the Choctaw's motivations for maintaining a friendship with him were purely for mercenary reasons, he no doubt took the opportunity to share his beliefs with them (JR 68:197). At the very least, Choctaw visitors to French posts would have observed the prayers or masses held by Catholic priests and they probably spoke with other Indians who lived among the French as slaves, concubines, or wives, or as "free" dwellers. Some of those Indians, particularly those held in bondage, had been baptized or married in the church (Baudier 1939, 128). They no doubt learned of Jesuit attitudes toward polygamy, divorce, and women in general and they would have shared this knowledge with the Choctaw.

The Choctaw, however, had many opportunities to experience directly Jesuit ideas about women. From the beginning of French contact, when the explorers traveled the Mississippi without women, the Choctaw became aware of a different attitude toward women. This awareness became more immediate when the missionaries moved into Choctaw country. From the *Jesuit Relations* we know that it was a Jesuit practice to limit their contact with women. Father Le Jeune decided that it was not becoming for the Jesuits to receive women in their houses, which as Carol Devens noted, "effectively barred them from participation in most religious instruction" (JR 6: 143; Devens 1992, 20). In another instance, he said that they could not instruct the women because "they brought their little children, who made a great deal of noise" (JR 12:141). In this case we see women's responsibilities being perceived as an impediment to learning about religion. This same attitude apparently informed Fathers Zenobe and Hennepin's response to the Illinois. In his report, Father Hennepin described their visits to Illinois' homes to speak to the people. He wrote, "We took their children by the hand, and expressed our love for them with all the signs we could. We did the like to the old men . . . [We] discoursed with the chiefs" (Habig 1934, 45). Hennepin does not mention talking to women although this may have been an oversight on his part. More than likely, Fathers Le Petit and Baudoüin followed in their footsteps by carefully controlling their interactions with women.

The missionaries also had to contend with their ideas about women's nature. By the seventeenth century the idea that women were easily seduced by Satan and thus that many were incorrigible had been well ingrained in Jesuit thought (Anderson 1991, 58, 67). By depicting women as unnatural or cruel the missionaries demonized the women. In the case of the five Taensa women who sacrificed their children in order to appease an angry spirit, they were doing what was expected of them according to Taensa beliefs. They engaged in a religious act that extended the honoring of beloved leaders beyond the material world into the spirit world. The responsibility to the deceased among Southeastern Indians is evident in the Ouma practice of serving the bones of a deceased chief as he was served in his lifetime. In one case the Ouma gave a deceased chief a share of the presents that they had received from the French. Ouma women also wailed for the deceased while his or her body lay in state (McWilliams 1981, 122 n. 47). The same attention to the bones of the deceased is found in the Choctaw migration story and their burial practices. Although the Choctaw did not practice sacrifice, the decreasing presence of women in political and religious affairs throughout the Lower Mississippi Valley would have affected the Choctaw. As they interacted with Taensa or other groups they would have noticed the increasing absence of women, and in typical diplomatic fashion, they may have adjusted to the new protocol, as well as responded to increased dangers, by sending men to negotiate with other nations.

Missionary avoidance of physical contact with women, moral judgments about women's conduct, and the suppression of customs that directly affected women no doubt had an impact on how Choctaw society perceived and treated women. Women's dress and participation in acts that the missionaries found horrifying positioned women as the center of backwardness and immorality among the Choctaw. Thus women who continued to behave according to Choctaw tradition rather than in a French Catholic way represented backwardness. When Choctaw women did take on French habits, especially those who married French men, they risked alienating themselves from their own people. The Choctaw, no doubt, recognized that the Natchez deliberately kept women out of their meetings because they feared their loyalty. Such actions may have aroused suspicions about intermarried Choctaw women. Out of deference to the station of the missionaries as beloved people and as spokespersons for the French and Choctaw, the Choctaw also may have chosen to keep women away from certain activities.

However, some roles of women simply disappeared. As Christian ideas about sin, evil, and eternal punishment became part of the worldview of native people, along with the introduction of slaves as chattel, practices such as restitution by torture until death and sacrifice had to undergo mutations. Those customs that did survive in some form may have changed so drastically that a place for women no longer existed. Those practices that disappeared completely probably did not leave behind an alternative way for women to gain honor. For example, although both men and women could no longer sacrifice themselves for religious reasons—that is, they could not fulfill responsibilities to the deceased by killing themselves—men could continue to sacrifice themselves through acts of war and be honored as warriors. In other words, whether through religious or military means, women could not become beloved through acts of sacrifice. Issues of morality and politics came together in the missions of Louisiana Territory in ways that removed or limited the means by which Choctaw women could gain honor as beloved people.

4

Struggle for Survival

When the French began occupying the Lower Mississippi Valley, the Choctaw eagerly met with them in hopes of developing a trade in firearms in order to protect themselves from English slave-dealers and their Indian allies. In a meeting with Iberville in 1702, they told him that they had lost eighteen hundred people because of tribal warfare instigated by English slave-dealers and that another five hundred had been taken captive. Iberville's promise to arm all the Choctaw, Mobilian, and Tohomé if the Chickasaw did not drive the English from their villages pleased the Choctaw, as did the many presents he gave them (Usner 1992, 18–19; McWilliams 1981, 172–73). However, the Choctaw's hopes for a beneficial trade relationship quickly began to falter as the French failed time and again to produce promised goods or gifts. In fact, the French often could not meet their own needs and had to turn to native people for assistance.

Transported to an alien land with little knowledge of how to survive in the humid, hot climate of the Gulf region, many French and Canadian citizens found themselves caught up in a cycle of destitution. The conditions of French towns and forts forced individuals and colonies to turn to native people in order to survive. Oftentimes their solutions involved displacing and dehumanizing native people, who became economic and social property for the benefit of the colonists. Women, in particular, became the slaves and concubines of civilian and soldier alike. Choctaw people, like other native groups in the Lower Mississippi Valley, found themselves drawn into a world struggling with the social problems of poverty, alcoholism, and disease. In many ways the French struggle for survival in the seventeenth and eighteenth centuries became the Indian's struggle. Only by understanding the conditions that French colonists faced in the Lower Mississippi Valley can we fully appreciate the pressures they exerted upon Choctaw women's lives as a result of the Choctaw's alliance with the French.

Early French Settlements

From the very beginning of the French presence in the Lower Mississippi Valley, native people were forced to deal with the problems of the French. They provided food, labor, and military aid for the French. Women, who were responsible for much of the food supply, often found the fruits of their labor and their lives being appropriated for the benefit of the French, sometimes by force. French explorers often ran out of food during long voyages up and down the Mississippi, and at times felt compelled to take measures for survival that included seizing food and canoes when needed. For example, during La Salle's return trip from his first expedition down the Mississippi in 1682, he and his men, low on provisions, had been living on potatoes. When they neared the village of the Quinipissa, La Salle's men took four of their women captive. They then sent one of the women back to her village to inform the Quinipissa that they meant no harm. They only wanted provisions. After the Quinipissa agreed to provide provisions, La Salle set the other three women free. Although the Quinipissa kept their promise to provide provisions that evening, the next morning they attacked the French, whom they perceived as enemies (French 1946, 64–65). The French had threatened their well-being through aggressive acts toward their persons and theft of their food stores, and those acts had repercussions. To hold women hostage for provisions that women typically provided would have made no sense to native people in the Lower Mississippi Valley. Since Southeastern native protocol called for bands or clans to offer food to friendly visitors, the taking of hostages could only be perceived as the act of an enemy.

As exploration turned to settlement, the needs of the French multiplied and their dependence on native people increased. Unfamiliar with the environment, they established posts and settlements in areas prone to hurricanes, rains, flooding, and excessive heat. As a result buildings and fortifications rotted in the damp environment, creating undesirable living conditions and necessitating continuous attention to repair. The dampness and unhealthy living conditions contributed to widespread illnesses. For example, D'Artaguette reported that in November 1722 there were "ninety people sick at N.O., with fevers and with other diseases" (Mereness 1916, 39). In fall of 1739 Father Pierre Vitry wrote that "an epidemic had been raging in New Orleans that summer, and the troops brought the disease to the fort [de l/Assomption]" (Vitry 1985, 27). Lord Adam Gordon reported similar conditions at the Mobile fort in the summer and autumn of 1764, where nearly everyone was "ill of Fevers, Fluxes and Agues." During his visit in October he found two regiments "so ill, and Weak, as scarce to be able between them to furnish a Subalterns Guard" (Mereness 1916, 387–88). The same conditions that caused sickness among the colonists also caused disease among their cattle. In 1751 Vaudreüil wrote to Rouillé that "for three years the deaths have been continuing among the livestock of the colony, and the shortage is so great in everything" that they were forced to turn to the Spaniards for aid (MPA:FD 1984, 5:87).

In addition to unhealthy living conditions, the colonists faced constant food shortages (MPA:FD 1927, 1:212; MPA:FD 1932, 3:36, 137). The French who first settled at Biloxi Bay were interested primarily in mining and trading, and they made little effort to produce food crops. Instead they expected France to send them shipments of food. However, during the early years of the settlement, the War of the Spanish Succession and shortage of money prevented the French government from sending needed supplies on a regular basis (Delanglez 1935, 51; Surrey 1916, 136, 155). In one extreme case the desperate settlers in Louisiana struggled to survive as they waited for four years (1708–11) to receive supplies from France (Allain 1979, 41). When supplies did reach the colony, the residents were charged exorbitant prices and the food was often unfit for consumption (Giraud 1953, 1:222; MPA:FD 1984, 5:86; Surrey 1916, 136). Regular flooding also created problems with storage of supplies, transportation, and living quarters. In 1740 Joseph Dubreuil, who built the levee system for New Orleans, recalled that "The establishment of New Orleans in the beginning was awful, the river when it was high spreading over the whole ground, and in all the houses there were two feet of water, which caused general and mortal diseases" (Fortier 1904, 102–3).

In an effort to provide needed food, French colonial officers began bringing in settlers for the specific purpose of cultivating fields. However, despite repeated efforts to grow food, hurricanes and floods regularly destroyed crops meant for local consumption and for trade. One hurricane in 1723 lasted six days and "did great harm to the crops of rice, peas, and corn, and destroyed the greater part of the houses at New Orleans. The store-house . . . at Fort Louis was destroyed, with a great quantity of goods" (Fortier 1904, 72). Hurricanes also destroyed property, provisions, and crops at Balize, Biloxi, and Mobile on September 11 and 18, 1740, creating near-famine conditions (Fortier 1904, 128). Indian and black slaves probably suffered more, as is indicated in a report about the August 1732 hurricane that caused famine conditions. According to Bienville the garrison at New Orleans had been reduced to their last quarts of flour before the *St. Anne* finally arrived with supplies and "all the Indians and half of the Negroes" had been "living on reed seed during more than three months" (MPA:FD 1927, 1:212).[1] Despite the inhospitable conditions, the French chose to maintain those colonies rather than to seek more suitable areas.

Unable or unwilling to generate enough food and supplies from local resources, French settlers were highly dependent upon shipments from France. Although the governor regularly sent requests for aid to France, supplies often failed to reach the colony because of pirating, ships lost at sea, delays in shipping, or rotting during the long voyages. The lack of navigable harbors near the colonies also made it difficult for supply ships to unload goods. Incidents of ships running aground and losing their cargo were not uncommon. In 1721 Du Pratz wrote of New Biloxi that "he never could guess why they had chosen that place for the principal establishment of the colony, and why they had thought of building the capital there. The land is sterile, and it is exceedingly difficult to unload anything from the ships, as the water is so shallow near the coast" (Fortier 1904, 78). His fears became reality when in September 1725 a ship ran aground along the Louisiana coast and in order to free the ship the crew had to throw between three hundred and four hundred barrels of flour overboard (Surrey 1916, 163). Constant shortages of supplies, exorbitant prices, and mismanagement of resources forced the French colonists to turn to local Indians for solutions to their dilemmas.

The problems facing the colony went beyond the needs of civilians. Soldiers and officers also suffered from lack of adequate supplies and coinage as well as high prices. In the case of the Swiss troops, whose conditions reflected those of all the soldiers, they drew their food, clothing, and equipment from the Swiss warehouse in New Orleans.[2] Although the costs of those necessities continually rose, their pay remained the same. Thus many officers and enlisted men found themselves owing more money at the end of the month than they had earned. In the 1720s Company of the West officials in Louisiana and France tried to reduce expenditures by instituting pay cuts, which led to higher rates of desertion (Woods 1980, 86). Conditions became so bad that in 1739 the government had to cease the practice of making salary deductions for food.

Needy French and Swiss soldiers often sought aid from the Spanish or English. Although they could reach Spanish or English settlements within a few days, they often encountered native people along the way or spent time at Indian villages. Others moved to native villages, although missionaries and officers feared they might not return to their posts. In 1710, when Bienville did not have enough supplies to provide for his men, he was forced to allow some of them to go live among the Indians. One group of thirty soldiers led by Lieutenant Philippe Blondel chose to stay with the Choctaw (Fortier 1904, 54; Pénicaut 1953, 133). Many chose to escape the harsh conditions in French forts or towns by fleeing to Indian villages. Conditions became so bad that in 1712 D'Artaguette reported, "The distress is great; all those who are there are dissatisfied. The soldiers are deserting to the Indian enemies and from there are going to Carolina. . . . It is pitiful also to see them as they are all naked and most often living on crushed and boiled Indian corn with a piece of meat. . . . The colonists are languishing" (Brasseaux 1979, 49). For many French settlers (civilian and soldier), Indian villages became the last hope of survival.

Soldiers unable to meet their costs for food, uniforms, and equipment had to find other means of income. Some turned to the deerskin trade. They set out with loads of "trinkets for the Indian trade in furs" (Hardcastle 1978, 85–87). Even Fathers Le Petit and Baudoüin were forced to trade beads, knives, and other items with the Choctaw at Chickasawhay for corn and deerskins in order to survive (Usner 1992, 253; MPA:FD 1929, 594, 613). Although the French lacked the needed food and supplies to offer as trade items to the Choctaw, civilian and military officers encouraged the deerskin trade. By expanding the deerskin trade the French hoped to maintain the Choctaw as allies and as impediments to English westward expansion.

However, the shortage of merchandise and the poor quality of French goods seriously limited French trade with the Choctaw, who preferred the better quality items provided by English traders (Woods 1980, 81–83; 114–17). In March 1733 D'Artaguette reported, "The scarcity of food that has been prevalent here for a long time will make us make a bad beginning with the Indians. . . . They will ask for their presents and we are bringing but little" (MPA:FD 1927, 1:214). The Choctaw continued to trade with the French, however, because they desired their guns and "out of fear of the common enemy" (Giraud 1987, 492). Their trade relationship with the French eventually affected women's participation in the economic life of their communities and their safety.

Thus, from the very beginning of French colonization, native people had immediate interaction with French settlers who were in desperate need of aid. Some went to live or trade among native communities. Others, representing the French colony, offered meager or poor quality trade goods to their Choctaw allies. These early French refugees and traders brought new ideas, stories, and practices to the Choctaw that affected their conceptions about gender roles. At the very least native people must have wondered at the suffering of the French, who did not have many women with them, women who could care for crops and gather wild foods. The absence of French women was only one of many French actions that would draw Choctaw attention to the roles of women.

Populating the Colonies

French officials tried to solve the problems of their colony by drawing French citizens to Louisiana Territory. However, many of those immigrants failed to become farmers who would provide food for the colony. Native people noticed the arrival of French women who failed to take on the responsibilities of growing corn or gathering of wild plant foods. Instead they witnessed the enslavement of native women, who were forced to carry out household chores and provide pleasure for French men. The colonists needed native women because the French women brought to Louisiana Territory, like many of the men, could not survive the harsh environment. French officials had determined that the presence of French women would lead to marriages and that, in turn, would induce the men already in Louisiana

Territory to settle down. They also needed to attract workmen to teach their trades to native people and French colonists, and soldiers to guard forts. The Canadian backwoodsmen who originally fulfilled military duties were no longer in the service of the French, and the French did not have the means to provide them with any support. Therefore many of them who were not interested in farming chose to live among the Indians rather than settle down in French towns. French officials hoped the lure of women would draw and keep the men in town. They reasoned that having wives would give the men incentive to settle down, which would help the colony to prosper (MPA:FD 1932, 3:15–16).

Thus French colonial officers began sending requests to France for families and for reasonable, strong, or pretty girls for the French and Canadian men to be sent to the territory. However, few responded to the call to go to Louisiana Territory. Colonial officials knew that if they were to gain new settlers they would need to devise some means of drawing people to Louisiana. Since rumors of bad conditions in the colony kept the number of immigrants low, Iberville, in 1701, requested that 18,000 livres be provided to send about sixty poor persons from France to Louisiana Colony. He argued that only the poor who needed government help would be willing to leave France for the new colony (Allain 1979, 40). The following year he asked the French minister to send farmers to Louisiana who could till the land, not adventurers (Fortier 1904, 48). In 1704 twenty-two Parisian girls were convinced to go to the "promise land" as wives for the colonists (Delanglez 1935, 53; Giraud 1953, 1, 152–53). Six years later D'Artaguette wrote the Count of Pontchartrain that they needed girls, especially farm girls, in order to encourage the backwoodsmen to settle down. He repeated his request just two years later, stating that they could not attract backwoodsmen and hunters as colonists if they did not have women (MPA:FD 1929, 2:57, 68–69).

Unfortunately, many of the men and women sent to Louisiana were those who were marginal in their own country. They did not have the skills or desire to farm, they were not experienced in any trades, and their health was often so poor that many died shortly after arrival because of disease and environmental conditions. Some of those who survived eventually made their way back to France. Others deserted the colonies for Indian towns. As news of conditions in Louisiana spread throughout France, officials had greater and greater trouble convincing anyone to move to Louisiana

Territory. Horror stories of wretched living conditions and widespread corruption replaced tales of riches to be gained and excitement to be had by all.

As a last resort the French Crown turned the colony over to the company of Antoine Crozat in 1712 in exchange for sending two ships of supplies and ten girls or boys per year for fifteen years. As soon as Crozat realized that there were no profits to be gained from the colony, he began providing only minimal supplies for the colony and failed to meet emigration quotas. After 1714 he stopped supplying the colony altogether (Allain 1979, 42). The French Crown then gave the patent to the Compagnie d'Occident in August 1717.[3] John Law, director of the company, immediately began a propaganda campaign to entice French citizens to immigrate to Louisiana. His fantastic stories of mineral wealth, harmonious relations among settlers and with Indians, and fertile lands initially attracted some French concessionaires and indentured concession laborers and artisans, as well as German, Alsatian, and Swiss immigrants. However, only 302 skilled workers voluntarily migrated to the colony between the years 1717 and 1721 because of the colony's poor public image (Brasseaux 1979, 50–51).[4]

In response to the lack of volunteers willing to go to the colony, France initiated forced migration in 1717. In November 1718 France singled out beggars, vagabonds, and indigents as people who could be forcibly deported to Louisiana. France quickly expanded the policy to include army deserters who would have their sentences commuted to lifetime exile in Louisiana. According to Jean François Benjamin Dumont de Montigny, a commissioned officer for the Company of the Indies, who was placed in charge of the prisoners sent to the colony in 1719, three hundred of them were deserters (Delanglez 1985, 34). A few years earlier, Crozat, who had proposed using convicts to populate the colony, had argued, "men alone could not people a colony." He recommended that young women from the poorhouses of France be recruited to go to the colony for the purpose of marrying the *faux sauniers*. In 1719 the French began rounding up prostitutes and female criminals for deportation to Louisiana (Conrad 1979, 60–63). Early in 1720 sixty girls from the Hôpital-Général of Paris, a house of detention and correction, arrived at the Isle-aux-Vaisseaux across from New Biloxi. Prostitutes made up more than half of 1,215 women shipped to Louisiana between October 1717 and May 1721 (Pénicaut 1953, 240 n. 5). From 1717 to 1720, when Law's Banque Royale collapsed and the company's patent was withdrawn, 1,278 "salt smugglers, defrauders and exiles had been sent to Louisiana in lieu of duty on the galleys or imprisonment in French jails" (Brasseaux 1979, 51).

When the Company of the Indies regained its patent in 1723, it endeavored to colonize Louisiana by sending over prostitutes at its own expense, forcing them onto transports bound for the struggling colony. Those marginalized women who were forced to go to Louisiana married poor men also exiled to the colony, and they and their spouses, whom Chevalier de Champigny characterized as unfit for farming, soon died or returned to France. Those that returned spread "the most frightful accounts of the Mississippi" (French 1853, 131–32). According to an Englishman who was a long-time resident of Louisiana, in a letter dated December 10, 1751, "out of forty-four girls who were sent by force from France in 1722 by the *Mutine* . . . there is only one who has left any posterity, although all were married and had several children. Of several convicts who were sent in the beginning of the colony, I do not know of a single one who was established there" (Fortier 1904, 110).[5]

The Company of the Indies never profited from its patent, although it made every effort to populate Louisiana and to limit expenses. The attack on the French fort at Natchez in 1729, as well as the heavy cost of retaliatory military expeditions upon the already costly maintenance of the colony, forced the company to relinquish its charter. The king of France, having accepted the surrender of the company's charter in 1731, authorized a Council of Government to oversee the colony. The council began sending men and women of questionable character to Louisiana. They, too, did not fare well (Baudier 1939, 122; French 1904, 133). In 1751 sixty poor girls arrived in Louisiana at the king's expense, "the last that the mother country supplied." They married those soldiers whose good conduct entitled them to a discharge, and each couple received an allotment of land and "a cow and a calf, a cock and five hens, a gun, an ax, and a hoe; and during the first three years rations were issued to them, with a small quantity of powder, shot, and grain for seed" (Fortier 1904, 134).

The effort to populate Louisiana Territory with the marginalized populations of France failed miserably. Joe Gray Taylor, in his analysis of the forced relocation of French disenfranchised, said, "very few had any agricultural experience," and characterized most of them as having "had no desire to do any work at all" (Holmes 1978, 68). Of those who were recruited as soldiers, the governors of Louisiana had little positive to say. Typical of their complaints was Kerlérec's assertion "that his entire French force was composed of former deserters and misfits of whom the governor of Santo Domingo had rid himself, and that the civilian population lived in perpetual fear of brigandage and worse from the soldiers" (Hardcastle 1978, 83).

The same problems continued to exist after the Spanish took control of Louisiana. On August 29, 1780, the inhabitants of New Orleans sent a message to Don Martin Navarro, the intendant who at the time was responsible for the civil administration of Louisiana, about all their sufferings. They said that in the last two years they had experienced "war, two hurricanes, inundation, contagion, a summer more rainy and a winter more rigourous than had ever been known, the stagnation of commerce, the ruin of agriculture, the want of capital . . ." (Gayarré 1885, 3:152–53). In a plot to regain the territory, the king of France ordered his ministers to collect information on the resources of Louisiana. Joseph Xavier de Pontalba wrote in his memoir to Napoleon Bonaparte, which was presented, on September 15, 1801, just fifteen days before Spain agreed to retrocede the territory to France, "Louisiana wants working hands. Give her population, and she will become an inexhaustible source of wealth for France. Give her population, whatever be the means employed, but give her population" (Gayarré 1885, 3:442–45; Holmes 1978, 67).

As Louisiana officials struggled to find ways to keep their forts and colonies going, they took a number of measures that ultimately proved disastrous. As mentioned above, the men and women who arrived in New Orleans or Mobile were ill-prepared for the rigors of colonial life in Louisiana. Many arrived with social problems that continued to plague them in their new homes. Those problems also affected settlers who were already there. Prostitution, alcohol abuse, crime, and sickness flourished in the colony. These problems, however, did not remain confined to French colonists, but had far-reaching effects on nearby native people, including the Choctaw. As the colony struggled to prosper, many French turned to Indians as a way to relieve their distress, which in turn created problems leading to distress for the Indians. The native people of the area not only had occasion to interact with the French population as allies and enemies, but also provided refuge for those who either did not want to live under those conditions or could not survive. Those native people who went to New Orleans or Mobile encountered women who did not know how to farm and who survived by means not understandable to them. Instead of redistribution of goods to ensure that even the poorest farmer or hunter had something, French men and women who could not afford to buy goods had to resort to any means possible in order to survive. As the Choctaw began interacting more with the French, the redistribution of goods and matrilineal rules of conduct began to change under the influence of French practices.

Slave Labor

The early colonists' unwillingness to farm, as well as their difficulty in growing sufficient crops for consumption and trade, meant that laborers to work the fields were in great demand. Colonists, enlisted men, and missionaries turned to Indian slaves, many of whom were women. Although the French did not enslave the Choctaw who were their allies, the Canadians often took slaves from friendly Indian villages (Giraud 1953, 180). The Choctaw had occasion to come in contact with slaves from related nations through war expeditions, diplomatic visits to New Orleans and Mobile, adoption into communities, and the slave trade. The Choctaw became involved in the slave trade and were aware of French treatment of female slaves. Thus slavery provided another means of introducing French ideas into Choctaw worldviews, ideas about women that differed from Choctaw ones.

French colonists always had a small number of slaves. According to the 1704 census of Louisiana reported by Nicolas de La Salle from Fort Louis of Mobile, among the one hundred and eighty men bearing arms and twenty-seven French families, including three little girls and seven young boys from one to ten years of age, were six young Indian slave boys from twelve to eighteen years of age and five Indian slave girls from fifteen to twenty years of age (Hall 1992, 97; MPA:FD 1929, 2:19; Fortier 1904, 51). Four years later, on August 12, 1708, Commissary La Salle reported that out of 199 whites in or near the garrison, including priests, workmen, twenty-eight women and twenty-five children plus sixty Canadian backwoodsmen living in Indian villages, the French also held eighty male and female slaves from various Indian nations including friendly ones (MPA:FD 1929, 2:32; Fortier 1904, 54). Most of the Indian slaves did gardening or domestic tasks. Those few who worked in the fields proved to be unstable workers.

In an effort to solve the colony's persistent labor shortage, the officials of Louisiana repeatedly requested that France allow them to exchange Indians for West African slaves at the rate of two Indians for three West Africans. They petitioned France in 1706, 1707, 1708, and again in 1713 to allow trafficking in Indian and West African slaves, but their proposals were rejected each time for fear that friendly Indians would be enslaved and traded. French colonists, however, continued to traffic illegally in Indian slaves.[6] In 1712 the French Crown granted Crozat a patent that allowed for the purchase of West African slaves. Article XIV stated in part: "If for the cultures and plantations which the said Sieur Crozat is minded to make, he finds it proper to have blacks in the said country of the Louisiana, he may send a ship every year to trade for them directly upon the coast of Guinea ... he may sell those blacks to the inhabitants of the colony of Louisiana." That same year about twenty black slaves were reported in Louisiana Territory (Giraud 1953, 180–81; French 1857, 42; Fortier 1904, 56).

The number of West African slaves remained small until 1719, when the Company of the Indies began providing West African slaves to the colonies. The first large contingent of slaves arrived in June of that year (Conrad 1979, 63; Fortier 1904, 83; French 1853, 119n.). For several years thereafter slave-traders delivered anywhere from three to five hundred West Africans annually from the coast of Guinea. Although the French population did not increase much, the slave population increased significantly. Two years after the Company of the Indies began supplying West African slaves, the 1721 census report for New Orleans listed 523 black slaves and 51 Indian slaves.[7] By January 1726 the number of West African slaves had nearly tripled, to 1540, and the number of Indian slaves had more than quadrupled, to 229 (Fortier 1904, 101). By 1732, when the Company of the Indies surrendered its charter, approximately seven thousand West Africans had been transported to Louisiana Territory (Usner 1992, 34; French 1853, 119).

The adoption of slavery in the French colony had numerous implications for Indian people. Difficulty with Indian slaves led the French to request that they be allowed to trade Indian slaves for West African slaves in Santo Domingo. Escaping Indian slaves cost the French an "investment" but more importantly much-needed labor. Although France prohibited the export of Indian slaves, and specifically outlawed the practice in 1726, the colonists continued to send them to the French islands on a small scale (Hall 1992, 97). The trade for West African slaves, however, also meant that Indian people had occasion to interact with free and slave West Africans. Any interaction between Indians and West Africans was cause for concern among the French. They feared that Indians would provide refuge for West Africans, but more importantly, they feared West Africans would align themselves with Indians and convince them to attack the French, so they took drastic steps to keep the two separated.[8] In 1723 Bienville and his men threatened to attack the Great Village of the Natchez if the villagers did not return a black slave to them. The person in question was, in fact, "a free black, who, instead of settling among the French, had gone over to the Indians, and even made himself head of a party." According to Dumont, "it was justly feared that he would teach them our way of attack and defence, and it was thus absolutely necessary to get rid of him" (French 1853, 56). A network of escaping slaves led by two African-Indian couples found refuge among the lower-river settlements of the Choctaw. Some of the recaptured slaves said they had been welcomed by pro-English Choctaw as allies against the French (Hall 1992, 115–16). In fact, several West African and Indian slaves accompanied the Western Choctaw when they raided a German farm in 1748 (Hall 1992, 18; MPA:FD 1984, 4:318–20).

The issue of West African/Indian relations posed a conundrum for the French. On the one hand, they were concerned about West Africans teaching Indians French methods of warfare or inciting them to attack French colonies. On the other hand, the French needed Indian allies to keep those native people who were incensed by French policy in line and to keep British-allied Indians away. When the French attacked a native nation, their troops often included Indians and West Africans. In his 1736 expedition against the Chickasaw, Bienville's army consisted of 544 white men, 45 black slaves commanded by free blacks, and a large number of Choctaw (Fortier 1904, 121). In another expedition, when Bienville assembled an army in 1739 to attack the Natchez and Chickasaw, he had "about twelve hundred white troops, and double that number of Indian and black troops" (French 1853, 116 n.).[9] Since alliances between different towns and nations changed constantly, the enemies of the French had many opportunities to learn their military strategies. Nonetheless, blacks posed a threat to the safety of the French colonists. Whether they freely moved into an Indian town or were taken captive during battle, blacks could be adopted into an Indian community where they might share knowledge of French military tactics or participate in attacks upon the French.

In order to prevent alliances between West Africans and Indians, the French took steps to foment animosity between the two. In one case, when the French learned that some West African slaves planned to murder whites in New Orleans, the comptroller for the Company of the Indies believed that the recaptured West African slaves who had stayed among the Choctaw for eighteen months had influenced the conspirators (Hall 1992, 107). The French speculated that native people might have incited them or that the West African slaves wished to imitate the Indians in order to regain their liberty. Either way Perier contrived a plan to create hostile feelings between Indians and West Africans in order to keep them apart. He executed the leaders of the West African slaves and forced the others to "put to death seven or eight Chouachas Indians and to destroy their village" (Fortier 1904, 114; French 1853, 99–101). The French, familiar with Southeastern native ideas of captivity and torture, knew that the threat of restitution for the lives of the executed Chouacha[10] would keep West Africans away from Indians.

Indians were subject to slavery up until the Spanish took possession of Louisiana Territory in 1766. When General Alexander O'Reilly, the new Spanish governor, arrived in New Orleans in 1769 he initiated new policies, one of which stated that as of December 1, 1769, "it is not permitted that Indians be held in slavery; wherefore, from the date of the notification of these presents, no one shall buy, exchange, and barter, or appropriate to himself Indian slaves. They shall neither sell, nor in any way part with, those they now have (unless it be to set them free), until they hear further from his Majesty on this subject" (Gayarré 1879, 3:20). Bishop Penalver supplemented this decree by ordering its enforcement "not only for Indian parents but for their children as well" (Baudier 1939, 179–80).

Slaves, West African and Indian, were also subject to Catholic training. When Marie-Françoise de Boisrenaud, a Paris woman, was brought to Mobile to become a wife of one of the colonists, she chose instead to devote herself to instructing native women and children, who were most likely slaves, and to attending to their baptisms (Higginbotham 1977, 240–41). When the Ursuline nuns arrived in New Orleans in 1727 they were soon teaching classes for orphan girls from the surrounding area. They also organized classes for female slaves, whom they instructed in religion. Sister Madeleine Harchard wrote, "We conduct also a class to instruct the girls and women, Negro and Indian. They come every day between one o'clock in the afternoon and half past two" (Baudier 1939, 105). The best-known story is probably that of an Osage woman slave,[11] Marie Louise, who was freed by the late François Viard in 1729 in accordance with his will. He also left her ten pistoles to be used for Catholic instruction. Since the Black Code forbade a cash legacy to a slave, the money was allocated to the hospital and the Osage woman was sent to the Ursuline nuns (Baudier 1939, 106).

In addition to instruction, some Indian slaves were also baptized. When Saint-Denis returned to Mobile from a raid against the Chitimacha in 1707, he brought with him several male and female prisoners as well as twelve or thirteen young children, some of whom were sold as slaves to French colonists for two hundred livres each. The owners wanted the slaves baptized, but Father Henri Roulleaux de La Vente hesitated to approve their baptisms. However, when several of the Chitimacha slaves neared death, he changed his mind and baptized two female Indian slaves ages eight or nine and thirteen or fourteen. On June 30 he baptized another nine Indian slaves ranging in age from two to thirteen years. Unfortunately, the sick slaves soon died (Higginbotham 1977, 292, 301–2). Father Maximin, a Capuchin sent to Natchitoches post in 1728, also baptized "Indians in bondage or in the service of the whites" during his two-year tenure (Baudier 1939, 128). Sister Hachard, in a letter dated April 24, 1728, wrote that seven slaves at the convent were to be prepared for baptism and first communion, and that a large number of day scholars, "negresses and Indian women," came "two hours every day to receive instruction" (Fortier 1904, 106). Although the Ursulines had a difficult time convincing Indian girls to accept baptism, they still received instruction (Giraud 1987, 307). Thus slavery provided another means for Indian people, including the Choctaw, to learn of Catholic ideas about women.

Concubinage

For native women the slave trade also meant sex trade. The scarcity of French women in the colonies had always presented a problem for French officials and missionaries who were responsible for the moral behavior of their people. However, even the early explorers had to concern themselves with issues of sexual impropriety on the part of their men. In Abbé Jean Cavelier's account of one of La Salle's exploratory trips of the area around Matagorda

Bay, where he mistakenly landed while searching for the mouth of the Mississippi, he expressed concern about allowing approximately twenty men to spend time at a Cenis village. He wrote that although they were treated well by the Cenis, they quickly left the village because he and La Salle feared that the soldiers among them would "tamper with the women" (Shea 1861, 41).

Since few French women chose to move to Louisiana Territory, French men sought native women "to satisfy their passions" (MPA:FD 1929, 2:69). The accepted practice of having slaves to do the labor of the households provided French men the opportunity to have sexual relations with Indian women. Although missionaries and governors found these practices objectionable, they could not stop them. In 1713 Antoine de Lamothe Cadillac, then governor of Louisiana, wrote Pontchartrain that "the Canadians and the soldiers who are not married have female Indian slaves and insist that they cannot dispense with having them to do their washing and to do their cooking or to make their sagamity and to keep their cabins. If this reason were valid, it ought not to prevent the soldiers from going to confessional, or the Canadians either. Indeed, my lord, I cannot refrain from representing to you that ... a remedy for such disorder in which it will not be easy to attain success except by lodging the troops in the fort ... permitting them to have only male slaves and not female" (MPA:FD 1929, 2:169).

In reporting on the state of the colony on January 2, 1716, Cadillac complained that nearly everyone had "Indian women as slaves who are always with child or nursing" (MPA:FD 1929, 2:211). He said French masters accused male slaves of impregnating Indian women, but that the priests pointed out the falsity of their claims because the children were obviously mixed blood. Cadillac argued that the French men had enough male slaves to serve them and that they should sell the women slaves or marry them (MPA:FD 1929, 2:212). Father Raphael wrote the Directors of the Company in 1724 complaining that "Everything is full of disorders in the colony; persons married in France, who have remarried here; others who live in a scandalous condition with their slaves" (Baudier 1939, 98). As the Choctaw and other native nations shifted from an adoption or torture practice to one of selling Indian captives to the French, female captives became slaves that purchasers could then resell for profit or keep as wives (Mereness 1916, 142). As slaves, women were not treated as captives in the traditional native manner, but were sold as chattel or kept for sexual purposes.

French men occasionally established arrangements with Choctaw women with the consent of the women's families; however, they did not always fulfill their obligations. In 1749 Tchichoulakta, a beloved man from Bouctoucoulou Chitto, complained to Vaudreüil that Sieur de La Houssaye, while in command at Tombecbé, had promised him a cow but had left the post without giving it to him. According to Vaudreüil, when he asked him why he replied "that it was because he had enjoyed his daughter whom he had given over to him on that condition" (MPA:FD 1984, 5:21–22). Although Vaudreüil's rendition of the conversation suggests otherwise, Bouctoucoulou Chitto's reply indicates the exchange may have been the result of an arranged marriage according to Choctaw practice, whereby the man offers meat and the woman corn to seal the relationship. By failing to give Tchichoulakta a cow, La Houssaye humiliated the daughter and her family.

La Houssaye's failure to seal the marriage also had significant implications for Choctaw society. Among Southeastern native people the exchange of people through marriage or an exchange of goods were traditional methods for sealing peaceful relations or alliances (Merrell 1989, 198). By failing to provide the cow the exchange was never sealed. In Choctaw matrilineal society husbands could not develop relationships of authority within the wife's lineage. Responsibility for household and lineage activities belonged to the brothers of the wife. Thus, for the Choctaw, intermarried French men had no authority within their lineages, but were expected to treat relatives with love and kindness (Galloway 1989, 255–56, 264). La Houssaye, often drunk, reportedly "mistreated several Indians in his fort without any cause" (MPA:FD 1984, 5:22). By not sealing the arrangement La Houssaye had not obligated himself, according to Choctaw ideology, to treat the woman's family as relatives. In fact, he had undermined the system of exchanging people through marriage, a system that reinforced the importance of women's participation in maintaining alliances between nations.

Although officers were responsible for the behavior of their men and were expected to uphold the ideals of French society, the missionaries complained that "officers and soldiers everywhere, especially in the more distant posts," engaged in sexual relations with native women (Baudier 1939, 97). Some of the soldiers and colonists moved in among native people and soon became involved with Indian women. On July 19, 1721, Monseigneur

St. Vallier, Bishop of Quebec, issued a *pastoralin* in which he declared the common practice of concubinage a public scandal (Baudier 1939, 63). Among French Catholics ecclesiastical law forbade marriage with Indian heathen women without dispensation from the Holy See. Of primary concern was the marriage of a Catholic man with an unbaptized woman or one who had little training in Christian religion. Since abstinence was not likely and missionaries and officers were not free to urge soldiers and colonists who lived with native women to get married, they had little recourse in stemming concubinage. However, in Illinois Territory the missionaries chose to allow such marriages rather than have French men living in sin.

Although the French government seemed disinclined to approve of such marriages, during his third voyage Iberville received the following instruction from Louis XIV:

> His Majesty has examined the proposal made by Sieur d'Iberville, namely to allow the French who will settle in this country [Lower Louisiana] to marry Indian girls. His Majesty sees no inconvenience in this provided they be Christians, in which case His Majesty approves of it. His Majesty welcomes the opportunity to let him [d'Iberville] know with regard to this matter that his intention is that he should apply himself to prevent debauchery and all disorderly conduct, that he should protect the missionaries and that his principal aim should be to establish the Christian Religion. (Delanglez 1935, 394–95)

Apparently Iberville did not share these instructions with Bienville, who wrote to Paris in July 1706 that:

> Sieur de la Vente, under the pretext that he is vicar-general of the Bishop of Quebec, ordered the missionaries who are among the savages to perform marriages of Frenchmen with Indian girls, although he [Bienville] had warned these gentlemen that such is not the intention of His Majesty, because it was necessary to gather the Frenchmen who are scattered among the Indians, and not to authorize them to live there as libertines, under the pretext that they are married with Indians. (Delanglez 1935, 395)

Bienville was disturbed that Sieur de la Vente was fighting concubinage in Mobile by performing marriages between French men and native women even though such marriages were considered valid in France, "always provided the Indian was Catholic" (Delanglez 1935, 396).

Of primary concern to French leaders was that the French men who married native women might be induced to behave like Indians. These fears are clearly expressed in Joutel's journal of La Salle's last voyage when he described encountering two Frenchmen among the Cenis. They were sailors, one from Brittany and the other from Rochelle. According to Joutel, "They had, in that short space of time, so perfectly inured themselves to the customs of the natives, that they had become mere savages. They were naked, their faces and bodies with figures wrought on them, like the rest. They had taken several wives, been at the wars, and killed their enemies with their firelocks . . . As for religion, they were not troubled with much of it, and that libertine life they led, was pleasing to them" (French 1846, 154). Four years later La Salle reported that the 199 whites in or near the garrison plus 60 Canadian backwoodsmen living in Indian villages without permission from the governor "destroy by their wicked, libertine lives with Indian women all that the missionaries of the foreign missions and others teach them about the divine mysteries of the Christian religion" (MPA:FD 1929, 2:32).

They not only were concerned with French men who turned their backs on French culture, but also with the threat of a growing mixed blood population that might soon outnumber the French in Louisiana. Duclos, at the request of Pontchartrain, gave four reasons for opposing such marriages in a letter dated December 25, 1725. Among his reasons he wrote that Indian women would either return to savage life or their husbands will become Indians and that such marriages will cause the adulteration of "whiteness of the blood in the children." He argued that "experience shows every day that the children that come of such marriages are of an extremely dark complexion; so that in the course of time, if no Frenchmen come to Louisiana, the colony would become a colony of half-breeds who are naturally idlers, libertines and even greater rascals" (Delanglez 1935, 397–98).

Not only were French men using native women as sexual slaves and concubines, but they were oftentimes prohibited from marrying native women because of the color of their skin and their culture. In a matrilineal, matrilocal society where children identified with the clan and family of the mother, such attitudes defied Choctaw logic. The children of mixed marriages were considered fully Choctaw with an "affectionate and nonauthoritarian relationship with their French father" (Galloway 1987, 126). Perdue notes that among the Cherokee, who were also matrilineal and matrilocal, the children of mixed marriages were considered Cherokee if their mothers were Cherokee and not as "half-breeds" as whites did (1998, 143). Although the Choctaw probably did not understand the attitudes of the French, they recognized that the French treated native women in a manner not considered acceptable. The need arose to protect women from the disrespectful behavior of French men. However, as Choctaw women began to form relationships with French men, and later with American men, concern for their physical safety shifted to one of concern about their economic well-being, as French men had different ideas about gender responsibilities.

Intermarriage

One group of French men that spent extended periods of time among the Choctaw at the behest of the military was the interpreters. Although numerous interpreters resided at different times among the Choctaw to facilitate military and nonmilitary concerns, at least two had lived among the Choctaw on a long-term basis. Father Baudoüin mentioned an interpreter who had been among the Choctaw for twenty-five to thirty years, who, as Galloway points out, would have provided "substantial reinforcement to the influence of the missionary" (Galloway 1987, 120). French policy involved sending young French boys among Indian people to learn their language and to facilitate French goals. Those young boys, cut off from French influences, adopted much of the culture of the Indians they lived among. The French did not penalize the interpreters for their adoption of an Indian lifestyle because such acculturation increased the interpreters' ability to gain information from Indian people. In fact, a native leader might adopt a boy in order to prepare him to be the chief's speaker. Among the Choctaw such a role was formalized in the institution of the *fanimingo*, whereby they adopted a non-Choctaw, giving the person a significant kinship role, who in return represented the Choctaw in councils with the foreign group (Galloway 1987, 111, 125).

It is likely that these young boys who grew up among the Choctaw, as well as the nonresident interpreters, engaged in sexual relations with Choctaw women. Galloway, in her study of interpreters and diplomacy in French Louisiana, notes that it is not clear if marriages between official interpreters and Choctaw women took place; however, indications suggest that they probably did. She points out that there is evidence that friends of interpreters married Indian women and that at least one interpreter, Simon Favré, "may have had a second family that founded the large and influential Mississippi Choctaw Farve line." In any case, French interpreters and Choctaw women would have benefited from such relationships. The interpreters, who often carried on private trading with native people, would have had the advantage of kinship over other traders (Galloway 1987, 126–27). Choctaw women would have had access to European goods that they might not have had otherwise. However, in 1728 the Conseil Supérieur of New Orleans decided that a native woman could not inherit property that belonged to her French husband, although her children could. If she was childless, then the husband's property became part of the domain of the Company of the Indies. Although records do not exist of how the Choctaw reacted to the decision, many natives were aware of French policy (Giraud 1987, 464–65). Inheritance policies thus served to further highlight the differences in gender roles between the French and the Choctaw. Eventually the Choctaw would pass a law in 1826 that reflected recognition of male control of property (Kidwell 1995a, 123).

Although conjugal relationships between French men and native women were at times consensual, such alliances had a deep impact on the Choctaw and often endangered French-Choctaw alliances. Relationships between French traders or soldiers and Choctaw women could endanger hard-won alliances. In one instance Red Shoe, a Choctaw leader at Cushtusha, aligned himself with the English allegedly because he discovered a French trader from Fort Tombigbee in an adulterous relationship with his wife (MPA:FD 1927, 1:33 n. 1; Adair 1775, x, 335). Later, Red Shoe was accused of killing three French officers, and on October 13, 1746, Beauchamp tried to convince Tatoulimataha, chief of Tchanke, to give him the lives of Choctaw in exchange for the French who had been killed.[12] Tatoulimataha refused, saying he would never make an attempt on his brother's life. However, he said if the Abihka or Tallapoosa were to kill Red Shoe, he would not say a word. He suggested that the French were at fault because "if his brother had committed this evil act, it was only from the despair of . . . the bad treatment that he had received, both personally and in the matter of his wives." He asked Beauchamp if it was by the order of the governor that the chiefs and other Frenchmen sent to the nation behaved badly toward them and their wives. He told Beauchamp that the French behavior toward their women "gave them much pain and that red men would kill one another for such things" (MPA:FD 1984, 4:291).[13]

Relationships between French men and Choctaw women also affected deployment of troops. In his report on the distribution and rotation of troops for each of the posts in the Lower Mississippi Valley, Vaudreüil recommended in April 1751 that the garrison at the post of the Alabama not be rotated out and a new one sent in because the soldiers presently there were married men who had many children. He wrote, "we would have to fear that the Alabama might be opposed to it and that this change might lead them to detach themselves from us, since they have even declared several times that they regarded as their own children all the creoles of both sexes born on their land, who today number eighty or ninety" (MPA:FD 1984, 5:68, 71). He also noted that the rotation of the old companies had been interrupted in recent years because, among other things, "this small number of troops included a number of persons who were not at all suitable, in certain posts ... because of the Indians, among whom their conduct might have brought on consequences, as will inevitably happen again today because of the number of vagabonds" (MPA:FD 1984, 5:72).

While consensual intimate relations between some French men and Choctaw women led to tensions between French and Choctaw, sexual misconduct and dismissive attitudes toward women had a telling effect on the status of Choctaw women within their own communities. Improper conduct toward women compelled Choctaw communities to protect their women from French soldiers and civilians, thus constricting their movements. Protective measures became more invasive on the lives of women as contact with the French increased. Native people noticed how French men treated women. According to Father Baudoüin the Choctaw had little respect for the French officer in command at the post of the Yowani in 1732 because the officer exhibited "irregular conduct with reference to the Indian women" (MPA:FD 1927, 1:160–61). Although the Choctaw found French treatment of native women reprehensible, such behavior also, consciously or unconsciously, became a part of their perception of women. The lack of French respect toward Indian women as well as French concerns with the dilution of French blood and culture impacted Choctaw women directly and indirectly. The introduction of French inheritance practices also served to diminish Choctaw women's economic status within their communities.

Disease and Alcohol

Choctaw people observed French attitudes toward indigent women as well as the related problems of disease and alcohol abuse that soon affected Choctaw society. A paradoxical situation had been created in which the French desired women in order to promote stability in the colony. Yet the arrival of French women strained the ability of the settlements to survive, and this concern led some French to seek ways of eliminating their responsibilities to the women. Those women who were sick, widowed, or otherwise indigent were considered burdens on society. In 1723 the king sent De La Chaise as a special commissary to report on affairs in Louisiana Territory. As commissary general Le Chaise worried about the constant shortage of supplies and the resulting black market. In his effort to find ways to extend the supplies he wrote the directors of the Company of the Indies that a number of women and children received rations who did nothing but cause disorder. He stated that "the majority of these women are ruined with pox and ruin the sailors. It is necessary that you be so good as to order the Council to have them go into the interior among the Indians" (MPA:FD 1929, 2:304 n. 1, 315).

Whether these women were actually sent to native villages matters little as the diseases they carried were also carried by French men, as well as by the Spanish and British, who did go among the Indians. The result was devastating. In his letter to the bishop of Quebec, St. Cosme noted that in December 1698 they were saddened to find the Acansea [Quapaw] destroyed by war and smallpox. He wrote, "there was nothing to be seen in the village but graves. There were two [tribes] together there and we estimated that there were not a hundred men; all the children and a great part of the women were dead." In their travels down the Mississippi they also encountered the Tunica, who were dying of disease (Shea 1861, 72, 81). During Iberville's second trip to the Mississippi he wrote in the *Journal of the Renommee* that among the Taensa "the disease diarrhea, which had been in this village for five months, had killed more than half the people" (McWilliams 1981, 122).

Smallpox was particularly devastating to native people. In 1722 Pierre de Charlevoix found Natchez towns ravaged by an epidemic that was most likely smallpox. A year later, in 1723, D'Artaguette noted the devastation of smallpox among the Arkansas, a disease that he said did not exist among the Indians before the French came among them. The Choctaw were hard hit by the 1728 smallpox epidemic that swept through Louisiana Territory. By the end of the Choctaw civil war in 1747 approximately 1,000 to 1,200 children and adults had died of smallpox, more than twice the number of Choctaw who died as a result of fighting (Mereness 1916, 57; Woods 1980, 73, 90, 145; Galloway 1985b, 122, 152 n. 12). During times of epidemic outbreaks people could not carry out their usual duties. The women who were sick could not care for their cornfields, gather wild foods, or even care for their homes. Those who were not stricken by smallpox, or had survived, had their hands full caring for the sick and dying. Their inability to provide food also affected the ceremonial life of the Choctaw, which revolved around the planting and harvesting of crops. The loss of such ceremonies meant the loss of an opportunity to recognize the contributions of Choctaw women.

Alcoholism was just as insidious a disease as smallpox and diarrhea. Although the French government did not approve of alcohol as a trade item, and alcohol does not appear among French records as an item of trade, many of the barrels and casks of wine and brandy sent to the colony found their way to native people. The fact that the Superior Council had to create an ordinance forbidding the trading of wine, and imposed a one hundred–livre fine for violation of the ordinance, indicates the trade of alcohol to native people had become a problem (Woods 1980, 117–18). Michel complained that "The soldiers, in violation of the police regulations, take wine and rum out of it [canteen] and resell it to the negroes and Indians" (MPA:FD 1984, 5:101). In a letter dated November 17, 1750, Father Louis Vivier wrote that "the brandy sold by the French, especially by the soldiers in spite of the King's repeated prohibitions, and that which is distributed to them under the pretext of maintaining them in our interest, has ruined this mission" (Biever 1924, 50; JR 69:201). Alcohol became a trade item as well as a tool of trade. The English, in an attempt to gain a foothold in the deerskin trade with the Choctaw, offered them rum (Surrey 1916, 358–59).

Alcohol contributed to abuses among native people and violence toward others. When drunk, native people fought among themselves and often tried to break into the homes of French soldiers and missionaries (Surrey 1916, 359). Father Louis poignantly described the changes caused by alcohol. The Indians "who are the gentlest and most tractable of men, become, when intoxicated, madmen and wild beasts. Then they fall upon one another, stab with their knives, and tear one another. Many have lost their ears and some portion of their noses, in these tragic encounters" (Biever 1924, 50–51). Abuse of alcohol led to death for some. Vaudreüil commented in his 1750 report to Rouillé that "It is regrettable that some of them are perishing every day because of the illness that is caused them by the trade in liquor, which cannot be suppressed because of the want of merchandise of the qualities [that we have] long asked for without being able to obtain them" (MPA:FD 1984, 5:47). Although little information is available on the effects of the trade in alcohol on Choctaw women, it is reasonable to assume that increased violence also included violence toward women.

In December 1758 Kerlérec submitted a report on the state of the Indian nations that had relations with the colony of Louisiana. About the Tunica he said, "This nation was formerly very numerous. It is at present reduced to about sixty warriors . . . The drink that has been so liberally lavished upon them for more than twenty years has reduced this nation to the number at which it is at present." He said the same of the Houma, who "were formerly very numerous, but they are, like the Tunicas, greatly reduced by the quantity of drink that has been traded to them . . . It [nation] is very lazy and debased by this drink" (MPA:FD 1984, 5:212). And of the Chitimacha he wrote, "[we] can today count about eighty warriors, unfortunate remnants of a numerous nation likewise reduced to this figure by the trade in drink and the close proximity of the French" (MPA:FD 1984, 5:213). The Apalachee fared even worse. He said they had been reduced to about thirty warriors "by the quantity of drink that has always been traded to them" (MPA:FD 1984, 5:224).

Choctaw women would not only have been affected by alcohol abuse among their own people, but also by that of French soldiers and deerskin traders. Drinking was so problematic among the soldiers that Michel, who wanted to disparage Vaudreüil's leadership, reported that "uncleanliness, filth, and corruption infect the soldiers in them [barracks], who besides do everything there that they wish to do. Others run about night and day. . . . They are permitted to do anything, provided that they go and drink at the canteen" (MPA:FD 1984, 5:100–101). In September 1752 Michel wrote Rouillé that "the soldiers that his Majesty has just sent will be almost a total loss for the colony [at New Orleans]. The majority have already run away or died of drunkenness, of debauchery of all sorts, and of venereal diseases" (MPA:FD 1984, 5:116). These same soldiers went among the Choctaw and other native people, leaving behind a trail of abusive behavior toward native women and men. Deerskin traders added to the problem not only because they used rum to manipulate trade with native people, but also because they kidnapped native girls (Surrey 1916, 362). The combination of binge drinking, venereal diseases, and uncontrolled behavior no doubt had a devastating effect on Choctaw women. At the very least they had to try to protect themselves from such behavior, which circumscribed their participation in society.

The Lower Mississippi Valley people including the Choctaw recognized that the French brought disease among them, but the way in which disease affected their conception of the French and themselves is not clear. Although the French also died of disease, many recovered. The missionaries often sought to administer prayers to the sick and often ridiculed indigenous methods of healing. Apparently native people equated missionary prayers with their own healing formulas. In any case some submitted to baptism on their deathbeds. The effects of disease and alcoholism on native women are not known. Reports by the French documented disease and death among men as warriors but not women. However, venereal diseases were of concern to the French and Indians. The threat of venereal disease may have been what led the men of the Arkansas to warn women not to engage in relations with French men or they would die (Mereness 1916, 58). Even in the absence of documentation there can be no doubt that Indian women suffered from the effects of alcoholism and venereal disease, particularly considering their consensual and nonconsensual relations with French men.

Undermining Choctaw Women's Autonomy

The hardships French colonists faced in the Lower Mississippi Valley, along with their attitudes and behaviors toward native women, produced conditions that dehumanized and alienated women within their own communities. Some of the by-products of French colonization such as slavery, disease, and alcohol had very real and observable effects on Choctaw women. As the French struggled to survive, native women became the victims of their solutions to their problems. Indian women, captured and sold as chattel, suffered abuses as labor and sex slaves. Whether as slaves or in their own villages, they also suffered the ravages of disease and alcohol. Even in the case of consensual relationships, French men often ignored their own social rules of behavior as well as those of native people. All of these factors contributed to a breakdown of the social structures of Choctaw society, which had supported the lives of all Choctaw. In the case of women the introduction of slavery and French inheritance practices threatened their well-being and their roles in society. In both cases their independence could be taken away from them.

Choctaw people were aware of how the French treated their own women. Whereas the Choctaw often traveled as a community, the French only sent men among the Choctaw. According to Vaudreüil, whenever the Choctaw went to the post at Tombecbé they would go "there in a troop with their wives and children" (MPA:FD 1984, 5:23). The presence of women and children along with the men bothered the French because they felt imposed upon to provide supplies from their meager stores to those they considered burdens. However, for the Choctaw, everyone was entitled to share in the resources of the community, and men and women traveled together as both were needed to carry out the same responsibilities that they fulfilled at home.

The French also appeared to perceive elder women as burdens on society and thus expendable. In one telling case Bienville and his men, who were on their way to attack the Natchez, encountered an old woman, whom Dumont described as "probably more than a hundred years old, as her hair was quite white." Bienville questioned the woman about the location of water since his troops were dying of thirst, and once she told him, he "abandoned her, as a useless burthen [*sic*] to the earth, to a little slave of his, who scalped and killed her" (French 1853, 53). Although the Choctaw also might kill an elder woman of another nation, they typically did so not because she was a burden, but because she represented the enemy.

The effects of French colonization on the roles of Choctaw women went beyond observable ones. As the Choctaw became aware of differences between their societies and that of the French, they had to reconcile those new ideas with their own. Although the Choctaw tried to maintain traditional gender responsibilities, changes were inevitable as they had to consider adaptations in accordance with the changing world in which they lived. French practices and missionary teachings about women influenced Choctaw ideas about the roles of women. For example, the French practice of ridiculing a man by referring to him as a woman affected the way in which native people perceived women. In one case, the "Great Chief" complained that Mr. Diron, who was in charge at Mobile, called him "a woman and that he did not wish to see me any more" (MPA:FD 1927, 1:33). The Great Chief retaliated to the insult by accepting a gift from the English, saying that the French did not give the Choctaw what they needed, but instead said he was a woman in front of the Little Chief of the Yellow Canes and several others. The Great Chief lamented that "the Frenchman has not always spoken thus of me" (MPA:FD 1927, 1:34).

Of course Choctaw people also humiliated men into action by accusing them of acting like women. In one instance Tonty, chief of the Mobile, who was angry with the French, told the Tohomé that they could not get ammunition from the French at Mobile. He warned them "that if they had war with any nation they would be defeated like women since they did not have any ammunition to defend themselves" (MPA:FD 1927, 1:24). However, we do not know if such threats had the same meaning to the Choctaw as they did to the French. We do know that Choctaw ideas about gender differed in many respects from those of the French. To be an Indian woman meant to engage in peaceful activities such as farming or cooking. Thus to be called a woman indicated that one did not have the skills attributed to men. In other words, one could not fulfill one's expected role in society, a serious shortcoming in communal societies where everyone needed to fulfill his or her responsibilities for the well-being of society. Thus, to be called a woman was an insult, not because women were disparaged, but because women did not train for battle. In any case, the French clearly insulted Choctaw men by referring to them as women whom the French did not take seriously. Although the effects of expression of such attitudes are difficult to quantify, there can be no doubt that the interaction between the French and Choctaw had a reciprocal effect on each other's behaviors.

In any case, the presence of French colonists among Choctaw people necessarily had an impact on both groups. The fear that the French who lived with Choctaw women might become more Indian-like reflected on Choctaw women. The actions of French men, particularly those who spent long periods of time among the Choctaw such as the interpreters or traders, had the potential to influence the lives of Choctaw women as in the case of inheritance laws. When the actions of colonists such as traders, interpreters, and slave owners are considered in conjunction with missionary and military actions, the overall impact on Choctaw gender roles takes on tremendous significance. Choctaw people not only altered roles in response to the effects of colonization, they also experienced new ideas about women, many of which would be realized in the form of laws and regulations in the nineteenth century.[14]

5

When the Dancing Stopped

If the idea of Choctaw beloved women was common during the time of early French colonization, then the use of that designation, but not necessarily the associated roles, must have passed out of use fairly quickly. By the end of the eighteenth century references to beloved women are no longer found. Even if the appellation were used infrequently, as the rarity of documented accounts would suggest, the question of why the title disappeared still remains. We know that Choctaw women's roles underwent significant change during the French colonial period, which in turn led to loss of status and conceivably any associated titles. However, we also know that beloved women continued to exist in other Southeastern cultures that underwent similar colonial contact. One reason for the different histories is that the structures that supported the status of women survived in one group and not the other. By examining how particular structures of society sustained women's status, or conventions such as the bestowal of titles like beloved woman, and what happens to those conventions when the structures supporting them break down, we can understand how the concept of Choctaw beloved women passed out of use so quickly.

The structures that support the conventions of society may take the form of rules, practices, or customs that can be flexible in response to environmental factors. For example, among the Choctaw it was customary for men to hunt and for women to farm. However, during the most crucial periods of farming, planting and harvesting, men assisted the women, but they did not lose status by doing so (Pesantubbee 1999, 405). During the rest of the year the expectations for male and female responsibilities continued until or unless another critical event occurred that required adaptations. Not until the nineteenth century, under American and Protestant pressure, do we find Choctaw men taking over farming responsibilities, an action that affected the status of men and women.

Choctaw encounters with the French required adjustments in Choctaw society, some of them voluntary, others necessary for survival. Many of the changes that affected women's roles might not have happened so quickly and thoroughly if some of the structures of Choctaw society had not been stressed by a myriad of factors in a short period of time. Issues of safety, morality, and interpersonal relationships between Choctaw people and multiple segments of French society, including explorers, military and civil officers, missionaries, interpreters, and traders, created numerous intersections of stress on Choctaw society. If Choctaw people had had to deal with only one segment of French society at a time, or one issue, then the structures of their society might have adapted to the introduction of new ideas and practices. However, as is the nature of society, the general actions and concerns of each French group paralleled and reinforced those of the others in ways that required dramatic reorganization of women's activities. Whether it was the avoidance of women by missionaries or aggressive behavior by French colonists toward women, both actions forced awareness of relations between men and women in new ways and required changes in behavior.

In the case of French colonization, we have seen how the alliance between the French and the Choctaw led to changes in the handling of captives and the distribution of property in the case of intermarriage, both of which affected women's roles and status in their communities. In both cases the Choctaw continued the practice of taking captives and supporting matrilineal, matrilocal inheritance rules, but changes also took place in those customs as a result of French influence. In this chapter we will look at how changes in one practice, the Green Corn Ceremony, a major Southeastern ceremonial, affected Choctaw women, and how the resultant changes in women's roles, in turn, affected the ceremony. However, unlike other Choctaw structures that survived through adaptations, the Green Corn Ceremony as a religious practice ceased to exist among the Choctaw. By examining the interdependent, interactive relationship between Choctaw women and the Green Corn Ceremony we can gain insight into how a designation like beloved woman could disappear so quickly.

The process of decline that took place in the usage of beloved woman is perhaps best illustrated through the use of the Green Corn Ceremony because it is unquestionably the central ceremonial practice of Southeastern native people. The decline in the celebration of the Choctaw's annual Green Corn Ceremony also occurred primarily during the period of French colonization. Among the Cherokee, who continued to use the title of beloved woman, the Green Corn Ceremony survived for a much longer period of time. Although the Choctaw ceased practicing the Green Corn as a religious ceremony by the end of the eighteenth century, they began holding fairs during harvest time that many contemporary Choctaw consider to be a modern form of the Green Corn Ceremony, where one can eat traditional corn dishes or observe stickball games and social dances. The first documented fair among the Mississippi Choctaw took place at Tucker community in the fall of 1935, and the Oklahoma Choctaw have been holding their annual Labor Day festival at the capitol grounds since 1884 (Ferguson 2002; Pesantubbee 1994, 68; Kidwell 1995b, 206 n. 23). Although the fairs help to retain Choctaw culture and identity, it is the loss of the ceremony itself that is important to understanding changes in Choctaw women's roles in the eighteenth century.

Green Corn Ceremony

The Green Corn Ceremony was a harvest celebration that generally took place in September when the corn had ripened. To consider the Green Corn Ceremony "as merely an agricultural rite," however, would be, as James H. Howard, an anthropologist who studied Southeastern native people, said, "as erroneous as to regard the present-day American Christmas solely as a religious commemoration of Christ's birth" (1968, 81). For eighteenth-century Southeastern native people the Green Corn Ceremony was the heart of their social and ceremonial world. It was a time of renewal and forgiveness, of sharing and thankfulness, a time to feast and dance in celebration of the harvest, to ensure success in hunting and warfare, and to welcome in the new year through purification and regeneration of the sacred fire. The ceremony

Fig. 2. Frontal view of Keller Figurine. Female kneeling behind basket with a cornstalk remnant to the right of basket. Used with permission of Illinois Transportation Archaeological Research Program, University of Illinois.

strengthened social bonds by uniting towns and recognizing the contributions and significance of everyone, men and women, children and elders. Through this ceremony Southeastern native people reinforced and emphasized the socioreligious ideals of balance, restitution, reciprocity, and consensus, all beloved values.

For the Choctaw the roots of the Green Corn Ceremony extend back to the origin of corn, when they first received corn from Ohoyo Osh Chisba,

Fig. 3. Side view of Keller Figurine. Female kneeling on ears of corn or mat of reeds. Used with permission of Illinois Transportation Archaeological Research Program, University of Illinois.

The Unknown Woman, a beloved being. The plant grew out of the very ground that Ohoyo Osh Chisba had stood upon. Its roots reached deep into the ground, the place of the Below World, where death, fertility, and certain powerful spirits resided. Its stalk rose toward the Above World, the home of "Hosh-tal-li" or Aba, the one above, and the place of the powerful sun, moon, stars, lightening, and thunder. Corn itself not only provided sustenance for the people of this world, but through its roots and stalks tied the three parts of the world together—Above, Below, and This World.[1] Because the corn plant crossed the boundaries of the three worlds it was considered powerful. It was beloved. It was beloved woman. And because women had primary responsibility for the corn, they were the mediators between the fertility and power of the corn and the Choctaw people. They nurtured the corn, which in turn provided food and medicine for the people and offerings for Aba.

The association of women with beloved corn and other domestic plants has a long history in the Southeast. Evidence of the importance of women in the agricultural cycle of Middle Mississippian peoples, progenitors of the Choctaw and other Southeastern peoples, is provided in the form of clay figurines found throughout the Southeast. Two such figurines were found in 1979 during excavations initiated by the University of Illinois. Archaeologists uncovered two fireclay (flint clay) sculptures in what is known as the BBB Motor site, which is located near the outskirts of Cahokia, an expansive Mississippian mound center located across the Mississippi River from St. Louis. The figurines are associated with the Early Stirling phase of the Middle Mississippian period, which dates their manufacture sometime between AC 1050 to AC 1200 (Emerson 1982, 3; Emerson 1997, 195; Prentice 1986, 240).

One of the statuettes, the Keller figurine, is a woman with a sloping forehead kneeling on a series of contiguous rectangles, some of which have vertical lines enclosed in shallow arcs on their upper portions (see figures 2 and 3). Thomas E. Emerson, an archaeologist, believes the incised lines may represent ears of corn or bundled reeds woven into a mat. Corn is a likely interpretation since there appears to be a basket in front of the woman with a cornstalk base next to it. The box in front of her is a rectangular, box-like object composed of vertical rods with a smooth cover. The figurine obviously represents the fertility of crops, but she may also represent a deity patting a rain cloud (the smoothed, loaf-shaped object also identified as a basket cover) from which rain is falling (the vertical rods) (Emerson 1982, 8, 10; Emerson 1997, 196, 201–2).

The other image, the Birger figurine, represents a kneeling woman who rests her left hand on the head of a carnivore-headed serpent, while her right hand hoes or tills the serpent's back. The serpent curls about the woman's knees and on her left side it bifurcates into two plant vines with three fruits each. The lips of the woman are curled back to bare her teeth. The features of the Birger figurine look similar to a trophy head because the facial muscles of the victim would relax, leading to the hanging of the jaw (see figures 4 and 5). Emerson believes that the woman symbolized agricultural fertility and the serpent depicted a water monster, a figure common in Southeastern cultural traditions. The serpent with a head like a panther represented the Below World of water and earth and This World, which is the place of animals. In addition, the three fruits that Emerson described as depicting the various stages of plant growth, the larger lower gourd being the older fruit and the smoother, smaller gourd on top the newer growth, could also represent the three worlds, Above, Below, and This World (Prentice 1986, 240–45; Emerson 1982, 5). The vines reaching toward the sky, like the cornstalk, connected This World to the Above World and the roots extending down into the soil attached This World to the Below World.[2]

Interestingly, the connection between the figurines and fertility is also suggested by Ramey Incised pottery found at the BBB site. The Ramey Incised pottery is unusual in that it was scarce, it was of general high quality, and it was not found just among the elite, suggesting that it was a special-purpose ware that was used by people across classes (Emerson 1989, 48–49, 63–64). Galloway raises the possibility that Ramey Incised pottery was used by menstruating women or was made by menstruating women while secluded in menstrual houses, which would account for their distribution across classes, but also their limited use. She also notes the presence of jimsonweed (*Datura stramonium*), which could have been used for abortions, and a large red crystal with a striking red impurity (1998, 208). If her interpretation is correct, then, as she suggests, the BBB site may have been the location of a menstrual house where activities related to female fertility such as childbirth, puberty rituals, and purification rituals took place. Emerson points out that a bottle found on the same site has what appears to be a female figure whose right arm ends in a bulbous fruit rather than a hand. The emanation of a fruit from her arm could symbolize fertility and birth (Emerson 1997, 207). If some of the archaeological sites like BBB were actually places for menstrual seclusion and fertility ceremonialism rather than elite ceremonial or purification sites for men, then such sites are arguably evidence of the importance of women's fertility within native societies (Galloway 1998, 204–5).

In any case, the two figurines indicate the importance of women and agriculture to Mississippian cultures, and later to the Choctaw. Recent evidence indicates that the fireclays used in making the figurines came from

Fig. 4. Frontal view of Birger Figurine. Female rests left hand on head of serpent while her right hand tills the serpent's back. Used with permission of Illinois Transportation Archaeological Research Program, University of Illinois.

several sources near St. Louis. The identification of the source of the fireclay is important for its implications. Emerson points out that flint clay deposits found in Southeastern Missouri are consistent with a pattern of using materials from this area in much of American bottom Mississippian trade (Emerson 1997, 195–96). Associations between the fireclay figurines and the Choctaw can also be seen in the historical Choctaw practice of flattening the forehead

Fig. 5. Rear view of Birger Figurine. Serpent wraps around back of female figure where its tail bifurcates and transforms into vines with gourds. Used with permission of Illinois Transportation Archaeological Research Program, University of Illinois.

of an infant, which led to a long sloping forehead as depicted by the Keller figure (Emerson 1982, 8). Interestingly, William Bartram and Bernard Romans identified only male infants as having their heads artificially flattened by bags of sand (Bartram 1928, 404; Romans 1775, 56). Adair, however, did not single out men as the only ones having their foreheads flattened. He wrote that "the Choktah Indians flatten their fore-heads" in order to beautify themselves

(1775, 9–10). In any case, the Keller figurine indicates that Mississippian women at one time also had their foreheads flattened and one has to wonder when the practice may have ceased for female infants.

By the time the French encountered the indigenous peoples of the Lower Mississippi Valley, native people had been growing corn for over five hundred years. By AD 1200 native people had begun cultivating not only corn, but also beans. The Choctaw raised as many as three varieties of corn, and prepared many different kinds of corn dishes, including sagamite, which was often mentioned by the French (Woods 1980, 4). Antoine Simon Le Page du Pratz, one of the earliest European commentators on native agriculture, identified the basic native corns as "a flour corn with a white, flat, shriveled surface, four kinds of 'hominy corn,' and a small early corn that ripened so quickly that the Choctaws got two crops of it in a season. In addition to these varieties, the Choctaws, by their own account, possessed a popcorn, a variety of the original tropical flint corn" (White 1983, 19; Du Pratz 1774, 226; Campbell 1959, 16–17). The Choctaw produced enough corn to provide for their needs. Romans estimated that the lands along the Tombigbee and Mississippi Rivers could produce up to eighty bushels per acre, and that even poorer sandy soils could yield fifteen to twenty-five bushels an acre (1775, 83).

As we have seen, responsibility for corn lay with the women among the Choctaw. Men assisted with planting and harvesting, but throughout the rest of the season women cared for and guarded the beloved plants. In the "Relation de La Louisianne," a small bound manuscript apparently written in the earlier part of the eighteenth century, the unknown author wrote that women "work the ground, sow, and harvest the crop" (Swanton 1931, 139).[3] Several times during the summer women hoed the soil, which they built up into hills around the corn to secure the plants from the wind (White 1983, 21; Du Pratz 1774, 184). The soil represented the land of This World and the fertility of the Below World, a boundary crossing that indicated a place of power. The French witnessed the power that the native people associated with the soil each time they rubbed their hands in the dirt wherever beloved people had walked.

When we understand the significance of corn in the Choctaw world, then we begin to see how women's responsibility for corn gave them influence in all aspects of Choctaw society. Roughly two-thirds of the Choctaw's food supply came from cultivated crops including corn, beans, and squash (White

1983, 26). Women provided the corn that nourished their families. They prepared the corn that fed visitors to their villages and diplomats that sought peaceful relations with them. A woman's family provided the gift of corn for their daughter's wedding. The corn they grew could be used as medicine that drew on the power of all three worlds to bring health to the Choctaw.[4] It is also likely that the Choctaw sacrificed corn to the fire during the Green Corn Ceremony as an offering of thanks to the spirit of the sun. The Choctaw recognized fire as an informant to the sun, who possessed the power of life and death. The practice of offering corn to the fire was common among other Southeastern native peoples, and it is likely the Choctaw had a similar custom (Campbell 1959, 18; Howard 1968, 83–84; Swanton 1931, 132, 138, 195–97).

Through the celebration of the corn harvest Choctaw people paid homage to and reinforced all the desired acts of human beings. Just as women, through their labor, provided the corn needed for renewal of Choctaw society at harvest time, the Green Corn Ceremony acknowledged and celebrated those tasks carried out by women. Since Choctaw women provided corn and engaged in activities that embodied desired values, it makes sense that those women entrusted with the most important and sacred of those activities, if not all those involved, would be respected. A decline in the practice of the Green Corn Ceremony meant fewer opportunities to formally recognize the contributions of women, and as the roles of women changed or disappeared so too did their contributions that made the ceremony possible.

Although accounts of the Choctaw Green Corn Ceremony provide few details about the ceremony itself, similar ceremonies were held throughout the Southeast and we can draw from accounts of those ceremonies to construct a reasonable picture of the Choctaw ceremony.[5] We can also study accounts about the Choctaw ceremony to determine how or why the Green Corn began to decline among the Choctaw. According to James Adair, the Choctaw of the 1740s had not celebrated the Green Corn for several years. He attributed the break in the practice to the fact that "the Choktah, by not having deep rivers or creeks to purify themselves by daily ablutions, are become very irreligious in other respects, for of late years, they make no annual atonement for sin" (Adair 1775, 325).

Adair's comment raises questions about his reasoning because ample sources of water for purification existed in Choctaw country. A rich river system consisting of the Mississippi, Yazoo, Big Black, Pearl, Leaf, Chickasawhay,

Tombigbee, and Alabama Rivers flowed through the region that was home to the Choctaw. Adair, in fact, contradicted himself when he described Choctaw country as generally abounding "with springs and creeks, or small brooks . . . Their towns are settled on small streams" (303). It may be that Adair, who had spent several years among the Cherokee, was familiar with their daily practice of going to water that involved completely submerging themselves in moving water. At times the springs, creeks, and brooks in Choctaw country may not have been deep enough to allow for total submersion, or the Choctaw practice may have been based on a cycle other than that of the rising sun. However, as Mooney noted, the Cherokee might also perform the purification rite by dipping their cupped hands into the water and then pouring the water over their heads and breasts (1982, 31; 1891, 335). If the Choctaw followed the latter practice, then the depth of their waterways might not matter.

Adair's statement that the Choctaw were not always able to go to water, a necessary act prior to entering sacred space, because of the lack of adequate waterways, therefore, suggests that other factors contributed to a decline in the practice of going to water. Possibly the Choctaw had ceased daily practices of going to water because warfare or epidemics forced them to constantly move away from certain waterways. At times it may have been too dangerous to travel outside the safety of villages in order to purify themselves. Or, in the case of epidemics, ritual leaders may have been too sick to lead the rites, or as often happens during epidemics, the elders most knowledgeable of the rite may have succumbed to disease before they could pass the needed knowledge to the next generation. Another possibility is that at times some streams may have become too low for submersion because of drought. More likely, all of these factors contributed to the cessation of the practice. As one mixed blood Choctaw told Adam Hodgson in 1820, at one time children were made "to plunge in the water" in the morning and at sunset, after which an elder would relate the traditions of their ancestors, but the practice had been abandoned due to the great changes that had taken place (1823, 278–79). Since purification was part of the Green Corn Ceremony, the decrease in the practice of going to water would have contributed to or reflected a decline in the annual harvest ceremony.

The observations of Du Pratz, a sometime trader and planter among the Natchez in Louisiana in the 1720s, suggest similar reasons for the decline in the Green Corn Ceremony among the Choctaw. In his recollections about native ceremonies in Louisiana Territory, he noted that since the arrival of the French religious ceremonies had lapsed "since their numbers have been greatly diminished" (1774, 351). Apparently population reduction resulting from disease, slave raids, civil war, and intertribal wars due to French and English actions impaired native people's ability to carry out ceremonies. The Green Corn Ceremony required the contributions of the entire community and often included neighboring towns. One's clan or family determined responsibilities, especially those belonging to white towns or peace towns. If those clans or families suffered losses, their ability to carry out their duties may have been impaired. As the ceremony became less frequent, and those most knowledgeable about the ceremony died, the ceremony itself would have become less elaborate and of shorter duration, eventually disappearing.

Evidence that the Green Corn Ceremony was still extant among the Choctaw in the mid-eighteenth century lies in an ambiguous statement made by William Bartram, a botanist who traveled through the Floridas, Carolina, and Georgia in 1773. Bartram had many opportunities to meet Creek, Cherokee, and Choctaw people during his travels. Among the Creek he observed that "some of their most favourite songs and dances, they have from their enemies, the Chactaws." They sought songs and dances from the Choctaw because they had to have "at least one new song, for exhibition, at every annual busk" (1928, 396). Although Bartram does not refer to the Choctaw when describing the Creek busk, or Green Corn Ceremony, not having been to the interior of Choctaw territory, his reference to the Choctaw as a source of new songs for the busk suggests that the Choctaw also held Green Corn ceremonies.[6] At the very least they composed songs that one would assume they sang at their own Green Corn dances.

Interestingly, Reverend Alfred Wright, a missionary to the Choctaw in the 1820s, reported that "it is extremely difficult to ascertain what the traditions of the Choctaws were." According to him a "difficulty in ascertaining their ancient traditions, arises from their unwillingness to divulge them, especially to foreigners" (1828a, 178). Wright also attributed the difficulty to the loss of knowledge of traditions that had occurred since contact with whites. He wrote that the few elders who retained knowledge no longer seemed to be transmitting that knowledge to the youth and children through the art of storytelling (1828a, 178). Wright may have been correct about the Choctaw's unwillingness to share information about the Green Corn Ceremony. David

I. Bushnell learned from the Choctaw at Bayou Lacomb that the Choctaw in times past never permitted whites to observe their dances. The Choctaw told him that if they "suspected a white man was watching them they would extinguish the fires at once and remain in darkness" (1909, 22).

According to Chahta immatahah, whom Gideon Lincecum interviewed from 1823 to 1825, he learned from his elders that the Choctaw were already holding annual new fruits ceremonies when they received the gift of corn. When the first crop of corn matured they held a five-day dance and feast called *Tanchi Okchamali Hihla*, Green Corn Dance. They held the dance annually in early summer until the Europeans brought them alcohol and people began to get drunk instead of dancing (1861, 20–26).[7] The women prepared several dishes including *tanch hiloha*, or green corn roasted on the cob, *tan fula*, a thick corn soup that was a hospitality food, and *tan hlabo*, a corn and meat stew that was eaten during the annual Green Corn Dance. Unfortunately, as T. N. Campbell noted, Lincecum did not provide much in the way of descriptions of the ceremony although it is clear from his writings that he believed "it was a focal point in their ceremonial life" (Campbell 1959, 17–18, 21 n. 2).

Obviously the Green Corn Ceremony existed among the Choctaw, but by the 1820s it was in such a state of decline that it may be that some Choctaw did not know of the ceremony while others chose not to mention it. According to David I. Bushnell, by 1908 the Choctaw of Bayou Lacomb no longer had any ceremonies although they had a series of seven distinct dances that they performed at night. The last dance was always the *siente hitkla* (snake dance) in which a singer led everyone around the dance ground in serpentine fashion (1909, 20–21). This and the other dances may have once been part of Green Corn ceremonies as similar dances are found at contemporary Creek busks (Howard 1968, 110, 114).

Decline in the Production of Corn

We may never know if the Green Corn Ceremony was in a state of decline or development among the Choctaw at the time of French contact. However, we do know that French colonization marked a time of great change in the Lower Mississippi Valley that no doubt affected the viability of the Green Corn Ceremony. To understand how the Green Corn Ceremony disappeared, it is perhaps best to begin with corn, for it was the success of the corn crop that gave cause for celebration and thanks. It was also the failure of the corn crop that contributed to the loss of the ceremony. Corn crops failed for reasons beyond human control. They also were lost because of intentional destruction by enemies, or because conflict prevented Choctaw people from planting or harvesting their crops.

Natural disasters such as drought often meant the loss of corn crops. Summer droughts were not unheard of in the Lower Mississippi Valley. The French reported crop failures in 1713 due to a drought that may have also affected the Choctaw. In 1734 a drought did destroy the Choctaw corn crop (White 1983, 28). The Choctaw had a memory of droughts, and Horatio Bardwell Cushman, who spent much of his life among or near the Choctaw, recounted their story about a drought followed by three years of famine that took place long ago in the days of their ancestors. As he retold it,

> ... the Tombigbee River, together with all the lakes and ponds, were completely dried up; that the river ceased to run, the water standing only in holes here and there, that all the larger game left the country going west; that the buffalo, then inhabiting their country, never returned. (1899, 306)

During times of drought, streams dried up, which meant the loss of fish from their diet. To avoid starvation they had to leave their towns for the woods in order to hunt for game and wild foods. With increased dependency on game and extended hunting periods, Choctaw were forced to remain away from their towns for most of the year (White 1983, 29–31). Thus the Choctaw not only would not have corn during times of drought, they also would not be residing in their towns where they held their ceremonies. Worms and hot winds like those that occurred in 1737 damaged crops. Records indicate that the Choctaw harvest failed completely in 1760 and was poor in 1777 and 1778. In 1782 and 1792 drought again destroyed their crops (White 1983, 28). The failure of corn crops or poor harvests might have meant the cancellation of the annual Green Corn Ceremony or might have convinced Choctaw people that the Green Corn Ceremony was needed more than ever in order to ensure the success of future harvests. However, such natural disasters coupled with the intentional destruction of their crops by their enemies may have made the former more likely.

Summer, the season for growing corn, was also the time for warfare (Perdue 1998, 87). French and English intrigues contributed to intra-tribal and intertribal warfare that brought not only the danger of death and captivity, but also destruction of crops. Indian allies of the British ravaged or burned Choctaw cornfields. Attacks by their enemies often prevented Choctaw towns, especially those on the north and eastern border, from cultivating their crops (Higgenbotham 1977, 219–20; Galloway 1995, 188, 196). When English-allied Indians attacked the Chickasawhay, the Chickasawhay lost more than two thousand warriors; to avoid complete defeat they abandoned their villages, leaving behind their crops (MPA:FD 1927, 1:156). Hostilities between different groups of Choctaw also led to destruction of crops. During the civil war between the Eastern and Western Choctaw in 1749, the Eastern Choctaw destroyed the Western Choctaw's corn crop (Woods 1980, 157). Such intra-tribal violence was not conducive to holding ceremonies that typically required the cooperation of friends and relatives.

Violence extended beyond the destruction of crops to the captivity and enslavement of women who tended fields that lay outside the boundaries of their towns. During times of extreme danger they may not have been able to plant or tend their crops, especially if the men who usually provided protection while the women were in the fields were away at war. The constant threat posed by the French and English may have been so overwhelming to some Choctaw that they chose to abandon their fields rather than live with the fear of attack. Chahta immatahah provides us with a telling line from one of the Choctaw dances, which they called the terrapin or turtle dance because the valley they fled to had thousands of terrapin that were good to eat and could easily be gathered by women and children:

> A life in the wilderness with plenty of meat, fish, fowl and the luksa hihla [turtle dance], is far better than our old homes, and the corn, and the fruit, and the heart melting fear of the dreadful Nahullo [white people]. (Lincecum 1861, 134–35, 148)

If, as the above lyric suggests, some Choctaw chose to survive by primarily hunting and gathering food rather than by farming, the implications for women and for the Green Corn are enormous. Women would no longer have the influence they once had through their association with corn. Not only would the ceremonial that celebrated corn, the product of women's labor, no longer be necessary, but also women's major contribution to the economic and political life of the community would be gone. Women would have to find new ways to contribute to the economic and political life of the Choctaw. The relationship between men and women would be out of balance until or unless their relationships were reconstituted in new ways to restore balance.

Whether or not Choctaw chose to abandon fields for forests, adaptation to a changing world may have affected the way in which they formed communities. In the case of the Cherokee, historian William G. McLoughlin noted that by 1809 their towns had changed considerably. "The traditional kind of compact community, centered around a single council house and ceremonial ground, was virtually gone" (1986, 170). Little information exists as to the layout of early eighteenth-century Choctaw towns. J.F.H. Claiborne described a council square or open space generally in a central location where people met for council meetings, national assemblies, stickball, or dances (Claiborne 1880, 490–91). Roullet, who visited the Choctaw in 1732, wrote of several towns that were situated on plains surrounded by natural barriers like a bayou or hills, or in one case a palisaded fort for protection. According to him their cornfields lay in the plains, and in the case of Yazoo village, their houses were built around the plain (Swanton 1931, 76). At the time of Adair's travels among the Choctaw in the mid-eighteenth century, he noted that barrier towns were compactly settled for social defense, "but the rest, both in the center, and toward the Mississippi, are only scattered plantations, as best suits a separate way of living" (1775, 302). Disease, war, and natural disasters may have forced Choctaw people away from their towns, or they may have adapted a form of community best suited to farming. In either case, they like the Cherokee may have become too dispersed to support the Green Corn Ceremony.

Disease may also have played a part in the decline of the Green Corn Ceremony. Although figures are not available, disease clearly affected the life of towns. In 1699 Iberville reported numerous Indian towns on the lower Pascagoula abandoned due to disease (Galloway 1994, 406). In March of the same year he found among the Bayogoula "possibly about 200 to 250 men and few women and children." According to his report one-fourth of the Bayogoula had died from smallpox, which was still spreading among the survivors (McWilliams 1981, 63). Galloway suggested that Soto and his men might have brought the common cold and tuberculosis, as well as "a truly remarkable disease vector in the shape of their ever-growing herd of pigs." Those diseases may have been communicable to humans as well as to deer and turkeys that were an important part of the Choctaw diet (1994, 399). She points out that workers today who are routinely exposed to live animals or the flesh of slaughtered animals are concerned about the transmission of diseases from infected animals, and she suggests that such transmissions of a range of diseases were possible in the past (1995, 133). Although men hunted, women generally processed the meat and hides, putting them at risk for disease. The loss of family and clan members due to illness may at times have left Choctaw towns without sufficient labor to plant or harvest crops or to carry out the lengthy Green Corn Ceremony.

Women provided the corn and contributed to the labor that made the Green Corn Ceremony possible. As the Green Corn Ceremony became less frequent, the opportunity for publicly reinforcing the significance of women's contributions also declined. As the activities of women that once supported the ceremony began to be curtailed or circumscribed, then the Green Corn Ceremony itself declined. The activities of women and the Green Corn Ceremony, caught in an interactive interdependent cycle of decline spurred by French colonization, reinforced each other's slide toward disappearance. To understand how changes in the Green Corn Ceremony and the roles of women brought about changes in each other, we must, one, identify outside forces that effected change in each and, two, trace how those external changes operated internally, within Choctaw structures, in an interactive, interdependent way that fostered a process of change that ended only with the cessation of the Green Corn Ceremony and the loss of memory about the ideal of beloved women.

The violence that surrounded French and British colonialism in the Lower Mississippi Valley affected both the Green Corn Ceremony and women. The Green Corn Ceremony, a time of diplomacy, of demonstrating and extending friendships to allies and neighbors, required a temporary setting aside of bad feelings or hostilities. The ceremony involved purifying the community of the societal pollution that had accumulated for the past year as a result of humans being unable to live up to social ideals (Wetmore 1983, 51). It brought people together on the white path of peace and harmony, and anything bloody and violent was to be set aside for the time being. If the

Choctaw were in the midst of conflict (civil or international), as they often were during the time of French colonization, then they might not have been able to set aside those conditions long enough to allow for the ceremony. Or they might not have had the labor necessary to carry out the ceremony because of war and the slave trade. In the case of the eastern Choctaw village of Scanapa, enemies killed the men, enslaved the women and children, and destroyed the village (Galloway 1994, 406). Not only did the larger Choctaw community lose a village of people who would have participated in a Green Corn Ceremony, they also were thrown into a state of mourning that was antithetical to a life-praising ceremony of thanksgiving. Such attacks also required able men to travel away from their communities in order to exact reparations for the deaths of their relatives.

Each time the Choctaw failed to carry out the ceremony, they missed the single most important opportunity to validate and reinforce the values that informed their social relations. Some of those values included recognition of women's contributions to the food supply of the community as well as their importance to the maintenance of Choctaw social, political, and religious structures. One of the primary functions of the ceremony included greeting honored visitors and feasting them with an abundance of food including corn and venison. Such magnificent feasts required the contributions of both women and men as each respectively supplied corn and venison. If cornfields were destroyed or women were not able to harvest the ripened green corn, then women could not produce the indispensable offering of corn to Aba or the expected corn dishes. The very reason for the ceremony no longer existed. The Green Corn Ceremony expressed thanks for the abundance of the earth and it ensured future fertility. Without the Green Corn Ceremony the Choctaw had no assurance that their people and the plants and animals they depended upon would flourish in the coming year. Not only were women at those times not able to provide the primary food for the ceremony, but also the symbol that connected women to the power of the fertility of the earth was missing.

The most powerful means for Choctaw people to contribute to and demonstrate the key ideals that informed and bound together Choctaw society had been taken from them. War and mourning meant that at times women could not plant or harvest corn; at other times, the Green Corn Ceremony could not be carried out. Both these activities were carried out at home. Men, however, as providers of game and as warriors did not engage in hunting or initiate attacks at home, and thus could continue to carry out some of their responsibilities even when cornfields were destroyed or villages abandoned. Thus in many ways the loss of the Green Corn had a greater impact on the reinforcement and recognition of women's roles than it did on those of the men.

Impact of the Deerskin Trade

Changing economic conditions also likely contributed to a decline in the practice of the Green Corn Ceremony. The French, in an effort to encourage Choctaw dependence and alliance, encouraged the deerskin trade. By 1725 the French had traded for more than fifty thousand hides, including four thousand deerskins from the Choctaw. In an effort to curtail the English trade among the Choctaw, French officials in 1732 reported to France that they were buying up all the deerskins the Choctaw could supply. In just two months they obtained 2,200 skins (Surrey 1916, 348–50). The French paid dearly for the skins when they could in order to maintain control over Choctaw trade. In 1754 Governor Kerlérec traded French items worth 62,000 livres for Choctaw peltries worth 30,000 livres. The French collected hides from the Choctaw although many of them rotted due to the heat and humidity or were destroyed by mites and other insects. In spite of the losses, during the war years, 1744–48, when supplies of French goods were limited, an estimated 1,600 Frenchmen engaged in the deerskin trade (Woods 1980, 40, 84; Surrey 1916, 360–62).

In order to facilitate the deerskin trade, the French focused more on hunting paraphernalia as trade and gift items than they did on the domestic necessities of women. Although the French occasionally provided limbourg cloth and blankets and occasionally kettles that could be used by women, an examination of their trade items shows they provided significantly more in the way of guns, ammunition, axes, knives, and shirts. In 1720, M. Pellerine, who hoped to profit from the proposed development of the deerskin trade in the Mobile area, ordered four hundred light muskets, two thousand weight in balls, three thousand ells of cloth, two hundred small hatchets, and forty sabers, which he planned to trade with the native people for skins (Woods 1980, 84). The French also provided cloth and awls that allowed women to substitute cloth clothing for bark or deerskin clothes, the deerskins being needed for the French trade. In the 1740s, the French traded bullets, powder, guns, knives, needles, razors, vermilion, cloth, ribbons, blankets, shirts, mirrors, hardware, and watered-down brandy for skins (Surrey 1916, 357–58). When the French tried to encourage Choctaw men to kill their own kinsman, Red Shoe, they offered a bounty consisting of "2 pieces of limbourg cloth, 48 blankets, 10 guns, 4 pounds of vermilion, 100 pounds of powder, 200 pounds of balls, 40 shirts and an assortment of trinkets" (Woods 1980, 155). The Choctaw desperately needed guns and ammunition, a need that Governor Vaudreüil took advantage of by prohibiting the trade of arms or ammunition to any Choctaw until they made reparations for the deaths of three French men by killing Red Shoe (Bossu 1962, 175).

Even before the development of the deerskin trade with Southeastern native people, French explorers tended to provide hunting and military paraphernalia rather than domestic items. On February 14, 1699, Iberville reported leaving "two axes, four knives, two packages of glass beads, a little vermillion" at his campsite where native people could find them. On several occasions in February and March he gave similar presents to the Biloxi for the Choctaw at Chozeta, the Bayogoula, and the Annocchy (McWilliams 1981, 43–47, 55). In his list of intended presents for native people dated March 26, 1700, Iberville included "some kettles" along with 200 livres each of powder, bullets, and game-shot as well as 12 guns, 100 axes, 150 knives, and gun flints. Less than three weeks later he reported arming all the chiefs and their men with guns and providing them with hooded cloaks, shirts, and other trifles (McWilliams 1981, 171–73).

Iberville apparently ordered iron pots from France to be used as presents or for trade but how many he actually received is difficult to estimate considering the irregular flow of goods to French settlements (Woods 1980, 6). One hundred middle-sized brass kettles were ordered in 1701 and three hundred pounds of brass kettles in 1703. By the 1730s France was producing a large number of cast-iron kettles and in 1733 Louisiana ordered five hundred for cooking. The heavy cast-iron kettles were not easy to transport. A large number have been recovered from Tunica sites where the French could have easily transported them by water (Brain 1979, 134, 164). James Taylor Carson notes that Choctaw archaeological sites reveal a "profusion of potsherds" throughout the eighteenth century, indicating that women continued to make and use their own pottery (1999, 52).

The deerskin trade impacted the Green Corn Ceremony and women in a number of ways. To begin, Choctaw men began hunting more to provide deerskins to the French than for food for their families. As Choctaw and other native people depleted the game animals in their areas, they had to travel farther and farther to hunt. In the 1730s Choctaw hunters from Shumotakali set up their camps about two miles from town. By the end of the eighteenth century Choctaw hunters were traveling west of the Mississippi in search of game (Usner 1992, 173–74). Romans wrote that by the time he arrived among the Choctaw in the early 1770s, he found that "game was so scarce, that during my circuit through the nation we never saw any" (1775, 58). As deer and other wild game were depleted in the Choctaw hunting territory, Choctaw people became more dependent upon crops. However, crops were also failing in the 1760s and 1770s because of drought. Thus women had to extend their energies beyond that of agriculture and wild food gathering. They soon began raising chickens and cows that the French brought as early as January 1699 (McWilliams 1981, 20, 36). At first they would not eat chickens, which had taken on a sacred aspect for the Choctaw and soon became abundant in Choctaw villages (Swanton 1918, 67). On March 14, 1699, Iberville reported visiting the temple of the Bayogoula where he saw figures of animals including that "of a cock painted red" (McWilliams 1981, 61–62). According to Swanton, Choctaw

> believed that the chicken had been put into their yards to give them a friendly warning of danger. If a chicken crows outside of its usual time, it is because it foresees bad weather. If one comes up to the doorstep or into the gallery and crows, it means hasty news. If a chicken flies up on the roost and crows after reaching it, there will be trouble in the family. If a hen crows, that means that the women of the neighborhood are going to fall out. (1931, 199)

The Choctaw initially also would not eat hens because they ate filth, which meant they behaved differently from most other birds and thus would be considered powerful and sacred.[8] Eventually the Choctaw, probably as much out of necessity as diplomacy toward the French, began to eat them (Swanton 1918, 67). As they did the chickens, the Choctaw, like other native people, let cows run loose (JR 69:211, 219–20).

The introduction of domestic animals also meant new diseases. If animals spread disease among other animals, plants, and humans, then women were likely more susceptible than men to such contagions because they handled and prepared the meat. For example, during hunting trips they remained in camp to dress the game and carried the meat home on the backs of horses introduced by the Spanish in the seventeenth century. At home they prepared chicken or beef as well as wild game. If women contracted diseases from animals, they would have suffered chronic and debilitating illnesses that would have made it difficult for them to care for the fields. In any event, women may not have been able to carry out responsibilities to the extent they had prior to the introduction of foreign diseases. If the crops failed or were poor, then the Green Corn Ceremony suffered.

The deerskin trade also affected the balance between women and men. At first the early French colonists needed food from native people that women often provided. Although French colonists would eat Indian corn when necessary, they preferred familiar French vegetables. In order to continue to participate in the trade economy, Choctaw women began cultivating leeks, garlic, cabbage, and other garden plants that they did not eat but sold to the French. They also sold chickens, carrying them up to 120 miles to Mobile (Romans 1775, 57). Romans described another interesting way in which some women obtained desired goods. According to him women would watch the men as they drank. When the men began to get intoxicated, the women would accept drinks from them, and upon taking a drink, they would surreptitiously pour the remainder into gourds that they had concealed under their cloaks. They would add water to the rum, and later, when the men ran out of rum, they would trade them their own watered-down rum for desired items (1775, 55).

Choctaw men, however, provided skins for trade with the French. As Choctaw males increasingly began to respond to French demands for skins, more attention began to be paid to male contributions of skins rather than to vegetable produce. The French emphasized male contributions by requesting deerskins, although they seldom made any kind of profit from the trade. In fall 1744, Sebastien-François-Ange'-Lenormant, the new *commissaire ordonnateur*, ordered commanders at trading posts not to trade with native people unless they had skins to trade.[9] Although his order was not enforced, it is indicative of the central role of the deerskin trade in French-Choctaw relations (Woods 1981, 152).

As women did not hunt as part of their contribution to the economy of the community, even if the French were inclined to trade with women, women were not likely to have control over skins to trade for such gifts. Thus Choctaw men gained status through trade items that they could redistribute to family, friends, and important members of Choctaw society. Women, on the other hand, became dependent on the status of their male relatives or husbands for their own status. The emphasis on the deerskin trade distorted the balance between women and men. In her study of French-Indian relations, Patricia Dillon Woods pointed out that as the economic base of the Choctaw became more dependent upon the goods that hunters were able to provide through trade rather than on crops, women began to lose status. The Western Choctaw, who traded more with pro-English Chickasaw than the Eastern Choctaw, received earlier and more English goods. Thus their greater dependence on European goods, she argued, led to an earlier decline in importance of women and their lands than for those in the east (1981, 167).

The emphasis on the deerskin trade also had the potential to affect acts of diplomacy among the Choctaw during the Green Corn Ceremony. Women were already being excluded from diplomatic exchanges with the French, particularly the explorers and military men, primarily as a result of the changing political climate in the Lower Mississippi Valley. More than likely this change carried over to the Green Corn Ceremony. European items such as beads, cloth, knives, rifles, and so forth became desired trade items that could be redistributed to friends and allies. Women could continue to provide corn and other foodstuffs as trade items, but the changes taking place in the Southeast contributed to a greater desire for those objects that the men could provide.

Both military and trade concerns led to the rise of medal chiefs. Whereas earlier leadership had focused on redistribution of goods, it now depended upon those who had medals. Recognition came not only through individual acts, but also to a great extent through recognition as a medal chief. The impact on women can only be guessed at, but as the French began to treat medal chiefs as the leaders of Choctaw society, other Choctaw were disadvantaged, particularly in French/Choctaw trade relations. The medals distributed by French leaders affected the status of Choctaw individuals and changed the system of leadership among the Choctaw. The medal chiefs received goods or gifts from the French that they could then redistribute among their friends and families. The French further affected the balance within Choctaw communities by appointing chiefs to govern the Choctaw, because they did not appoint women (*Westward Expansion* 1983, reel 6, vol. 72).

According to Father Baudoüin, the position of Great Chief of the Choctaw was not an ancient one. It had been in existence for only twenty to twenty-five years through French influence; in order to ensure the recognition of the Great Chief, they provided him with "a very considerable annual present which he shared with the principal chiefs of the different Choctaw villages which he attached to himself thereby maintained in his interests." The French, however, manipulated Choctaw leadership even more by providing presents to lesser chiefs who then did not have to attach themselves to the Great Chief because they had their own gifts by which to encourage a following (MPA:FD 1927, 1:156). The French could then leverage allied chiefs against those that might present a problem. Father Baudoüin noted that Chicacha Oulacta was "created and recognized" as the first Great Chief of the Choctaw Nation by the French (MPA:FD 1927, 1:158). He apparently killed Conchak Emiko, a beloved leader, in order to appease the French, who were angry at the presence of English traders among the Choctaw (MPA:FD 1927, 1:157).

The impact of French influence in the determination of Choctaw leadership was also felt during the Green Corn Ceremony. The annual ceremony included a time for councils in which leaders discussed issues of import to the Choctaw. Those leaders tended to be male for a number of reasons. For one, as women withdrew from the political arena of warfare and diplomatic endeavors, they forfeited the means by which they could earn the privilege of entering councils. According to Adair, "those who have not successfully accompanied their holy ark . . . dare not even enter the sacred square, when they are on this religious duty" (1775, 49). If, like other nations in the Southeast, the Choctaw ingested black tea during councils, then they probably also could not drink it unless they had proved themselves brave warriors (Bossu 1962, 142; Adair 1775, 49 n. 22). As women withdrew more and more from war-related activities, they had less opportunity to earn the right to enter the sacred square or to drink the black tea, which restricted their participation in councils. However, they may have been able to become part of councils based on criteria other than participation in war-related activities. Bossu relates one case among the Alabama, who had the same restrictions, whereby "the wife of a great chief used to attend these assemblies as a warrior because of her quick and penetrating mind" (1962, 142). Since menstruating women also could not enter council grounds, those warrior women who did participate may have been postmenopausal. The susceptibility of elders to repeated disease episodes, however, may have also reduced the number of women eligible to participate in councils.[10]

The deerskin trade also impacted the Green Corn Ceremony through the prevalence of rum as part of trade negotiations. In a letter dated August 26, 1770, the Englishman Charles Stuart wrote that white people contributed to the Choctaw's troublesome behavior "by giving them rum in exchange for whatever they may have to dispose of both here & in the Nation, and when the poor wretches get drunk, they of course do mischief for which they are blamed by the very people who gave them liquor. It is indeed incredible the vast quantities of liquor that has been distributed amongst Indians for these twelve months past, too I verily believe that four fifths of what has been purchased in that time from Indians, has been with Rum" (*Westward Expansion* 1983, reel 6, 5.72). Choctaw Captain Houma during a council with the British in 1772 complained that "the cause of all the disorders & quarrelling between us & our white men. It is rum it pours in upon us like a sea from Mobille, and from all the plantations & settlements round about particularly from the House of Simon Favre, who is settled upon this river" (*Westward Expansion* 1983, reel 6, part i, 5.73).

What part rum played in the demise of the Green Corn Ceremony may not be clear. However, according to Chahta immatahah the Choctaw people had become so affected by alcohol that they had "lost the truth." Old and young got drunk and the traditional teachings stopped (Lincecum 1861, 7). In the case of the Cherokee, disputes arose as some of them wanted to consume liquor at ceremonies. It may be that rum also disrupted Choctaw ceremonies or in a sense replaced the ceremony as people gathered together to drink. As Chahta immatahah told Lincecum, the "Tanchi Okchamali hihla (green corn dance) . . . and feast was annually celebrated by the red people, until the white man came and made them all drunk" (Lincecum 1861, 26). Real or fictional account, the effects of alcohol among native people are well known. Unfortunately, observers tell us little about the impact of rum on Southeastern native women. We do not know if they also drank heavily, or if they became the targets of men's troubling behavior.

Cycle of Decline

The changing conditions in the Lower Mississippi Valley exerted enormous pressures on the functioning of the Green Corn Ceremony as well as on Choctaw women's roles. In the case of the Green Corn Ceremony, violence, natural disasters, introduction of the deerskin trade and medal chiefs, and changing women roles, to name but a few influences, impeded the ability and desire of Choctaw people to continue the ceremony. Each time the Choctaw had to forgo the ceremony or alter or eliminate some element of the ceremony, the ceremony became less viable as an instrument for sustaining the early contact culture of the Choctaw, including the values that supported women's roles. The same process held true for Choctaw women's roles. All of the elements that affected the Green Corn Ceremony, changes in the ceremony included, forced adaptations in women's roles, sometimes leading to alteration of roles, other times to elimination of roles.

These changes did not occur in isolation. Choctaw society functioned in an interdependent, interactive way that was expressed through such ideals as balance, restitution, reciprocity, and consensus. Choctaw society achieved balance, not in a one-to-one relationship, but in a multifaceted way that required contributions from all members of society in order to function optimally. In the case of restitution, for example, if someone caused the loss of a life, a life that contributed to a family, a community, and a moiety, then the responsible person gave his or her life to the family of the deceased in order to restore balance to that family. If restitution was not made or accepted, the violence could go on endlessly. In other words, the means existed in Choctaw society to maintain or restore balance whenever events threatened that balance. One of the primary ways of instilling the values of balance in society is through ceremony. For the Choctaw that ceremony was the Green Corn Ceremony. The Green Corn Ceremony marked the beginning of a new year, it reminded people of how to live their lives, and it restored them, at least for the moment, to a state of balance.

The Green Corn Ceremony and the roles of women, like all elements of Choctaw society, also interacted in a reciprocal and an interdependent, interactive way. The roles of women assured that certain parts of the ceremony took place. Men, elders, and children had their responsibilities for other aspects of the ceremony. Various rituals of the Green Corn Ceremony recognized and reified the respect and need for women's roles that helped assure the success of the Green Corn Ceremony. As Chahta immatahah remembered the story, once when the Choctaw reached a new place the women planted only a portion of their seed because they did not know if it would flourish there. When harvest time came they only gathered eighty ears of corn, leaving the rest for seed. The *miko* praised them for their thoughtful and good sense. He told them that on the day of the feast they should distribute one kernel of corn to each person, and although they had much meat and little corn, it would be "as if the feast had consisted wholly, of green corn" and the sun would be just as pleased (Lincecum 1861, 169–71).

As the practice of the Green Corn Ceremony declined, stories like the one above would have begun to lose currency. Without the Green Corn Ceremony, the story of how women saved the ceremony through their resourcefulness no longer had relevance, especially to those young people who never witnessed the ceremony. And when people stopped telling stories about the Green Corn Ceremony, thinking about the ceremony also ceased. Recognition of influential women's roles faded along with the stories and ceremonies because it was the stories and ceremonies that vivified women's importance in Choctaw society. Men, elders, and children were also affected by the changes in the Green Corn Ceremony, but when one takes into account the centrality of corn and feasting, it becomes apparent that the loss of the Green Corn Ceremony had the potential to affect women's influence in Choctaw society in dramatic ways. In the case of men, their responsibilities as hunters did not change. With the demise of the Green Corn Ceremony they no longer provided venison or other game meats for the ceremony. However, they continued to reinforce their prestige through hunting by providing the trade items desired by the French and British, who in turn provided European goods that Choctaw hunters could then distribute to their relatives and supporters.

As women's roles changed or became more circumscribed, they no longer participated in key events during the Green Corn Ceremony such as councils or distribution of goods except through their husbands, fathers, or uncles. As women's responsibilities changed, they contributed in different or lesser ways to the Green Corn Ceremony, thus contributing to its decline because their activities no longer balanced those of men as they once did. Without the traditional contributions of all members of Choctaw society, their ability to carry out ceremonies (civil and religious elements) was impaired, and as the ceremony declined, so too did the primary means for reinforcing the ideal of balance in society. The ceremony and the values it embodied and expressed about some of women's contributions were lost. Reciprocally, as the contributions of women became more restricted, so too did the ability of Choctaw society to continue the Green Corn Ceremony. Caught in an endless cycle, the decline of each reinforced and hastened the decline in the other. Eventually the appellation, ideal, or office of the beloved women disappeared along with the Green Corn Ceremony.

6

Restoring Balance to the World

By the time the French ceded Louisiana Territory to Spain in 1762, native people throughout the Lower Mississippi Valley had experienced "the most bitter phase of colonial rivalries" and intertribal warfare in the Southeast (White 1983, 98). Entire towns had disappeared, some completely destroyed by war or disease, others abandoned to be reestablished closer to other towns for safety, and some absorbed into nearby nations, their distinctions lost to history. The violence surrounding the Choctaw contributed to the loss of their Green Corn Ceremony, which, as described in chapter 5, had been a major ceremonial for recognizing and reinforcing the contributions of women. The loss of the Green Corn not only meant the loss of an organized practice for recognizing women's status, but also the loss of a means for earning status through their contributions to the ceremony.

Although the annual Green Corn Ceremony did not survive the chaos of the French colonial period, other practices did. Those practices changed over time in response to the same stresses that led to the loss of the Green Corn Ceremony. More importantly, those practices continued to reinforce many of the same values that they had reinforced before. Some of those values were so foundational to the way of life of the Choctaw that they were embodied in all their practices including the Green Corn Ceremony. Of course, the surviving practices could never replace the Green Corn Ceremony, but they did provide a source of continuity for Choctaw values. One of the practices that survived is the *yaiya*, or funeral cry, of the Choctaw. The mortuary practices of the Choctaw reflected their values about life and the afterworld, and those who carried out the necessary functions were highly valued. Mortuary practices, then, can provide us with a means for tracking developments in women's roles and status within Choctaw society. In other words, whereas the Green Corn Ceremony collapsed, taking with it a significant means for recognizing women's importance to the community, mortuary practices have continued up to the present time, providing us a mechanism for assessing Choctaw women's status in the light of change. In the previous chapter we demonstrated how the collapse of the Green Corn Ceremony was intimately related to the loss of beloved titles for women. In this chapter we will use mortuary practices to show how some Choctaw women continued to garner respect and honor albeit without accompanying titles. Understanding the Choctaw response to colonization is vital to understanding why one ceremony disappeared and another did not.

Catastrophic Change

For the Choctaw the first half of the eighteenth century brought new knowledge and experiences that led to drastic alterations in women's behavior that paralleled and reflected much deeper changes taking place in the very fabric of Choctaw society. These changes occurred relatively quickly, more like a response to catastrophic disaster than a longer process of acculturative adaptation that we often associate with cultures in contact. The intense, rapid changes swirling around the Choctaw mirrored in many ways the chaotic "disruption of normal structural arrangements within a social system" that often follows a major disaster such as a hurricane or earthquake (Barkun 1974, 51, 55). In the same way that a disaster population experiences a temporary sense of confusion as their traditional authority relationships are rendered less capable, the Choctaw found many of their social structures being challenged or threatened by French and British interests (Barkun 1974, 55). As a result, some of their structures changed in accordance with conditions or, like the Green Corn Ceremony, collapsed.

Unlike their neighbors the Cherokee and the Creek, the Choctaw lost their major ceremonial, the Green Corn Ceremony, in the first half of the eighteenth century. The Cherokee continued to hold their Green Corn ceremonies throughout the nineteenth century and, according to John Witthoft, elements of the ceremony were still being observed by some conservative Eastern Cherokee in the mid-twentieth century (Wetmore 1983, 47). The Creek busk, or Green Corn Ceremony, remains extant today.[1] All three of these indigenous nations faced similar contact experiences from European colonialists, such as epidemic disease, slavery, warfare, and trade. Yet of the three only the Choctaw lost the Green Corn Ceremony. The Chickasaw also had a Green Corn dance in the mid-eighteenth century but soon lost it, probably because of similar stresses as experienced by the Choctaw (Cushman 1899, 406; Speck 1907, 56; Swanton 1928c, 262; Adair 1775, 105–17).

We cannot, of course, offer an inclusive explanation for why one nation responded one way and another a different way under relatively similar conditions, much as we cannot fully explain why some indigenous groups experience revitalization movements in the face of colonization and others do not. Almost all native groups experienced comparable contact situations; however, each group "innovated tradition and initiated new ways of life within the world created by contact" according to their own motivations and capabilities (Martin 1991, 684). However, we can look at specific cases and identify elements that contributed to the loss of ceremony in a particular situation. In other words, we can identify those factors that led to change among the Choctaw and the ways in which the Choctaw changed. Other Southeastern nations may have responded to the same colonial relations in different ways for a variety of reasons. Positive and negative experiences, new visions, and hopes all come together in myriad ways to create different outcomes for each group (Martin 1991, 684).

The Choctaw experience of French colonization differed in some respects from the experiences of the Cherokee or Creek with the British and Spanish. Although the Choctaw had some contact with the English and Spanish, primarily through slave-raiding Indian allies of the British, they did not have the sustained interaction that the Cherokee and Creek experienced. As the British and Spanish pushed westward toward the Mississippi River, the Cherokee and Creek found themselves increasingly interacting with the growing white population. These nations could retreat westward toward Choctaw territory as they gave up lands to the British and Spanish. They also became allies of the British and Spanish and carried out attacks against the Choctaw on their behalf. The Chickasaw, encouraged by the English, also sent slaving expeditions south into Choctaw territory.

The Choctaw, however, were caught between the French, who claimed territory along the Mississippi from New Orleans to St. Louis, and the British and Spanish and their allies, including the Chickasaw, Cherokee, and Creek. The British and Spanish wanted access to the Mississippi River and thus created westward pressures as they sent allied native nations to try to open trade with the Choctaw or to capture Choctaw people for the slave trade. The French, however, did not seek access to the Atlantic. They already had control of the Mississippi River and the Gulf region. Rather, they wanted alliances, and they needed the Choctaw as a buffer between themselves and the British and Spanish colonialists and their Indian allies. They encouraged the Choctaw to engage in conflicts with those native nations that the French considered enemies. Although the Choctaw, for the most part, remained allies of the French, the overtures of the British who wanted to expand their deerskin trade created internal dissension among the Choctaw, some of whom engaged in trade with the British, thus putting the Choctaw alliance with the French at risk. As a result, the Choctaw suffered civil war as well as external conflicts with British-allied Indians from the north, east, and southeast and threats from the French.

Just as any community would find itself in a state of chaos following a catastrophic event, the Choctaw faced chaos as contact with Europeans led to rapid changes in their political, economic, and religious world. The Choctaw, like the survivors of a catastrophic disaster, found themselves surrounded by decimated towns and nations, and by emigrations of people seeking refuge from disease, warfare, and slavery. By 1726 the region's population was less than half of what it had been in the 1680s (Usner 1992, 44). These changes came on the heels of a major restructuring sometime between the 1560s and 1670s when neighboring cultures came together to form the confederacy known as the Choctaw (Galloway 1995, 28, 142, 170, 267). Choctaw structures may already have been in an unstable state at the time of the arrival of the French and thus were not as capable of responding to rapid changes as the Cherokee or Creek. Or, a strong, charismatic leader who could keep the traditions going, much like we find in revitalization movements, may not have arisen. In the case of the Green Corn Ceremony, it is possible that it might not have been as established among the nascent Choctaw at the time of French exploration in the 1680s as it was among the Cherokee or Creek. In any event, as we have seen, the Green Corn Ceremony did not survive the changes taking place during the French colonial period.

Under such catastrophic conditions, the Choctaw lost many of their elders who were the carriers of knowledge. Each succeeding generation of children grew up experiencing fewer aspects of their culture like the Green Corn Ceremony than the previous generation, until only vague memories remained. That catastrophic change began in the early years of French contact, intensified by British and Spanish intrigues. By the middle of the eighteenth century, in the closing years of French colonization, the Choctaw, in a sense, began a new epoch. Their history, their cultural knowledge, began not with the pre-French colonial period or the French colonial period, but with those elements that survived the French colonial period. It is as if they lived one history from the time of the formation of the Choctaw confederacy to the height of French colonization and began a new history in the closing decades of the French colonial period. The new history for many Choctaw did not include memories of some aspects of their earlier culture, including the ideal of beloved woman and the Green Corn Ceremony.

Thus, by the time British and French writers of the mid-eighteenth century and later observed the Choctaw, some aspects of their culture were no longer a part of the experiences of the young and were rapidly dying out along with the lives of the elders. The better known English authors included Bernard Romans, a civil engineer who surveyed Choctaw Territory in 1771–72 (Romans 1775, 202–21); James Adair,[2] a trader, who attempted in 1745–46 to a develop a trade relationship with the Red Shoe faction (Adair 1775, x); and William Bartram, a naturalist who spent time among the Creek from 1774 to 1775 (Bartram 1928, 304). French naval officer Jean-Bernard Bossu, who traveled up the Mississippi Valley and through present-day Alabama in the years 1751–62 (Bossu 1962, 156–76), also wrote of his observations of the Choctaw. These European chroniclers wrote of a Choctaw world that survived French colonialism and was still in a state of chaos and recovery, where those with memories of earlier roles or ceremonies chose not to share them with outsiders and adaptations had become normative among the young.

Not only were these mid-eighteenth-century writers observing a confederacy whose collective memory began with those aspects of culture that survived

French colonization, they were also observing a male version of the Choctaw world. As Theda Perdue noted in her study of Cherokee gender and culture change, "male European observers had virtually no access to the private lives of women or to women's culture" (1998, 4). Therefore they could not with any certainty learn much about women's roles. Europeans limited their interaction with the Choctaw primarily to men who probably had little knowledge of women-specific behaviors or rituals or who felt that it was not appropriate to speak of such. In addition, European authors often interpreted women's behavior according to their understanding of the eighteenth-century European world and not Choctaw culture and history (Perdue 1998, 3–5).[3]

Later, Horatio Bardwell Cushman and John R. Swanton would write their own ethnographic histories of the Choctaw based on the writings of earlier English and French authors and on the experiences of contemporary Choctaw. Cushman, a missionary who spent much of his life near or among the Choctaw, described women as slaves to their husbands who did all the drudgery work around the house (Cushman 1899, 174). Swanton, drawing primarily on contemporary Choctaw Christian informants and the observations of eighteenth- and nineteenth-century Europeans and Americans, quoted descriptions of women that depicted them as oppressed and without influence in a ceremonially-poor Choctaw society. Cushman and Swanton were influenced by the image of the ideal Southern Anglo-American woman of the nineteenth century (Welter 1966, 151). This "true woman" did not participate in the ambitious, selfish, and materialistic world of men (Perdue 1985, 35–36). Neither author had reason to question earlier descriptions of Choctaw women because they could make sense of Choctaw women's roles in light of Anglo-American conceptions of Southern women's roles. Beloved women did not exist, nor would consideration of such a role arise, because in both the Choctaw and white worlds beloved had become associated with leaders in the political, economic, and religious world of men. Women were relegated to the domestic domain, submissive wives to their husbands.

Although the appellation, title, or office of beloved woman had disappeared, Choctaw women continued to garner respect based on the same values that they always had. Those values, however, were being expressed under new conditions and changed practices. In order to trace the continuity of those values back beyond the boundary of the new Choctaw history, we must look for those social elements or structures that survive catastrophic change under any circumstance. Economic systems can undergo drastic changes during and following periods of chaos and thus may not provide viable practices for tracing elements that survive catastrophe, as was the case with the Choctaw Green Corn Ceremony. However, some elements of society continue to exist among the survivors of any catastrophic event as they begin rebuilding their societies. People continue to be born, to live, and to die. Thus structures must be in place to deal with childcare, domestic concerns, and death. These structures change over time relative to conditions, but the basic elements or values that inform those structures can survive a catastrophic event. By examining women's roles in mortuary rites (although any of those three structures would serve our purpose), it is possible to trace the ways in which those values most respected by Choctaw people continued to be expressed and reinforced by Choctaw women.

Choctaw Values

A number of values, including balance, restitution, community, and reciprocity, informed eighteenth-century Choctaw society. Each aspect of Choctaw society balanced other parts of society in order to accomplish some task or to achieve some goal. For example, Choctaw society was divided into two moieties that interacted with each other in a reciprocal manner. Members of one moiety married members of the other, and when someone died members of the opposite moiety carried out the mourning ritual for the other moiety (Swanton 1931, 76–78; Halbert 1900, 365; Halbert 1902, 438; Cushman 1899, 306).[4] In the case of unnatural death such as murder, balance was restored through restitution. The one who caused the death forfeited his or her life for the deceased. In that way the one who killed restored balance to the family, the community, and the moiety that had lost someone.

Choctaw maintained balance in their society through a system of interdependent relationships. Each gender or aspect of society contributed to the functioning of community (home, village, or society) through specific roles that depended upon others' fulfilling their roles for the completion of a task or goal. Thus, although women handled domestic affairs such as cooking and providing vegetable foods, Choctaw diets were rounded out by male contributions of game meats. Women and men did not spend equal amounts of time on agriculture and hunting, nor did they provide equal amounts of corn and meat; however, both contributions were needed to provide an adequate diet. Nor did people responsible for similar tasks have similar rates of success. The Choctaw used a system of reciprocity whereby those who had more shared with those with less, thus ensuring a degree of balance in the community.

Participation by everyone was needed to ensure that the system of interdependence worked effectively. Young and old, male and female contributed in some way to the functioning of the community. The contributions of one group balanced those of another. In such a society it is not likely that one gender would have total responsibility for carrying out tasks that affected the entire community. Thus women's and men's participation or contributions might differ, but the proper functioning of a community required the participation of both. So closely were the actions of women and men integrated and co-determinant that when a pregnant woman was near delivery the father fasted during the day, avoided salt and pork, and limited his activities in order to avoid harming the baby (Swanton 1931, 116–18).

With the understanding that women and men contributed to every aspect of society, we can next identify the ways in which women participated in Choctaw mortuary practices. We can also identify the ways in which Choctaw values were expressed through women's contributions to mortuary rites and trace the continuity of those values through the various changes that mortuary practices underwent in the eighteenth and nineteenth centuries. In other words, we can determine if certain women carried out functions highly valued by Choctaw society, indicating that they were honored people, or if they could earn recognition through their participation in funereal ceremonies.

Fertility and Death

We begin by examining the logic of women's involvement in mortuary practices, first by identifying the earliest possible expression of values associated with life or fertility and death, and second by determining women's association with those expressions. Those values deriving from Choctaw cultural narratives or historical practices would have been considered beloved values. Thus those women who carried out tasks associated with those values would have been held in high esteem. By tracing the manifestation of those values through changing mortuary practices, we can demonstrate a pattern of continuity that derives from Choctaw antecedents. Such a pattern will provide one explanation for how Choctaw women continued to garner the respect of their communities.

Like the Green Corn Ceremony, funeral ceremonies reinforced values held dear to the Choctaw. The Green Corn reinforced values associated with fertility and life, while funeral rites reflected beliefs about death and the afterlife. Women, as the cultivators of plants that went through an annual cycle of life and death, were associated with that cycle. By providing corn for their families each year, women reenacted that primordial act of Ohoyo Osh Chisba, The Unknown Woman, who first brought corn to the starving Choctaw. Like Ohoyo Osh Chisba, corn was considered powerful because as a plant it crossed the boundaries of the Below World, This World, and the Above World (Hudson 1976, 122). The roots of corn reached into the Below World, the world of fertility (or life) and death. For the Choctaw the Below World was not a world of punishment, of hellfire, but one of power that was also dangerous. Women were associated with that power because Ohoyo Osh Chisba, a woman, became corn, and women of This World were responsible for the cultivation of corn as well as other plants. They also embodied the power of fertility and death through their menstrual cycles.[5]

The association made between women, fertility, and death can be traced back to Middle Mississippian (1050–1200) mortuary practices. Two fireclay female figurines recovered by archaeologists symbolize the relationship between women, plants, and the Below World of death. The Birger figurine, described in the previous chapter, was uncovered in a site considered to be of a burial/ceremonial nature, indicating that the item was placed there at the time of interment. Thomas E. Emerson and Guy Prentice suggest that the drooping facial features of the Birger figurine, as well as the serpent that is part of the Below World and a source of plant life, represent death. They also believe the basket may represent containers for transporting souls or bones as well as seeds (Prentice 1986, 240, 244–47; Emerson 1982, 3, 5, 10; Emerson 1997, 211). The face of another female figure recovered from Mound C at the Etowah site is painted black, which Adair and Mooney identified as a common Southeastern symbol of warfare or death (Adair 1775, 191; Mooney 1891, 342; Prentice 1986, 248). Both figures were intentionally broken, which Prentice interpreted as a symbolic killing preceding burial (248).

Breaking the figurines may symbolize the act of sacrifice whereby the spirit of the figurine is released to accompany the spirit of the deceased to the afterworld.[6] Since it was not uncommon in the early eighteenth century for spouses, close friends, or servants to sacrifice their lives in order to accompany the deceased to the next world,[7] the earlier Mississippian practice of symbolically killing the female figures may represent a similar act. The idea that someone or something could accompany the deceased to the spirit world is later demonstrated when the Choctaw sacrificed the deceased's favorite horse (introduced by Europeans) or dog to be buried alongside the deceased. It also became common to deposit beads or gorgets in the grave of a woman or place food, drink, and favorite items next to the deceased so that the deceased's spirit would have everything she or he needed in the next world to carry out the same acts that she or he did in this world (Swanton 1931, 170–71, 180; Halbert 1900, 358; Cushman 1899, 302; Claiborne 1880, 503).

Archaeological evidence also indicates that some of the cultures occupying the areas around what became the Choctaw homeland practiced a two-stage burial process in which a temporary burial took place shortly after death, followed by a secondary burial when the remains of the first burial were placed in a permanent burial site with the remains of ancestors or relatives. Two Late Mississippian–period mound sites, Winterville and Lake George, located in the lower Yazoo Basin, had provisional burials as well as secondary burials.[8] There is also evidence indicating that secondary burials occurred during the Moundville period throughout the Alabama-Tombigbee drainage, particularly at the Moody Slough and Big Prairie Creek sites (Galloway 1995, 283–85, 290). Although archaeological investigations have not provided conclusive findings about the extent of two-stage burial processes, the two Late Mississippian–period examples suggest that eighteenth-century Choctaw mortuary practices had antecedents from that period.

According to Robert Hertz, who wrote a study on temporary burials, the waiting period during which the body decomposed took place because of the vulnerability of the corpse, the discomfort of the dislodgement of the soul, and the "pollution" inhering in material things and the deceased's relatives. He concluded that burials that involve a provisional burial and a secondary burial (bone house) occur because death is viewed as a process, terminated only by complete bodily dissolution and the entry of the soul into the afterlife. The final transfer of the remains to a permanent burial place thus represents the incorporation phase in which the corpse is placed with the bones of its ancestors and the soul gains admittance to the land of the dead. Balance is achieved through the final burial rite, at which the mourners are then reincorporated into the community (Hertz 1909, 33–34, 47, 55, 58, 62, 64; Galloway 1995, 277). Thus those responsible for the execution of both burials held the comfort and restoration of balance of the spirit and society in their hands.

Choctaw Mortuary Practices

Among the Choctaw responsibility for burial of the deceased belonged to the entire community although a few select people handled the processing and disposition of the body. Those responsibilities shifted somewhat as mortuary practices changed among the Choctaw during the eighteenth and nineteenth centuries. Even with the changes in Choctaw mortuary practices over the years, particularly during the time of Protestant missionization, the necessity for some kind of funerary practice provides us with a context in which to identify and trace changes in women's roles as well as the perpetuation of religious values that informed women's roles in Choctaw society. Women lost an important role as part of these changes, but they also continued to carry out important responsibilities that reflected Choctaw values including those associated with earlier conceptions of fertility and death.

At the time of French exploration Choctaw funerals involved a practice often referred to as bone-picking or bone-gathering whereby the bones of the deceased were cleaned and later gathered together in one charnel house.[9] As that practice died out the Choctaw replaced it with a pole-pulling ceremony that involved removing poles that had been placed around the grave of the deceased. By the end of the nineteenth century that practice also ceased to exist as Choctaw adopted a more Christian-inspired form of funeral services. Both versions included a cry, or yaiya, during which the mourners wailed for long periods for the deceased, an aspect of the funeral in which women had a dominant role.[10]

The earliest description of a Choctaw funeral is provided by the anonymous French officer quoted in Swanton's book on the social and ceremonial life of the Choctaw. Swanton believed the author was describing the funeral as it was practiced sometime after 1731 but before 1755. According to the anonymous author, when a sick person neared death, the women prepared the dying person by washing his body, painting him, daubing his face, and dressing him in his finest clothes.[11] After death the body of the deceased was placed in a raised cabin shaped like a coffin and left to decompose for five or six months.[12] After the body had sufficiently decomposed, all the relatives assembled and the "honored woman (*femme de valleur*) of the village who has for her function (*distrique*) to strip off the flesh from the bones of the dead, comes to take off the flesh from this body, scrapes the bones well, and places them in a very clean cane hamper." The bones were then wrapped in linen or cloth and the flesh was thrown into a field. The honored woman then served food to all the mourners. After the feasting and singing, the mourners carried the bones to the charnel house where the bones of others lay, until the house was full. Then all the bones were taken out and interred in a mass grave (Swanton 1931, 170–71; Galloway 1995, 299–300).

Bossu, Adair, Bartram, and Romans gave similar descriptions of the two-stage mortuary practice with a few minor differences. According to Bossu the mourners did not sing or dance, but maintained "a mournful silence" (1962, 166–67). Adair mentions that "formerly when the owner of the house died, they set fire to it, and to all the provisions of every kind; or sold the whole at a cheap rate to the trading people, without paying the least regard to the scarcity of the times" (1775, 136). Bossu also added that the Choctaw held an annual ceremony at which time the families of the deceased returned to the cemetery to weep for their ancestors, after which they held a great feast (167).

None of these authors, whose collective time among the Choctaw ranged from 1745 to 1776, mentioned female bone-gatherers, although they did describe male officials. Romans described five members of "a certain set of venerable old Gentlemen" who "constantly travel[ed] through the nation" to determine when the time was right for the cleaning of the bones which they then undertook to complete (Romans 1775, 61). Louis LeClerc de Milford, who published his *Memoir* in 1802, wrote that every morning the nearest female relatives of the deceased wept while circling the scaffolding upon which the body had been placed.[13] Once the women had determined that the body had decomposed enough, they informed the person responsible for cleaning the bones, who then undertook the task (Milford 1956, 202; Swanton 1931, 174, 265).

The mortuary practice of the Choctaw gives us some indication of their understanding about the spirits of the deceased and the afterworld. From their migration stories we know that the Choctaw venerated the bones of their ancestors. They took great care to ensure that the spirits of the deceased traveled safely to the spirit world to join those relatives who had died before them. According to Adair, the Choctaw were so careful with the bones of their relations that they would not place the bones of a relation in the bone house of others and never in that of an enemy (Adair 1775, 192–93). Bossu, apparently impressed by the intensity of the cries, said that the Choctaw's love for their deceased relations could "be seen in the tears that are shed when their dear ones have departed" (1962, 167). The display of grief was so important that some Choctaw went so far as to hire mourners "to magnify the merit and loss of their dead" (Adair 1775, 196).

One can assume from the care with which the bones of the deceased were handled that the Choctaw entrusted beloved people to clean the bones and to wrap them carefully and place them in bone houses. Only the anonymous French officer spoke of an "honored woman" who cleaned the bones of the deceased (Swanton 1931, 171, 243).[14] We do not know if the French officer observed an atypical practice or whether he observed the last female practitioner in a changing system. That women at one time served as bone-gatherers makes sense in light of their association with fertility and death through their cultivation of plants and their monthly cycles. It is also consistent with their roles as the determiners of a captive's fate. Women, who gave birth to all members of a community, also decided whether captives became part of the community through adoption or were tortured until death. The death of a captive served to free the wrongly killed person's spirit so that it could enter the afterlife, thus restoring balance to the spirit world, and in turn, This World.[15]

The importance the Choctaw attached to the process of sending the spirit to the afterworld is also reflected in their attention to the funeral ceremony. Everyone attended these ceremonies, including chiefs. When Major Beauchamp met with some Choctaw in 1746 to demand restitution for the killing of three Frenchmen, he reported that Alibamon Mingo left the talks to go mourn the death of Choucououlacta, a ceremony that he said the Choctaw observed religiously (MPA:FD 1984, 4:282). Any relative or visitor who happened to come to visit participated in the mourning by weeping over the grave before entering the house. The family of the house would also accompany the visitor and thus might weep many times over the grave in the course of a day (Halbert 1900, 354, 360). Galloway suggests that the funeral ceremony, like the Green Corn Ceremony, may have also been an occasion for celebration, feasting, and important political activities (Galloway 1995, 300). However, unlike the Green Corn Ceremony, which required everyone to behave in a peaceful way, the funeral may have allowed people to pursue the red path.[16] When Sonakabetaska promised "to avenge the death of Sieur de Verbois at the time of the first boning," he was, according to Galloway's interpretation, referring to the time of the cleaning of the bones of the deceased (MPA:FD 1984, 4:284; Galloway 1995, 300).

Although women apparently no longer served as honored women who cleaned and gathered the bones of the deceased, they continued to participate in the ceremony in significant ways. For example, Romans, while writing of his experiences among the Choctaw from 1771 to 1775, noted that during the period of intense wailing the women were there constantly, and sometimes they fainted from their exertions in the corrupted air and heat of the sun, obliging other mourners to carry them home (1775, 61). Such dedication would have earned those women the respect of their communities. He wrote that the men also mourned in a similar manner, but only "in the night or at other unseasonable times, when they are least likely to be discovered" (61). The women also wailed as they walked in the procession to the site of the burial (Cushman 1899, 166). Those women apparently had primary responsibility for letting the relatives and the spirit of the deceased know how much he or she would be missed.

The women also participated in the ceremonial procession when the relatives of the deceased carried the bones to the common charnel house. According to Milford, after the bones of the deceased had been cleaned and wrapped, the women lit pitch pine torches that signaled the relatives to start their procession toward the charnel house (Milford 1956, 203; Swanton 1931, 174, 265–67). The role of signaler was not an inconsequential responsibility. Among Southeastern native people fire was deemed sacred and had to be treated respectfully. According to Creek sacred laws, they "must always respect the fire." A Chickasaw prophet told Adair that they knew that the "giver of virtue to nature resided on earth in the unpolluted holy fire" and in the sun where it was "attended by a great many beloved people." The Choctaw believed that fire acted as informant to the sun, who had the power of life and death (Gregory and Strickland 1971; Adair 1775, 97; Swanton 1931, 195–96). Clearly, only someone highly respected would be given the honor of handling the torch.

Sometime near the end of the eighteenth century the practice of placing the body of the deceased on a scaffold and cleaning the bones began to give way to a pole-pulling ceremony and burial. Halbert believed the pole-pulling ceremonies were introduced after the Choctaw abolished the bone-gathering custom. However, many Choctaw protested the abolishment of the custom of placing the dead on scaffolds and continued the practice for many years (Halbert 1900, 355, 357; Cushman 1899, 167, 303). According to Reverend Lorenzo Dow in his *Journal*, "it seems certain that this custom still prevailed in 1804 among the Six Towns Choctaws" (Halbert 1900, 357). Halbert estimated the bone-picking ceremony ended sometime between 1800 and 1812, but according to Horatio Bardwell Cushman a few bone-pickers were still traveling from town to town around 1818 when Protestant missionaries first arrived (Halbert 1900, 357; Cushman 1899, 167). The practice apparently survived even longer among some Choctaw, because General Sam Dale, who participated in the Choctaw removal to Indian Territory in the 1830s, reported that some of the deceased were still on scaffolds and the relatives of those dead stayed behind to bury the bones and to sing mourning songs (Swanton 1931, 181; Claiborne 1860, 175–76; Claiborne 1880, 493).

As the practice of placing the dead upon scaffolds began to decline, Choctaw replaced it at first by burying the deceased in a sitting posture and later by laying the deceased in a coffin. They also added a pole-pulling ritual (Cushman 1899, 167, 303; Swanton 1931, 183). Two of the oldest men in the community, officially called *hattak in tikba* (headman), one from each *iksa*, supervised the preparations for the burial and appointed seven men as *fabussa sholih* (pole-bearer[s]) (Cushman 1899, 167–68; Halbert 1900, 357–58).[17] The pole-pulling ceremony began with a procession led by the seven men, who each carried a red painted pole that they set up around the newly dug grave. Six of the poles were about eight feet high, and the seventh about fifteen. Thirteen hoops made of grape vines were attached to each other to form a kind of ladder that was suspended from the top of the tallest pole where a small white flag had been fastened (Cushman 1899, 167; Claiborne 1880, 489; Swanton 1931, 177).[18] H. S. Halbert, who described streamers of white cloth or a red handkerchief at the top of the pole, said that they let passers-by know that it was a grave and they were expected to halt and weep for the deceased (1900, 359). According to the description provided by Henry C. Benson, a Methodist missionary to the Choctaw, the hoops had been replaced with flags by the 1840s (1860, 294). After the pole-planting work was finished, men and women surrounded the grave, knelt down and covered their heads, and then wailed for a long time (Halbert 1900, 359).

The Choctaw had an extended period of mourning. Cushman said mourners would return to the grave for thirteen consecutive moons and cry, and at the end of each cry they removed a hoop. During the cry, as many mourners as possible would kneel in a close circle around the grave, draw their blankets over their heads, and wail until they could cry no more. Each time someone got up and left, another mourner from one of the nearby groups replaced her. According to Adam Hodgson, who observed the Choctaw around 1820, three Choctaw women covered with blankets mourned at the grave at sunrise, noon, and sunset for approximately twenty minutes each time, for ninety days, or three moons (Swanton 1931, 179; Cushman 1899, 145, 168; Hodgson 1823, 270).

Reverend Israel Folsom told Swanton that during the period of mourning both men and women "remained silent and subdued, ate very sparingly, and abstained from all kinds of amusements, and from decking themselves out in their usual manner" during the days or months of mourning. Cushman said the women "remained at home prostrated with grief—their hair streaming over their shoulders, unoiled and undressed, being seated on skins close to the place of burial or sacred fire. . . . For a long time they would continue to visit the grave regularly morning and evening to mourn and weep" (Swanton 1931, 180; Cushman 1899, 302).[19]

In the same manner as the feasting held at the conclusion of the Green Corn Ceremony, a large feast followed the removal of the last hoop and/or the pole-pulling. The men brought venison and the women large kettles full of hominy (Swanton 1931, 176, 178; Halbert 1900, 361). The venison and hominy were distributed to all the groups attending the cry. Interestingly, men recognized women's contributions of hominy by giving them venison. According to Halbert, "It is customary to give to all the contributors of hominy a small quantity of venison for their private use, which they can carry home with them. This is intended as a remuneration [act of reciprocity] for their contribution of hominy for the public use" (Halbert 1900, 361–62).

However, he does not mention women distributing hominy to the men who brought venison. It may be that since foodstuffs such as venison and hominy were the responsibility of women who did the storing, cooking, and serving, and since husbands lived in the homes of their wives, it would not make sense to give hominy to the men (Searcy 1985, 35). Or, as Theda Perdue explains in her study on Cherokee women, women's working cooperatively in the field comprised a communally based pursuit, whereas although hunting involved some cooperation, the hunter who killed a deer owned that deer alone until which time he divided it among family members, friends, or the most needy (1998, 83). The act of remuneration, or reciprocity, also recognized the importance of women in providing the labor for their primary beloved food source, cultivated corn.

After the feasting the mourners danced until just before daybreak. About two hours before daybreak one of the mourners, either a woman or a man, would begin to wail. The other mourners approached the person wailing, covered their heads with their blankets, and wailed for about ten minutes. The pole-pullers then pulled up the poles (Halbert 1900, 362–64). Next, according to Halbert, "an old woman of the iksa opposite to that of the dead comes forward with a pair of scissors in her hand, and cuts off a single lock of hair from the heads of the women of the mourning family. An old man, likewise of the opposite iksa, in the same manner, approaches the males of the mourning family and trims off their long hair." This ended the ceremony (Halbert 1900, 365). At the time Halbert wrote this article he said the practice of cutting the hair continued among the women, but had ceased among the men and that the ceremony as he described it continued in nearly all the Choctaw communities, in spite of Christian opposition, until about 1883 (Halbert 1900, 365; Swanton 1931, 194).

Beloved Responsibilities

The funeral ceremony was a necessary part of the ceremonial cycle of the Choctaw. Through the ceremony the mourners expressed their sympathy and care for the relatives of the deceased, as well as for the deceased, and ensured the successful journey of the spirit. To properly care for the body and the spirit, the body had to be prepared, the bones cleaned, and the remains properly interred in a temporary charnel house and later in a permanent one with the bones of all their relatives. Great care went into the funeral ceremony itself. Cushman, apparently as impressed as Bossu with the intensity and elaboration of the funeral, wrote, "no people on earth paid more respect to their dead, than the Choctaws did and still do; or preserved with more affectionate veneration the graves of their ancestors. They were to them as holy relics, the only pledges of their history; hence, accursed was he who should despoil the dead" (Cushman 1899, 191). The care with which the Choctaw prepared the deceased for the afterworld indicates that they would entrust only beloved people to handle the body and bones of the deceased, and according to the anonymous French officer, "honored" women once held that role.

However, even as the funeral ceremony changed and men became the sole bone-gatherers of the deceased and later the pole-gatherers and pole-pullers, women continued to carry out major functions during the ceremony that reflected their contributions to the well-being of the deceased's spirit and of the survivors. Throughout the eighteenth and nineteenth centuries, Choctaw women continued their cries for the deceased. Although men also mourned at funerals, women participated in a more intense manner. They went to the charnel house or the grave more often than men, sometimes up to three times a day, for as long as twelve months (Cushman 1899, 144–45). Cushman pointed out that the women might mourn near the grave or the sacred fire. For the Choctaw the fire was the sacred informant to the sun, to which they "ascribed the power of life and death" (Wright 1828a, 179–80). During their councils and national assemblies, they convened around "The Council Fire" where one could do no wrong lest the fire inform the sun. Like the Cherokee, the Choctaw probably offered the first fruits of the harvest to the fire during the Green Corn Ceremony, thus assuring that the sun would send corn in the future. Thus, by mourning next to the fire, the women were petitioning the "Creator Being above" to aid the living and the deceased as the spirit made its way to the afterworld (Cushman 1899, 147–48, 246; Corkran 1955, 34; Adair 1775, 20).

The women also helped the dislodged spirit to journey safely to the afterworld, a journey that entailed crossing a slippery sweet-gum log and passing two guardian spirits before it was welcomed by the spirits of friends and relatives who had passed on before. The Choctaw believed the spirit remained for some time around the place where the body lay. According to Claiborne the spirit remained until after the last pole had been pulled. Prior to the 1800s the Choctaw also believed that a person had two spirits, one that went to the afterworld and one that remained on earth restlessly wandering about its former habitation. The anonymous French officer explained that the Choctaw believed that if the spirit did not have everything it needed to travel and live in the afterworld, it would remain behind as it sought those desired items. In addition to the favored tools or belongings placed in the grave of the deceased, women also often placed a little corn and venison in the grave so that the deceased would not be hungry during the long journey to the afterworld (Cushman 1899, 167–68; Claiborne 1880, 489; Wright 1828a, 182–83; Swanton 1931, 215–20). In other words, through mourning and the provision of food women assisted the spirit of the deceased in its journey to the afterworld.

Women also had primary responsibility for preparing the feasts, just as they had for the Green Corn Ceremony. Families contributed food and labor for the preparation of the feast although women did most of the cooking and serving. The feast served to reinforce ideals of reciprocity and community as they promoted group interaction and solidarity (Searcy 1985, 43). It also served as a way of ending the mourning of the friends and relatives of the deceased and reincorporating them back into everyday life (Hertz 1909, 63–64). Food provided sustenance for the living, and corn, the symbol of community effort, recalled the relationship of women to fertility and life. By providing food for the feasts, women helped the mourners to return to the world of the living, thus restoring balance to society.

The women may also have continued to carry on the values of Choctaw society through dances. Interestingly, dances at funerals are mentioned primarily by nineteenth-century sources although they indicated the mourning ceremonies they were describing included practices from earlier times.[20] In the early 1820s Reverend Cyrus Byington collected one of the earlier accounts from an elder white man who spent most of his life in the Choctaw nation. According to the elder white man, while members of one moiety cried for the deceased, the other danced. The next day the moieties would change places (Byington 1829, 349–50). Henry C. Benson, another missionary to the Choctaw from 1843 to 1845, wrote that the dance following the feast lasted often until morning (1860, 294–95). In Cushman's account, he identified the dance as the "grand *Aboha hihlah*, home dancing" wherein the people danced the spirit of the deceased to the afterworld (Cushman 1899, 169).[21] A more recent account was obtained from A. L. Tinsley of Philadelphia, Mississippi, a close neighbor of the Bok Chito Band of Choctaw, who told Swanton he observed them dancing after the feast, probably sometime between 1908 and 1909 (Swanton 1931, 186).

Only Halbert, who was writing in the late 1860s, described the dances in any detail. According to him, after the feast but before the pole-pulling, the young people gathered at the *ahihla*, dancing ground, which had been previously prepared for this purpose.[22] Six long dances took place, beginning with *nakni hihla*, the men's dance in which only the men danced. The women then chose their partners for the next five dances in the following order: *shatanih hihla*, tick dance; *nita hihla*, bear dance; *yahyachi hihla*, trotter's dance; *ittisanali hihla*, dance of those who oppose each other; and last, *ittihalanli hihla*, the dance of those who hold each other (1900, 362–63).[23]

There is no question that dances were held at the conclusion of funerals; however, we do not know if the nineteenth-century practice was a new innovation or a continuation of an older practice that went unnoticed by earlier observers. We do know that Choctaw ceremonial practices included dances. According to Swanton, some Choctaw said that they historically had a *pishofa* dance (healing or curing dance) similar to that of the Chickasaw, while others denied it (1931, 221). We have already noted the existence of Green Corn ceremonies that included dancing. The likelihood that the Choctaw had dances is also indicated by Bartram's observation that the Choctaw were "very eminent for poetry and music" and "every town amongst them strives to excel each other in composing new songs for dances" (1928, 396).

The Choctaw might have concealed their dances from outsiders or ceased holding them because of the conditions surrounding them during the French colonial period or because of missionary disapproval. The anonymous French officer wrote that the Choctaw no longer held the dance of the young people, "the French having made them conceive too great horror for it" (Swanton 1931, 222). Protestant missionaries also considered dancing an abomination. In one of his letters printed in the *Missionary Herald* in December 1828, Calvin Cushman, assistant missionary to the Choctaw, described pole-pulling ceremonies as a site of "great rioting and dissoluteness" that ended with "feasting, drinking, and great disorder [most likely dancing]" (1828, 380). French Catholic and Protestant missionary attitudes toward dancing, which they viewed as immoral, contributed to its suppression.

Whatever the cause for the lack of accounts in the eighteenth century, the existence of dances in the nineteenth century provided another means for women, as well as men, to physically express Choctaw values. Although

Halbert identified only six dances, there may have been more at one time. Since men contributed game for the feast and women provided corn or hominy, it makes sense that the songs and dances used to break ceremonial time and to reincorporate the mourners back into the community would include hunting and corn themes (just as they did in the Green Corn Ceremony).[24] David I. Bushnell, who studied the Choctaw of Bayou Lacomb in 1908 and 1909, said they had a set series of seven dances that they always danced in the same order. Frances Densmore, who recorded Mississippi Choctaw songs in 1933, recorded the songs of thirteen dances but said none was connected with any ceremonialism (Bushnell 1909, 20; Densmore 1943, 134). It may be that the Choctaw had a much greater repertoire of dances and songs, as indicated by Bartram, and that they were all connected to ceremonies at one time, but eventually they telescoped down into one set of six or seven dances. The remaining songs may have been eventually dropped from the repertoire of dances as their ceremonial cycle ceased to exist.[25]

In any case two of the songs collected by Densmore demonstrate the significance of corn to Choctaw people, and it is possible that they were once part of ceremonies, including funeral ceremonies. The first dance song is identified as a "Pleasure Dance Song" in which "the men are in one row and the women in another row, facing them. They move their hands up and down, as though shaking corn in a basket, all moving their hands together" (1943, 176). The second song, titled "Hunting Song," recorded by Lysander Tubby, suggests some connection to funeral ceremonies.

> Go and grind some corn, we will go camping,
> Go and sew, we will go camping,
> I passed on and you were sitting there crying,
> You were lazy and your hoe is rusty. (Densmore 1943, 177)

This song underscores the division of labor among the Choctaw. The women were primarily responsible for cultivating and preparing corn and sewing clothes; the men left home to go to hunting camps. The first two lines suggest three plausible scenarios: both men and women are getting ready to go to the hunting camps (Searcy 1985, 44), or the women stay home and carry out their typical responsibilities while the men go hunting, or the women prepare provisions for the men to take on their hunting trips. The last two lines are more ambiguous. Line 3 could be interpreted to mean that a man left to go hunting, leaving his wife behind (passed on), who then cried. In which case line 4 might indicate he left her behind because she was so lazy her hoe rusted from lack of use. Or, consistent with a particular genre of stomp dances, the singer might be singing that while he is at camp his wife is so lonely for him she is crying and is unable to do any work. However, I would like to offer another interpretation. Line 3 may indicate that the hunter died (passed on) and his wife was mourning for him. If line 3 is about death, line 4 might indicate that the woman, overwhelmed with grief, did not work during the time of mourning and that the mourning period lasted so long her hoe got rusty.

The original meaning, assuming there was only one interpretation, may never be known, as Densmore learned when she tried to get a translation for the words of a "Tick Dance Song." She noted that much discussion went on between her Choctaw translators as they offered different translations (1943, 139). The "Hunting Song" does suggest that the work of women was recognized through song and dance, and if such a song were sung at the conclusion of funerals, it provided another means for the continuation of the values that were associated with beloved people. They not only helped the spirit of the deceased and the mourners at a crucial time in the life of the community, they also helped the community to return to a normal state of affairs through feasting and dancing that drew on the symbolism of life-giving corn. They continued the ideals of society by showing respect and concern for the deceased's spirit, the relatives of the deceased, and the community. If beloved people embodied the values of society, then women continued to carry out those values through their acts of mourning and preparation of food.

Continuity and Loss

Through mortuary practices Choctaw women expressed many of the values embodied by Ohoyo Osh Chisba. Like Ohoyo Osh Chisba they provided corn for their families and communities, and by doing so they reinforced the ideals of balance, community, and reciprocity. Through crying and dancing they helped the spirit to unite with ancestors in the utopian afterworld and they helped reincorporate the mourners into everyday life. They restored balance to the world of the spirits and the world of the living just as they did in earlier times through their decisions about how to complete restitution for those who died unnatural deaths. In other words, their acts represented the ideals most valued by Choctaw society, those that were considered beloved.

Although Choctaw women continued to fulfill necessary functions at funerals, they also lost important positions that reflected a general curtailment of women's roles that began in the late seventeenth century and continued throughout the eighteenth century. Bone-gatherers and pole-pullers served in specialized positions that set them apart from other mourners. Women's exclusion as bone-gatherers coincided with the suppression of the practice of replacing the life of the deceased with that of the one who killed the deceased. In both cases women ensured the release of the spirit from this world so that it could enter the utopian afterworld. They helped the spirit to complete its cycle of life and death just as they aided the living through the cycles of planting and harvesting the corn. Their loss of roles as bone-gatherers also occurred at a time when women no longer entered the sacred square or council where the beloved fire burned. Yet they continued to sit near the sacred fire while in a state of mourning.

If males took over positions once held by women too, then women lost specialized roles that would have gained them recognition as beloved. However, women continued to contribute to the mourning rites of the Choctaw. Bone-gathering had ceased as a mortuary practice in the eighteenth century, but the body still had to be prepared for interment, which women continued to do as late as the 1920s. Juanita Jefferson, Choctaw tribal judge, described how her father used to construct coffins while her mother prepared bodies the traditional way for funerals (Jefferson, telephone conversation). According to Bertram Bobb, chaplain of the Oklahoma Choctaw Tribal Council, many features of the cry still exist in rural areas. Wakes are often held in the home of the deceased and feasting is still part of the funeral (interview 1990). A seminary student told me that in Choctaw Parish it is not uncommon for participants at three-day meetings to hold a memorial much like the one-year anniversary of the funeral cries (anonymous interview 1993). Women continue to care for the spirit of the deceased as well as the spirits of the living through mourning, preparation of feasts, and participation in dances.

The funeral ceremony, like the Green Corn Ceremony, embodied and reinforced Choctaw values. Both ceremonies ensured the survival of Choctaw communities by restoring balance to society. Reverend Calvin

Cushman may have realized the importance of funeral ceremonies when he said of the Choctaw pole-pulling ritual, "Perhaps no one thing tends so much to debase the people or presents so powerful temptations to those who are somewhat disposed to give up their dissipation [harmful or frivolous practices]" (1828, 380). He recognized that even those Choctaw who were drawn to Christianity would often ignore his admonitions and attend pole-pulling ceremonies. The Green Corn Ceremony provided for an annual renewal that purified society of all the pollution that arose as a result of daily living. The funeral also purified society in that the spirit of the deceased was released through mourning and the people restored to balance through feasting and dancing. Although Choctaw funeral ceremonies underwent many changes and each community had its own version of the ceremony, balance and reciprocity between genders continued, but it was expressed in new ways. Women continue to carry on the values of Ohoyo Osh Chisba in Choctaw society much like women of earlier times once did.

Conclusion:
The Legacy of Corn Woman

We may never know the extent to which eighteenth-century Choctaw recognized beloved women before the effects of French colonization led to changes in native women's roles in the Lower Mississippi Valley. However, when we recognize that everything valued and respected in Southeastern native societies could be referred to as beloved, from beloved speech to beloved land, it makes sense that Choctaw women as child-bearers and caretakers of corn would be considered beloved. That the Choctaw used this appellation in association with the female principle can be seen in their reference to Nanih Waiya as Iholitopa Ishki, or Beloved Mother (Swanton 1931, 30; Cushman 1899, 232; Lincecum 1861, 9). One of the earliest references to a Choctaw woman of status comes from Gravier's 1700 report in which he tells of a great female Houma chief whom he described as occupying the first place in all the councils (JR 65:147–49).[1] Thirty to forty years later, an anonymous French officer described "an honored" woman who stripped the flesh from the bones of the deceased. His use of the appellation "femme de valleur" suggests that the Choctaw referred to certain women as honored or beloved as late as the mid-eighteenth century (Swanton 1931, 170–71). When we look at the numerous ways in which women contributed to the well-being of the Choctaw, we can identify numerous ways in which they could have earned recognition as beloved.

Although "beloved" applies to anything or anyone highly valued or sacred, we have come to associate beloved people primarily with political leadership. I recall talking to a Choctaw relative who is highly regarded in the Choctaw Nation of Oklahoma about the absence of the idea of beloved woman among the Choctaw. Her response was that beloved people were part of councils and traditionally women were not on councils. Since we assume beloved are those who are in political positions, it is logical to examine the Choctaw political system for evidence of women's involvement. Scholars often have a tendency to focus their attention on political roles as a way of identifying powerful people who would also be beloved people, but such attention may reflect a Western bias and not necessarily an early contact-period Choctaw categorization.[2] Be that as it may, we can look to the political life of the Choctaw and find indications that women were part of decision-making processes, directly or indirectly. As such they likely could earn titles that reflected beloved status. If, as early French explorer accounts indicate, Lower Mississippi Valley native women were part of diplomatic envoys and war-related activities, then Choctaw women likely also participated in such affairs.

Some evidence exists of Choctaw women's participation in the political decision-making process of Choctaw society in the French colonial period. As noted in the introduction, during the council meeting at Dancing Rabbit Creek in September 1830, seven Choctaw female elders sat in the center of a circle of approximately sixty Choctaw men. The women participated in the discussion about the ceding of Choctaw land and removal to Indian Territory. When one of the councilmen, Killihota, expressed his willingness to give up their land and move west, one of the women, angered by his speech, accused him of having divided loyalties and threatened to cut him open with a butcher knife. Two other councilmen stood up and told Killihota that what the elder woman said about him was true (Halbert 1902, 382, 384–85).

The opening remarks by Middleton Mackey, the interpreter, suggest he was following a long-established protocol toward women council members. By addressing the women elders first and promising them that he would faithfully interpret to them everything said by the commissioners, he displayed recognition of the powerful place these women occupied in the council. In accordance with Choctaw restitution tradition whereby women decided the fate of captives, he told them that if he told a lie, they could cut his neck off

The Legacy of Corn Woman

(Halbert 1902, 382). Mackey displayed respect and honor toward the female elders, and he acknowledged the women's right to determine the life or death of someone who threatened the balance of Choctaw society. Interestingly, the women elders are not included in government reports, leading us to wonder how many times government representatives might have excluded women from their reports.

From Simpson Tubby, an Eastern Choctaw Methodist preacher in the early 1900s, we know that women held honored positions. For example, he told Swanton, "if the head chief or a captain died suddenly and the vice-chief could not be present at an assembly which had already been summoned, the wife of the deceased took his place. . . . When she rose to speak . . . all kept quiet and listened attentively" (Swanton 1931, 101). The respect given to those who spoke at councils can be found in national assemblies that began with the oldest males, called beloved men, or *hatak holitopa*, reciting all of the Choctaw's traditions and history to the attentive audience (Noley 1985, 95; Cushman 1899, 148). Women also could hold other important positions that involved the careful delivery of speeches or messages to Choctaw leaders. Tubby also told Swanton that there were female official messengers called *Mantema*, or someone "to go and carry or deliver something sacred or particular." Other titles women could hold included *Onatima*, "when you get there give it (to him)" and *Wakayatima*, "get up and hand it or deliver it." The wives of *mingoes*, or band captains, held the titles *Nompashtika* or *Nompatisholi*, both meaning "speaker" (Swanton 1931, 121). For an oral-based society in which the importance of speech was recognized and rewarded, the idea that anyone but the most trusted and valued of citizens would be allowed to deliver a message from one leader to another, or to speak on behalf of the people, is inconceivable.

These accounts of women's involvement in Choctaw political life could be construed as instances of atypical behavior that occurred under unusual circumstances such as negotiating for ceding of land. Atypical or not, the presence of the seven female Choctaw elders suggests that under certain conditions women could be and were part of councils. This seemingly isolated occurrence of women's participation in a council can be accounted for in at least two possible ways. One, their roles were vestiges of earlier activities of women in the seventeenth or early eighteenth centuries that chroniclers failed to note; or two, they were innovations or borrowings reflecting late eighteenth-century or early nineteenth-century conditions.

Evidence of Choctaw women's involvement in political affairs in the early eighteenth century comes indirectly from our knowledge of Natchez and Choctaw relations. Father Le Petit's observation that delegations to the Natchez always included six women suggests that Choctaw delegations to the Natchez also included six women (JR 68:159). The later absence of women in Choctaw councils may reflect the dynamics between white men and women in the nineteenth century rather than women's exclusion due to Choctaw protocol. French, British, and American men had long represented white interests without the presence of women. In fact, white women were taught that their contributions to society did not include political or economic concerns. Nor did white males acknowledge native women's presence in such matters. Instead the pressures were toward limiting women's participation and not for drawing them into the international political arena. The incongruity of not having women present during negotiations is indicated by Adair's recollection of a council of "a great many head-men of different towns" that he attended at the house of Choctaw leader Red Chief. A woman told him that she believed that the speeches made by the men were not good, as they did not allow any women or boys to hear it (Adair 1775, 313). Men were making decisions for the community, which was not consistent with ideals of participation and consensus or with communal orientations.

Choctaw women also may not have had an opportunity to speak publicly in front of French or English representatives because of the constant state of war in which the Choctaw found themselves. As early as 1702 the Choctaw Nation consisted of three or more districts, each of which was led by a peacetime or white leader, or, during times of conflict, usually a temporary seasonal situation, by a war or red leader. Ordinarily, a military leader, or *miko*, was subordinate to civil authorities and acted only with their consent. However, English and French slave-raiding interests and warfare, possibly beginning as early as 1700, forced the Choctaw into a nearly permanent state of war with the Chickasaw and other British-allied nations (Noley 1985, 96; Galloway 1985b, 125–27). Since Choctaw women did not typically engage in battle, and their participation in tribal negotiations with Europeans declined as the threat of captivity, rape, and death increased, their participation in war councils would have been unlikely. However, by the nineteenth century the Choctaw and United States were at peace with each other. Thus, at the time of the Treaty of Dancing Rabbit Creek, women would have been able to participate again in councils. However, by that time Choctaw gender roles and political structures could have changed enough to render women's participation in councils unusual or inappropriate.

Galloway raises the possibility that the French did not observe Choctaw women participating in councils because those councils tended to take place during ceremonies like the Green Corn or mourning rites. She notes that the French did not visit the Choctaw during ceremonial times and "that in fact the Choctaw always seemed to be unavailable at the time that they would have been having a green corn ceremony" (1986, 16). The noticeable absence of the Choctaw during ceremonial times would also account for the relatively few accounts of female political activity especially after the French colonial period.[3] Accounts exist of international councils involving the French, Choctaw, and other native nations, but very little has been written about domestic Choctaw councils. When the Green Corn ceased to be practiced, the opportunities for women to participate in councils may have been affected. It is, therefore, notable that Choctaw women were observed in the council at the Treaty of Dancing Rabbit Creek, which was held in September, the time of the Green Corn.

The likelihood that the involvement of seven women in the council at Dancing Rabbit Creek represented an innovation or borrowing from other Indian nations is highly improbable. The native nations of the Southeast were undergoing similar changes in their political systems. Among the Cherokee, for example, English pressure to move from village councils that included women to centralized intertown councils comprised mainly of men began as early as the 1730s. Men dominated the intertown councils primarily because foreign relations, typically their domain, became the primary concern of the councils. Intertown councils also required leaving home to travel to other locations, which the women often did not do because of their domestic and agricultural responsibilities. The English also enhanced the men's status in council by bestowing honors and gifts on them but not on the women. By the end of the century the practice of excluding women from Cherokee councils was well established (Perdue 1998, 93–94).

In addition to their political involvement, Choctaw women also carried out acts considered sacred or important. As producers of domesticated plant food and gatherers of wild foods, women contributed to a major portion of the Choctaw diet. The importance of domestic food was celebrated through the Green Corn Ceremony in which women participated through food and dance. The Green Corn Ceremony involved the sacred through purification, dancing, and feasting. Women also carried out sacred tasks during funeral ceremonies in which they might have specialized roles, and they participated in communal rituals such as dancing and feasting. Women's relationship to fertility is also recognized in rituals surrounding menstruation and childbirth. When we begin to broaden our gaze, we find that women also participated in healing rituals and war rituals in addition to their many domestic activities, all of which made them important to Choctaw society.

The pressures experienced by Choctaw society during the French colonial period arguably led to alterations in women's behavior. Women's economic, political, and domestic life had changed so much during the first half of the eighteenth century that ceremonies such as the Green Corn Ceremony did not survive. The instability of the Lower Mississippi Valley due to the threat of violence and enslavement, as well as the influence of missionaries, contributed not only to the suppression of such practices but also to changes in women's roles. Women no longer could participate in the activities or rituals they once did, thus limiting their opportunities to enhance their status. In addition, town leaders typically met during annual ceremonials such as the Green Corn Dance to discuss mutual concerns (Noley 1985, 94). The loss of the Green Corn Ceremony meant that alternative arrangements had to be made, arrangements that apparently excluded women and boys.

By the middle of the eighteenth century, Choctaw society had changed dramatically. The experiences of the French colonial period not only shaped the future of the Choctaw but also their memory of the past. We know that the Choctaw confederacy was already in a state of major reconstruction and adaptation to local conditions at the time of French exploration in 1682. The Choctaw ceremonial cycle may have been in a state of decline or development. The pressures of French colonization could have hastened any tendency toward decline or interrupted the development of a ceremonial cycle. Either way the effects of French contact (in conjunction with British and Spanish intrigues) contributed to the cessation of ceremonies like the Green Corn, which in turn lessened formal opportunities for relating cultural stories about beings such as Ohoyo Osh Chisba. By the time British and later American writers began reporting on Choctaw culture and history, the memory of earlier aspects were long forgotten by some and not revealed by others.

Thus, when Protestant missionaries entered the Choctaw Nation, they found a people susceptible to their messages about women and men's roles because their roles had already undergone dramatic change. The missionaries further contributed to changes in Choctaw social organization by continuing the legacy of challenging Choctaw concepts of gender roles. After 1819, a shift toward a patrilineal emphasis became apparent along with a breakdown of the clan structure (Eggan 1937, 42). Choctaw social organization no longer supported the participation of women in what were then becoming male-dominated roles. When American commissions wanted to deal only with men, they faced a society that had already experienced the exclusion of women from public roles such as participation in councils with the French.

In fact, the pressures of treaties and the concomitant threat of land loss and removal necessitated constant discussion and negotiation by the male-oriented political leadership of Choctaw society. Attention was directed to men because they were the ones that the Americans wanted to negotiate with, and not just any men, but those men who seemed most likely to be manipulated by American demands or threats. Political leaders became the most visible of the beloved because circumstances required political leaders to respond constantly to American pressures to cede land or remove west of the Mississippi River. Long before the American republic came into being, therefore, any reference to beloved women that might have existed was gone, and by the 1830s the association between beloved people and political leadership seemed to have become the norm.

However, women continued to carry out highly valued functions as seen in the case of funerals. From care of the deceased's remains to mourning, feasting, and dancing, Choctaw women ensured the continued balance within society and between the living and the spirits of the ancestors. They also continued many of their traditional domestic roles as caretaker of the home and children, the transmitter of language and culture to their children, and in some cases as the final arbiter of domestic concerns related to childcare and marriage. As American society became more focused on Choctaw men because of their political and economic activities, women continued to practice Choctaw traditional cultural ways without attracting too much attention.[4] Through domestic activities that white males, both missionaries and civilians, assumed to be innocuous and nonthreatening to the conversion and acculturation process, and through similar church-related activities, women could continue to teach Choctaw values, stories, language, and culture.

In contemporary Oklahoma Choctaw Protestant communities where acculturation is perhaps most evident, women are still recognized as the repositories and transmitters of Choctaw culture.[5] Through the revitalization efforts of the 1960s that continue up to the present time, Oklahoma Choctaw people are relearning many of the dances they had once lost. They are turning to their Mississippi Choctaw relatives to learn songs, dances, stories, and language. Both the Oklahoma and Mississippi Choctaw reinforce their culture through annual festivals, stickball games (demonstration for Oklahoma Choctaw and tournament for Mississippi Choctaw), and language. As the Oklahoma Choctaw, in particular, begin to learn more of their language and more of their stories through their annual festivals, schools, newspaper, and Internet site, it may be that they will also begin to remember the legacy of Ohoyo Osh Chisba, The Unknown Woman, who, according to their traditional stories, brought them corn. Through corn Ohoyo Osh Chisba nurtured the Choctaw and brought them together in ceremony, the Green Corn. The centrality of corn to Choctaw people today can be seen in the *tomfulla, banaha*, and *tanchi palvska* (corn dishes) found at community gatherings, church dinners, and family celebrations.

Today Choctaw women continue the legacy of nurturing family and community through language, food, childcare, stories, and ritual. They are also visible in the revitalization of Choctaw culture (as well as other native cultures) that began in the 1960s. For example, Billie Nowabbi, a Choctaw United Methodist minister, served on the planning committee for the first national seminar for United Methodist native women, held at Mills College in Oakland, California, in 1973. The seminar helped awaken women's awareness of native image and the role of a tribal theology of women in church, family, and community (*Advocate* 1973, 4; Pesantubbee 1994, 140–41). Juanita Jefferson, a Choctaw from Talihina, organized a group of Choctaw and other native senior citizens to teach them Indian sign language, native gospel songs, and powwow dance steps. These senior citizens, dressed in traditional clothing, performed for Choctaw Nation special events and for nursing homes and church gatherings throughout Southeast Oklahoma (Pesantubbee 1994, 138). Although gospel songs and powwows are not historically Choctaw traditions, the dress and language are, and together they help reinforce a sense of

Choctaw community and identity. When Choctaw Larger Parish, United Presbyterian Church, U.S.A., wanted someone to tell Choctaw stories at youth camps, they turned to an elder woman who researched and developed Choctaw stories that she told in English and Choctaw (Pesantubbee 1994, 247–48). As one young Choctaw man told me, "at several of our camp meetings during the summer, most of the leadership was women" (anonymous interview 1993).

In the last forty years Oklahoma Choctaw women have begun to move into more leadership positions within their communities, including in churches and in government. They are interested in learning more about the history of women's roles in Choctaw life. In August and October 2002 I was invited to speak to two different groups of native women, the first from Oklahoma and the second from several states in the Southeast. Both groups included Choctaw women. In each case Choctaw women had not heard of Choctaw beloved women, but they had a tremendous interest in learning about my research on Choctaw women's status in the eighteenth century. These women were seeking ways to create a more inclusive place for women in areas of leadership. They were not interested in returning to traditional ways, but in drawing inspiration and strength from the examples of their ancestors. They wanted to learn from history the ways in which they could effectively contribute to the leadership life of their communities that over the last two centuries had become the domain of men.

Choctaw women have always had an influential presence in their families and communities whether through domestic affairs or more public religious and economic concerns. In many ways they have come full circle some 150 years later by returning to the council where decisions are made concerning all members of the Choctaw Nation. Seven women have served on the Oklahoma Choctaw council since the late 1970s. They are Edna Belvin, Harriet Wright James, Lu Bauers, Lillian Sullivan, Lois Burton, Deana Cantrell, and Charlotte Jackson. Jackson is currently the only woman council member, and she has been serving since 1991 (Tate, telephone conversation; Jefferson, telephone conversation; Jackson, telephone conversation). In 1988 Juanita Jefferson became the first and so far the only woman Choctaw tribal judge, and she continues to hold that office. In 2001 she was honored as outstanding elder of the Choctaw Nation (Jefferson, telephone conversation). Perhaps the greatest indicator of women's return to the political arena happened in 1983 when Harriet

Wright James ran for chief of the Choctaw Nation of Oklahoma. She did not win, but she could be seen at Choctaw events like the annual festival sharing her ideas with the community.

Women are also serving as council members and judges among the Mississippi Choctaw. One Mississippi Choctaw woman, Linda Farve, served on the council from 1981 to 1984. She was elected again in 1999 and is still serving on the council. She is perhaps best known for her commitment to preventing the storage of hazardous waste on the reservation. When asked about Choctaw women that she would consider beloved, she identified her mother and her aunt, who is confined to a wheelchair, for their activism in fighting the hazardous waste storage plan (Farve, telephone interview).

These women contribute to the well-being of Choctaw society by embodying those attributes valued by Choctaw. They are not breaking new ground but are continuing the legacy of their grandmothers and of Ohoyo Osh Chisba. They are keepers of cultural knowledge and they are leaders in their Nations. They are, for all intents and purposes, Choctaw Beloved Women.

Notes

Introduction

1. See Swanton 1928b, 302–3, 423, for a discussion of Creek war leaders and ceremonial leaders as beloved. For information about Cherokee beloved women associated with war and ceremonial rituals, see Perdue 1998, 26–27, 36, 38–39; and Reid 1970, 187.
2. I do not use "Native American" or "American Indian" because I associate those descriptors with the post-1776 era. Issue can be taken with all of these terms, the misnomer "Indian" perhaps more so. However, native people, local and extended, grassroots and academic, commonly use the term "Indian" intra-communally to designate both specific and general ethnicity. The term "Indian" is not acceptable usage for non-Indians; however, those who have a history of similar experiences with Euro/Americans use it among themselves to recognize their common distinction from the non-Indian majority society.

Chapter 1: In Search of Beloved Women

1. Although Hernando de Soto may have encountered Choctaw, the impact appears to have been minimal in comparison to later French and British colonization.
2. Patricia Galloway, written remarks to author, August 2002.
3. Adair was conversant in Chickasaw and probably Choctaw as the two languages are similar. The word *hottuk oretoopah*, for example, could be either the Chickasaw word *hattak hollittopa* or the Choctaw words *hatak holitopa* or *hatak holittopa* (Adair 1775, x; Byington 1915, 138; Munro and Willmond 1994, 111; Roberts 2002).

4. See Galloway 1994, "Confederacy as a Solution to Chiefdom Dissolution: Historical Evidence in the Choctaw Case."
5. The Mobilian were Muskhogean and believed to have been located near Choctaw Bluff on the Alabama River, but later settled near Fort Lewis. The Naniaba were located on the Tombigbee River, just above its fork with the Alabama River. McWilliams states, "they were almost certainly a Choctaw tribe." The Tohomé were also a Muskhogean group of the Gulf Coast that spoke a dialect of Choctaw. They had a settlement on the west bank of the Tombigbee, a few miles above the Indian town of Mobile located at the head of Mobile Bay (Hodge 1907, 1:916; 2:24, 771; Pénicaut 1953, 61 n. 3; Mereness 1916, 267 n. 1). Lusser listed the Tomé (Tohomé) as a group of Choctaw established on the Mobile River (MPA:FD 1927, 1:117). Rowland, Sanders, and Galloway note that "This incident helps to confirm the incorporation of the Tohomé by the Choctaw" (MPA:FD 1984, 5:25 n. 3).
6. The Chakchiuma once lived near the northern edge of Choctaw country, but later relocated near the southern edge of Chickasaw country (Galloway 1995, 193). The Alabama or Alibamu are part of the Koasati of the Creek Confederacy and were formerly located in South Alabama, although chroniclers of Soto located them in northwest or central Mississippi (Hodge 1907, 1:43, 363).
7. The Bayogoula lived on the west bank of the Mississippi. Iberville noted that the Bayougoula and Ouacha as well as the Ouma, Theloel, Taensa, Coloa, Chycacha, Napyssa, Choutymacha, Yagenechyto, Bylocchy, and Pascoboula spoke the same language or at least understood each other. The name Pascagoula comes from the Choctaw words for "bread people." They lived on Pascagoula River in southern Mississippi in intimate connection with the Biloxi (Hodge 1907, 2:205). McWilliams identifies the Colapissa as the Acolapissa from the Choctaw *okla pisa*. The Colapissa once lived on the headwaters of the Pearl River, but later moved to the north side of Lake Pontchartrain and various lagoons in the area (1981, 126 n. 61). The Tunica were originally located on the lower Yazoo in Mississippi (Hodge 1907, 2:838).
8. The Ouacha are a small Muskhogean nation who originally inhabited the lower part of Bayou Lafourche, Louisiana. In 1718, following the Chitimacha war, they moved to an area about three leagues above New Orleans on the Mississippi (Hodge 1907, 2:918–19).
9. Penman speculates that environmental conditions prevented long-term occupation and that earlier agriculturalists found the area unfavorable for maize production (1977, 304).
10. Galloway states that it is possible that the Soto expedition brought the common cold, tuberculosis, and a "truly remarkable disease vector in the shape of their ever-growing herd of pigs which infected Indians deep in the interior as well as deer and turkeys" (1994, 399).

11. Some versions include other nations such as the Cherokee, Shawnee, and Delaware. In one version the Cherokee, Shawnee, and Delaware sprang from the Choctaw rather than the Choctaw separating from the surrounding people (Swanton 1931, 32).
12. See Galloway for a discussion of the reliability of nineteenth-century versions recorded by whites (1995, 331–37).
13. Another version of the story attributes the gift of corn to a crow that drops a kernel of corn as it flew by the Choctaw people (Lincecum 1861, 24–25; Swanton 1931, 210).
14. According to Chahta immataha, the Choctaw of the early nineteenth century erroneously remembered their stories as saying their ancestors emerged out of Nanih Waiya, the mother of the race. He said he was told that they left from Nanih Waiya. In any case, the Choctaw came to refer to Nanih Waiya as Beloved Mother (Lincecum 1861, 9).
15. Although Ohoyo Osh Chisba translates as "The Unknown Woman," I refer to her as Corn Woman throughout this book. Throughout the Southeast First Woman or the provider of corn is known as Corn Woman. Among the Cherokee, Selu is also called Corn Woman, Corn-Mother, or Grandmother (Mooney 1900, 242–47; Kilpatrick and Kilpatrick 1964, 129–34; Payne n.d., 26–28). The Natchez also refer to the woman who provided corn as Corn-Woman (Swanton 1929, 230).
16. See *haloka, holitopa,* or *hatak holitopa* (beloved man) in Byington, *A Dictionary of the Choctaw Language,* 135, 138, 164. According to John R. Swanton, *haloka,* meaning sacred or beloved, was used in Choctaw to designate son-in-law, father-in-law, and mother-in-law (Swanton 1928c, 184). See also Swanton 1928b, 302.
17. For a discussion of war leaders who were also considered beloved, see Parker 1991, 122; and Swanton 1928b, 302–33.
18. The Hitchiti occupied the area now known as Alabama, Southern Georgia, and Northern Florida. They were considered the "elder brother" of other Southeastern nations; they spoke a Muskhogean dialect and were eventually absorbed into the Creek Nation (Hodge 1907, 1:551).
19. By institutional authority I mean the power given to a leader to impose decisions on a state. I am contrasting institutional authority to consensual authority among Southeastern people that allows for leadership as long as the people choose to follow that leadership.
20. The Taensa are related to the Natchez and originally occupied the area of present-day Tensas Parish, Louisiana. They later moved to Mobile, followed by another move to the Red River in 1764 to avoid English control. After another move they eventually settled on the northern end of Grand Lake (Hodge 1907, 2:668–69).
21. The Cahayrohoua are believed to have resided in Southwest Arkansas near the Red River (Hodge 1907, 1:184).

22. Iberville recorded that the Indians belonged to the nation of the Annochy and Moctoby. Hodge identifies the Annochy as Biloxi, a term apparently derived from the Choctaw language (1907, 1:147–48).
23. By the 1700s the Tunica resided on the Yazoo River in what is now Mississippi. They are part of the Gulf stock language group (Hodge 1907, 2:838; Kniffen et al. 1987, 5, 123).
24. Fort Maurepas was commonly known as Fort Biloxi.
25. The Cadadoquis or Kadohadacho, meaning "real Caddo," are part of the Caddo nation and they lived along the Red River in Louisiana. During the last quarter of the eighteenth century they moved near the Nachitoches (Hodge 1907, 1:638–39).
26. The Yowani, meaning "cutworm" or "caterpillar," were located on the Chickasawhay River south of present-day Shubuta, Mississippi. During the eighteenth century they were part of the Sixtowns people (Hodge 1907, 2:1001–2).
27. Some studies of the Choctaw indicate that women participated in social dances only. See Swanton 1931, 223; Cushman 1899, 156.
28. Ouma or Houma is from the Choctaw word *humma*, meaning "red." Iberville observed cranial deformation among some of the older Ouma men, a practice known among the Choctaw. They lived near the Bayogoula and Mougoulascha, who occupied the same village on the west bank of the Mississippi River. After more than half their people were killed by the Tunica, who had joined them in 1706, they moved close to New Orleans (Hodge 1907, 1:137, 577; Galloway 1995, 187).
29. The Yazoo were located on the lower Yazoo River in Mississippi. It is believed that they later integrated with the Chickasaw and Choctaw (Hodge 1907, 2:995).
30. Chickasawhay was located on the east side of Chickasawhay River, about three miles below the present town of Enterprise, Georgia (Hodge 1907, 1:262).
31. Marcel Giraud believes that Pénicaut did not go to Louisiana on Iberville's first voyage. Richebourg Gaillarde McWilliams, however, argues that he cannot exclude the possibility that Pénicaut went on the first voyage. See Pénicaut 1953, xxiv–xxv.
32. According to Galloway the Moctoby or Moctobi occupied the Pascagoula estuary and delta in Southern Mississippi along with the Biloxi and Pascagoula. They are believed to have been Siouan (1995, 309–10). The Pensacola were an Alabama River nation located to the southeast of the Choctaw (Galloway 1995, 311).
33. In McWilliams's translation of the Pénicaut narrative, Pénicaut writes that the Indians flogged everyone in the village until they bled. I chose to use the word *scratch* instead of *flog* because later ethnographies and contemporary Southeastern Indians refer to the practice as scratching.

34. The Cenis are the same as the Hasinai or "our own people," the name the Caddo give themselves. The Caddo are believed to have moved eastward from the Southwest to the Red River region of Louisiana and Arkansas, although their stories indicate that the Red River region was their place of origin. There are some interesting similarities to the Choctaw story, primarily the west to east migration and evidence that they either drove earlier occupants out of the region or that they themselves may have been forced back from the coast (Hodge 1907, 1:179, 182).

Chapter 2: A Violent Landscape

1. This observation is based on a study of the *Mississippi Provincial Archives*, vols. 1–5 (MPA:FD 1927; 1929; 1932; 1984) and the *Historical Collections of Louisiana*, vols. 1, 3, 5 (French 1846; 1853; 1857).
2. For example, see "Journal of Lusser" (MPA:FD 1927, 1:116–17); "Journal of Régis du Roullet" (MPA:FD 1927, 1:149–54); and "Memoir on Indians by Kelerec" (MPA:FD 1984, 5:225–26).
3. Concha is short for *Kunshak-bolukta* or "round reed-brake." It is a former important Choctaw town that was part of the northeast division. The town was originally located at the junction of the three primary Choctaw divisions in what is now the southwest corner of Kemper County, Mississippi (Hodge 1907, 1:334).
4. The Coweta (Kawita), Kasihta, and Okmulgee (Ocmulgee) were all Lower Creek towns. The first two were located near Chattahooche River in Alabama and the third near Flint River in Georgia (Hodge 1907, 1:661, 669; 2:105).
5. Abihka is an Upper Creek town near Upper Coosa River in Alabama (Hodge 1907, 1:1).
6. Tallapoosa is an eastern group of towns of the Upper Creek located on Tallapoosa River, Alabama (Hodge 1907, 2:677).
7. The Shawnee at one time were a leading nation of South Carolina, Tennessee, Pennsylvania, and Ohio (Hodge 1907, 2:530–31).
8. Bienville succeeded Sauvole as governor of Louisiana in 1702.
9. The Apalachee, believed to be from the Choctaw *A'palachi* [people] on the other side, lived in Florida, but were linguistically more related to the Choctaw than the Creek. The Chatot were related to the Choctaw and spoke the Choctaw language. The Tawasa are a Muskhogean nation first located by Soto in the neighborhood of Tallapoosa River, but they later moved further southeast (Hodge 1907, 1:67, 237; 2:704).
10. The Okeoulou were located in what is now Neshoba County and Newton County. Roullet translated their name as "Scarce Water," although it is often translated as "Beloved Water" (MPA:FD 1927, 1:96 n. 2).
11. See Reid 1970 for a discussion of blood revenge among the Cherokee.

12. From the Choctaw *Saktchi huma*, or "red crawfish." The Chakchiuma spoke a Choctaw-Chickasaw dialect and lived along the Yazoo River, Mississippi. They were probably the most populous of the Yazoo nation. Swanton believed the Houma and Chakchiuma were once part of the same people. Adair suggests that the Chakchiuma accompanied the Choctaw and Chickasaw on their migration from the west and settled between the two nations (Hodge 1907, 1:231; Swanton 1911, 292–93).
13. The German settlers were important to the welfare of the French colonists because of their success in farming in the Mississippi region.
14. Ofogoula is from the Choctaw *ofi okla*, or "dog people." They are believed to be a Siouan group who were located on the Yazoo River in Mississippi but later moved downriver to the Tunica (Hodge 1907, 2:108; Swanton 1911, 7–8).
15. According to Le Sueur, the Englishman, who had been encouraging Chickasaw to obtain slaves for him, only bought the women and children, for which he paid three hundred livres apiece. The men were killed (Tonti 1985, 220 n. 2).

Chapter 3: The Novel World of the Jesuits

1. Catholic missionaries in Louisiana included French Capuchins and Jesuits as well as Spanish priests. From 1882 to 1898 an Irish priest from Holland, Reverend B. J. Bekkers, served among the Choctaw.
2. For example, Fred Eggan states that "missions were established among them [Choctaw] as early as 1819 (1937, 41).
3. Romans does not explain why the Choctaw called the missionary a woman. It may be that he engaged in tasks considered the work of women, or they could have been referring to his clothing, his manner of dress, his celibacy, or his noninvolvement in male pursuits such as hunting or warring. The Choctaw may have also asked him to undo his baptism because of unsuccessful ventures that they blamed on his weak medicine (see Bossu 1962, 168–69).
4. Ymatahatchitou is Red Shoe, who apparently was responsible for the deaths of three French men.
5. In 1674–75 Bishop Calderon visited the Indian missions of Florida, where he apparently learned of the Choctaw although he probably did not visit them. Galloway points out that trade was carried on with the Indians to the west through Christianized Indians (1994, 405). Thus it is possible that Choctaw people had some knowledge of Spanish Catholics. In 1673 the Jesuit Jacques Marquette traveled down the Mississippi River with Louis Jolliet, but they did not travel beyond a point just above the juncture of the Arkansas and Mississippi Rivers (Kenton 1925, xlvii).
6. More commonly known as Quapaw, the Arkansas were located a short distance above the mouth of the Arkansas River at the time of Joliet's visit in 1673. A few years later they moved close to the entrance of the White River (Hodge 1907, 2:333–35).

7. The Coroa are possibly a Tunica group and they lived along the Mississippi River near the Yazoo River (Hodge 1907, 2:726).
8. Quinipissa comes from the Choctaw *kana* and *pissa* ("those who see" or "scouts"). The Quinipissa, a Muskhogean group that formerly lived in the vicinity of present-day Hahrville, later moved close to the Chickasaw, with whom they incorporated (Hodge 1907, 1:9–10; Swanton 1911, 279–80).
9. The Mongoulacha or Mugulasha lived with the Bayogoula on the west bank of the Mississippi. Their chief was also chief of the Quinipissa at the time La Salle and Tonty encountered them. In 1700 the Bayogoula attacked and nearly killed them all (Hodge 1907, 1:954).
10. Religious objects were not the only items to make their way into the Lower Mississippi Valley native world. When Iberville met the chief of the Mongoulacha he was wearing a cloak of blue serge that he said was given to him by Tonty (Fortier 1904, 38). It is likely that Tonty presented the Mongoulacha with other gifts. Among the Bayogoula Iberville found a double glass bottle, which Tonty had given them on an earlier trip, on an alter in their temple along with other presents to their deity (Swanton 1911, 275).
11. Tamaroa means "cut tail" or "he has a cut tail." They were part of the Illinois confederacy and occupied the region of the Mississippi River near the mouths of the Illinois and Missouri Rivers. Their village was a stopping place for the French during their trips up and down the Mississippi (Hodge 1907, 2:682).
12. Du Ru is also spelled Du Rue and Du Rhue.
13. Some of the missionaries who served at Mobile include Fathers Roulleaux de la Vente, Huvé, LeMaire, and Dominic Varlet. Many missionaries in Upper Louisiana Territory traveled the Mississippi River to New Orleans and had occasion to interact with native people. Some of those missionaries include Reverend Father Boulanger; Fathers Paul du Poisson, missionary at the Port of the Arkansas; John Souel, missionary to the Yazoo; and Doutreleau (Baudier 1939, 32, 89, 119; Shea 1855, 445).
14. Although Father Le Petit is typically credited with being the first missionary to establish a mission among the Choctaw, Shea notes that Mr. Noiseux, an "unreliable writer," mentions two earlier missionaries. According to Noiseux, Geoffry Thierry Erborie was a missionary among the Choctaw and Natchez from 1699 until 1709, when he returned to the Illinois. He also wrote that John Daniel Testu established a Choctaw mission in 1713, where he may have remained until his death in 1718 (1855, 441, 502).
15. Shea writes that Father Vitre, the Superior, recalled Baudoüin to New Orleans because of troubles with the English. In 1750 Baudoüin became Superior and "was taking measures to restore the mission." According to Shea the mission subsisted until about 1770 (1855, 451).

16. Chahta immatahah appears to be telling of the Apalachee experience with Spanish expeditions in the first half of the sixteenth century, although the description of the priest seems to be that of a Jesuit rather than a friar. The migration of some Apalachee to Mobile in 1704 and 1715 may account for the integration of Apalachee experience into Choctaw history. Soto may have encountered Choctaw during his expedition across the South. In any case, the storyteller has confused events across time and cultures. See Hann (1988) for a history of Apalachee experience with Spanish explorers and missionaries.
17. The Christian cross in which the vertical axis is longer that the horizontal axis should not be confused with the cross-in-palm symbol that represents the sun or the four logs representing the four directions (Kniffen et al. 1987, 258, 260).
18. La Salle's first expedition included seven Indian women, probably Mahican or Abnaki, but not French or Canadian women (Minet 1682, 42). Fortier states there were ten women (1904, 23). During La Salle's second expedition in search of the Mississippi from the Gulf of Mexico he encountered two Shawnee whom he had lost during his first expedition. When he tried to convince the Shawnee to join him again so they could return to their own country, they told him "that they were not unnatural enough to abandon their wives and children" (Cavelier 1861, 28–29).
19. Roger Baudier cites Pierre Margny but does not provide sufficient information to verify his citation.
20. For an excellent discussion of the history of Jesuit attitudes toward women, marriage, and divorce and their impact on their perception of native women, see Karen Anderson's *Chain Her By One Foot* (NY: Routledge, 1991).
21. Bossu mistranslated *Bras Piqué*, Tattoed Arm, as Stung Arm (1962, 45).
22. Dumont says that the Great Chief's little son was responsible for the mix-up in dates. The boy, imitating his father, had thrown two sticks into the fire (French 1853, 82). This version does not seem as likely because if they knew the child had thrown the sticks in the fire, then they would also have known that they did not have the correct number of sticks anymore.
23. Bossu tells of one Natchez man, Etteacteala, who refused to sacrifice himself upon the death of his wife. He fled the area and was able to return after the funeral had taken place. However, when a relative of his deceased wife also died, the Natchez chief determined he should be sacrificed, in part to rectify his failure to be sacrificed with his wife. He created such a commotion that the wife of the deceased told him that since life was so dear to him he should go away (1962, 32–33).
24. Carson suggests that the Choctaw took the Catholic paraphernalia because they initially held the missionaries in such high regard (60). In this particular case the religious artifacts were the spoils of war much like scalps and more likely represented a show of Natchez power, and then Choctaw power, because each was able to overcome their enemy's power and defeat them.

Chapter 4: Struggle for Survival

1. The Chevalier de Louboey reported on May 8, 1733, that "The colonists are obliged to send their Negroes into the woods to gather cane seed to keep them from perishing" (MPA:FD 1927, 1:218).
2. In the eighteenth century it was common practice for European governments to recruit mercenary soldiers. The government of France arranged for recruitment of Swiss soldiers for Louisiana. According to Hardcastle sometimes as many as one-fourth of all the troops in Louisiana were Swiss, and most of the time they constituted fifteen percent of the troops (1978, 82–85).
3. The company is also referred to as the Company of the West or the Mississippi Company. Later the company became the Company of the Indies.
4. In 1722, 4,200 settlers arrived in Louisiana and began cultivating crops. However, harsh weather and loss of ships or cargoes continued to plague the settlers.
5. Not all the women who arrived in Louisiana were from marginalized populations. Some, such as those who arrived in 1728, voluntarily emigrated in hopes of reaping the benefits of the new colony. Alceé Fortier describes them as being of "good character" and being placed under the charge of the Ursuline nuns until they were married (1904, 109). However, the women were also convinced to move to Louisiana by embellished stories of the wealth of the colonies.
6. Surrey stated that as late as 1752 a trader from Cape Francois bought three Indian men and two Indian women at New Orleans (1916, 230).
7. Surrey listed 110 Indian slaves held in the Mobile Valley and another 118 Indian slaves held along the Mississippi and in and around New Orleans in 1721. She stated that there were 73 Indian slaves in 1727 and 47 in 1731 (1916, 230).
8. See Swanton 1911, 235, for an example.
9. Bienville's army included Choctaw as well as native people from the Illinois Province and Canada.
10. The Chouacha was a small nation located on the east bank of the Mississippi River, a short distance below present-day New Orleans. After being attacked by some black slaves in 1703, they relocated to the west side of the river (Hodge 1907, 1:235).
11. The Osage call themselves Wazhazhe. They are a southern Siouan nation of the western division. In 1673 they were located on the Osage River. In 1701 Iberville located another group of Osage in the region of the Arkansas River (Hodge 1907, 2:156–57).
12. Tchanke is one of three Choctaw villages that attacked a community of German settlers and the Nachoubaouenya, allies of the French, in October 1748 (MPA:FD 1984, 5:26, 31).
13. For another translation of this incident as reported in the Journal of De Beauchamps, see Mereness 1916, 293–94.

14. See Kidwell for a discussion of laws passed by Mingo Hwoolatahoomah and his captains, many of which affected Choctaw women's sexual practices (1995a, 124; 1995b, 76–77). By the 1930s Choctaw kinship systems in Mississippi and Oklahoma had disappeared (Kidwell 1995a, 129).

Chapter 5: When the Dancing Stopped

1. For more information about the three worlds as conceived by Southeastern native people, see Hudson 1976, 122–25.
2. For a description of similar female figurines, the Figure at Mortar and the Schild effigy pipe, see Emerson 1989, 54–57.
3. Little is known about the author of this journal except a short notation, "Relat de Kened." Swanton notes that this relation appears to have been written in the early 1700s (1931, 243).
4. Tan fula, a soupy corn dish, was fed to the sick (Searcy 1985, 40).
5. The Natchez called their ceremony the Great Corn (Du Pratz 1774, 338); among the Creek it is known as the busk.
6. Bartram's statement does not clearly indicate whether he is referring to a Choctaw annual Green Corn dance or a Creek busk. However, since *busk* is a Creek term for the Green Corn, I interpret his statement as referring to the Creek. However, if one were to just as logically infer that he was referring to the Choctaw, then Bartram gives even greater proof of the existence of the Green Corn among the Choctaw.
7. Although Chahta immatahah's story has chronological problems, various aspects of the story correlate with other cultural narratives obtained by Swanton about the Choctaw and other Southeastern native people to lend some credibility to it. His story obviously incorporates events that took place among other native people possibly with the Spanish and French. Chahta immatahah was also a very old man who hinted at his own inability to recollect events correctly. Considering that Lincecum translated his notes some forty years after his interviews, it is not surprising that much cultural and chronological confusion exists in the story. In a personal communication Galloway notes that Chahta immatahah's ability to recollect far distant events and considerable medical knowledge, but not more contemporary significant events such as the Natchez war, raises questions about his narrative. Galloway also suggests that Lincecum's apparent lack of awareness that Chahta immatahah was an honorific title and not a personal name is evidence of the fabrication of this story. However, an examination of the 1831 registers of Choctaw claimants reveals a number of honorific titles being used as personal names (Lincecum 1861, 1, 3, 10, 56; Pesantubbee 1999, 392; Senate Exec. Doc. 512, 3:39, 51; Galloway 1995, 332).
8. See Hudson for an explanation of anomalous beings (1976, 139–41).

9. The French referred to trade items as gifts, probably because trade extended the earlier practice of exchanging gifts to secure alliances. Although the French continued to trade for deerskins in order to maintain alliances, the exchange involved pricing and thus was more like bartering than gift-giving.
10. Patricia Galloway, personal note to author, August 2002.

Chapter 6: Restoring Balance to the World

1. Many smaller nations lost their major ceremonies too. I chose to focus on the Cherokee and Creek because they represent two of the larger nations in the Southeast that also absorbed some of the smaller nations. Romans identified the Creek as the next largest nation after the Choctaw (1775, 62).
2. James Adair's nationality is not definitely known. He has been described as Irish, Scottish, and English. For biographical information see "Introduction" (Adair 1775, vii).
3. James Adair, for example, was convinced that native people were of Jewish descent and thus interpreted their culture in relation to his understanding of Jewish history.
4. The Choctaw originally were divided into two exogamous moieties. Some scholars and observers have used the terms *clan* or *iksa* (a division or group) interchangeably with moiety. See Swanton 1931, 76–78.
5. In a similar story about the origin of corn, some interpretations of the Cherokee story of Selu (Corn Woman) suggest that corn grew from her menstrual blood or from the blood of her body following her death (See Wahnenauhi Version in Mooney 1900, 248–49; Churchill 1997, 156).
6. In his study of mortuary customs, Hertz states that in order to enable a material object to pass from this world into the next, it must be destroyed (1909, 46).
7. See Natchez or Taensa practice of sacrificing the lives of relatives and friends of the deceased (Pénicaut 1953, 92–95; Mereness 1916, 47; Kniffen et al. 1987, 245; Claiborne 1880, 503).
8. Both sites included flesh burials and skull burials as well as bundle burials, which indicate a practice of primary and secondary burials (Galloway 1995, 283).
9. Halbert states that the *na foni aiowa* often translated as "bone-picker(s)" is incorrect, and that the proper translation is "bone-gatherer" (1900, 354).
10. Halbert identified two cries, the little cry "*yaiya iskitini*," which is held at the grave, and the big cry "*yaiya chito*," which is the last cry (1900, 361).
11. The author may have witnessed the funerals of men only. In any case, the use of male pronouns is consistent with the author's usage. Since observers did not write about women's burials, I am assuming their bodies were handled in the same way.

12. In Iberville's report for March 1700, he wrote that Father Du Ru observed a similar ceremony among the Ouma, who were close allies of the Choctaw and spoke a similar language. Father Du Ru reportedly said, "The women bewail their dead night and day. I was in the Great Chief's cabin where his body has been lying for more than two months. After his flesh drops from the bones, they will take them to the temple" (McWilliams 1981, 122).
13. Milfort's (or Milford's) memoir includes a significant number of questionable statements. However, in general his description of Choctaw funerals is in line with what other observers have noted. I have included his description because it contains some minor differences that can be attributed to regional or community differences.
14. Swanton wrote that the "bonepickers of the Choctaw might be male or female" (1928a, 700).
15. See John Middleton (1982, 145) for an explanation of the need to restore balance to society and the deceased when one dies a "bad death."
16. Among Southeastern native people it was common for a stickball game to be played during the Green Corn time. Sometimes referred to as little war, the game could become quite violent. However, if someone was killed during the game the rules of restitution did not apply. They did not replace a life with a life. The Red Path is the path of war, conflict, and danger (Hudson 1976, 235).
17. Halbert said there were six pole planters (1900, 357–58).
18. H. B. Cushman said the ladder of hoops provided easier ascent for the spirit to reach the top of the pole, from which it then went to the afterworld (1899, 167).
19. This description is a compilation of several versions of the pole-pulling ceremony that underwent changes during the nineteenth century.
20. During fieldwork among Protestant Choctaws, I interviewed several elders who told me they had never heard of any Choctaw dances. The Mississippi Choctaw continue to hold social dances, and in the 1970s some Presbyterian Oklahoma Choctaw went to Mississippi to learn some of the songs and dances. See Howard and Levine 1990 and Pesantubbee 1994.
21. Halbert states that there were never any "dancing-the-spirit-home" ceremonies as described by Claiborne (and later H. B. Cushman) (1900, 360). The italics in Cushman's account are mine.
22. Dance is also spelled *hila* or *hilha* (Byington 1915; Haag and Willis 2001, 335).
23. Densmore spells it *shatanni hila* (1943, 113). Bushnell spells it *tinsanale hitkla* (1909, 21).
24. H. B. Cushman described the concluding dances as a "jolly dance" (1899, 146).
25. Ruth Y. Wetmore describes a similar experience among the Cherokee, whom she said once had a ceremonial cycle that included six major festivals, but they eventually telescoped into one, the Green Corn Ceremony (1983, 46).

Conclusion: The Legacy of Corn Woman

1. Lincecum records a story told by Chahta immatahah in which the great Inki and Ishki, the Great male spirit and his wife, upon their return to the stars appointed a man and a woman to instruct and rule the Choctaw in their stead (1861, 21). Although this is the only known recorded version of this story, and its authenticity has been questioned, it does raise the possibility of women's having a leadership role according to Choctaw cultural narratives.
2. For example, see Carson 1997 and Cushman 1899.
3. Patricia Galloway, personal note to author, August 2002.
4. See my 1999 article "Beyond Domesticity: Choctaw Women Negotiating the Tension between Choctaw Culture and Protestantism" for a discussion of how Choctaw women could continue to pass on traditional culture to their children because their domestic activities were perceived as nonthreatening to the civilization and missionization programs of the missionaries and the U.S. government.
5. See my dissertation, *The Role of Choctaw Churches in the Revitalization of Choctaw Culture and Identity*, for more information on retention of culture in Choctaw Protestant churches.

Bibliography

Abbreviations

DCB: *Dictionary of Canadian Biography.*
JR: *The Jesuit Relations and Allied Documents; Travels and Explorations of the Jesuit Missionaries in New France 1610–1791.*
MPA:FD: *Mississippi Provincial Archives, French Dominion.*

Books, Articles, Papers, Dissertations

Adair, James. 1775. *History of the American Indians.* Edited by Samuel Cole Williams. London. Reprint, New York: Promontory Press, 1930.

Allain, Mathe. 1979. "French Emigration Policies: Louisiana, 1699–1715." In *Proceedings of the Fourth Meeting of the French Colonial Historical Society, April 6–8, 1978,* ed. Alf Andrew Heggoy and James J. Cooke, 39–46. Washington, DC: University Press of America.

Anderson, Karen. 1991. *Chain Her By One Foot: The Subjugation of Native Women in Seventeenth-Century New France.* New York: Routledge.

Anderson, Kim. 2000. *A Recognition of Being: Reconstructing Native Womanhood.* Toronto: Sumach Press.

Bakhtin, Mikhail M. 1981. *The Dialogic Imagination: Four Essays.* Edited by Michael Holquist. Austin: University of Texas Press.

———. 1986. *Speech Genres and Other Late Essays.* Translated by Vern W. McGee. Austin: University of Texas Press.

Bangert, William V. 1972. *A History of the Society of Jesus*. St. Louis: The Institute of Jesuit Sources.
Barkun, Michael. 1974. *Disaster and the Millennium*. New Haven: Yale University Press.
Bartram, William. 1928. *Travels of William Bartram*. Edited by Mark Van Doren. Macy-Masius, Publishers. Reprint, New York: Dover Publications, 1955.
Baudier, Roger. 1939. *The Catholic Church in Louisiana*. New Orleans: N.p.
Bekkers, B. J. 1902. "The Catholic Church in Mississippi During Colonial Times." *Publications of the Mississippi Historical Society* 6:351–57.
Benson, Henry C. 1860. *Life among the Choctaw Indians, and Sketches of the South-West*. Cincinnati, OH: L. Swormstedt and A. Poe.
Biever, Albert Hubert. 1924. *The Jesuits in New Orleans and the Mississippi Valley*. New Orleans: N.p.
Blitz, John Howard. 1985. *An Archaeological Study of the Mississippi Choctaw Indians*. Archaeological Report no. 16. Jackson: Mississippi Department of Archives and History.
Bossu, Jean-Bernard. 1962. *Travels in the Interior of North America: 1751–1762*. Translated and edited by Seymour Feiler. Norman: University of Oklahoma Press.
Bourne, Edward Gaylord, ed. 1904. *Narratives of the Career of Hernando de Soto in the Conquest of Florida as told by a Knight of Elvas and in a Relation by Luys Hernandez de Biedma, Factor of the Expedition*. Vol. 1. New York: A. S. Barnes and Company.
Brain, Jeffrey P. 1979. *Tunica Treasure*. Papers of the Peabody Museum of Archaeology and Ethnology Vol. 71. Cambridge, MA: Harvard University.
Brasseaux, Carl A. 1979. "The Image of Louisiana and the Failure of Voluntary French Emigration, 1683–1731." In *Proceedings of the Fourth Meeting of the French Colonial Historical Society, April 6–8, 1978*, ed. Alf Andrew Heggoy and James J. Cooke, 47–56. Washington, DC: University Press of America.
Braudel, Fernand. 1972. *The Mediterranean and the Mediterranean World in the Age of Philip II*. Trans. Sian Reynolds. New York: Harper and Row.
Bushnell, David I. 1909. *The Choctaw of Bayou Lacomb, St. Tammany Parish, Louisiana*. Smithsonian Institution Bureau of American Ethnology Bulletin 48. Washington, DC: Government Printing Office.
Byington, Cyrus. 1829. "Extracts from Letters of Mr. Byington." *Missionary Herald* 30, no. 11 (November): 346–50.
———. 1915. *A Dictionary of the Choctaw Language*. Edited by John R. Swanton and Henry S. Halbert. Smithsonian Institution Bureau of American Ethnology Bulletin 46. Washington, DC: Government Printing Office.
Campbell, T.N. 1959. "Choctaw Subsistence: Ethnographic Notes from the Lincecum Manuscript." *Florida Anthropologist* 12 (March): 9–24.
Carleton, Kenneth H. 1994. "Where Did the Choctaw Come From: An Examination of Pottery in the Areas Adjacent to the Choctaw Homeland." In *Perspectives on the Southeast*, ed. Patricia B. Kwachka, 80–93. Athens: University of Georgia Press.

Carson, James Taylor. 1997. "From Corn Mothers to Cotton Spinners: Continuity in Choctaw Women's Economic Life, A.D. 950–1830." In *Women of the American South: A Multicultural Reader*, ed. Christie Anne Farnham, 8–25. New York: New York University Press.

———. 1999. *Searching for the Bright Path: The Mississippi Choctaws from Prehistory to Removal*. Lincoln: University of Nebraska Press.

Cavelier, John. 1861. "Cavelier's Account of La Salle's Voyage to the Mouth of the Mississippi, His Landing in Texas, and March to the Mississippi." In *Early Voyages Up and Down the Mississippi by Cavelier, St. Cosme, Le Sueur, Gravier, and Guignas*. Introduction by John Gilmary Shea. Albany: Joel Munsell (Microfilm, Lamont Library, Harvard University).

Churchill, Mary. 1997. "Walking the 'White Path': Toward a Cherokee-Centric Hermeneutic for Interpreting Cherokee Literature." Ph.D. Diss., University of California, Santa Barbara.

Claiborne, J. F. H. 1860. *Life and Times of Gen. Sam. Dale, The Mississippi Partisan*. New York: Harper and Brothers.

———. 1880. *Mississippi as a Province, Territory and State, with Biographical Notices of Eminent Citizens*. Vol. 1. Jackson, MI: Power and Barksdale. Reprint, Baton Rouge: Louisiana State University Press, 1964.

Coker, William S. 1982. "The English Reaction to La Salle." In *La Salle and His Legacy: Frenchmen and Indians in the Lower Mississippi Valley*, ed. Patricia K. Galloway, 129–38. Jackson: University Press of Mississippi.

Conrad, Glenn R. 1979. "*Emigration Forceé*: A French Attempt to Populate Louisiana, 1716–1720." In *Proceedings of the Fourth Meeting of the French Colonial Historical Society, April 6–8, 1978*, ed. Alf Andrew Heggoy and James J. Cooke, 57–66. Washington, DC: University Press of America.

Corkran, D. H. 1955. "Cherokee Sun and Fire Observances." *Southern Indian Studies* 7 (October): 33–38.

Cushman, Calvin. 1828. "Extracts from a Letter of Mr. Calvin Cushman, An Assistant Missionary, Dated Sept. 1828." *Missionary Herald* 24, no. 12 (December): 380–81.

Cushman, Horatio Bardwell. 1899. *History of the Choctaw, Chickasaw, and Natchez Indians*. First abridged edition. Stillwater, OK: Redlands Press, 1962. Abridged edition, ed. and foreword by Angie Debo. New York: Russell and Russell, 1972.

DCB. *Dictionary of Canadian Biography*. Toronto: University of Toronto Press, 1966–.

Debo, Angie. 1934. *The Rise and Fall of the Choctaw Republic*. The Civilization of the American Indian Series, vol. 6. 2d ed. Norman: University of Oklahoma Press, 1961.

Delanglez, Jean. 1935. *The French Jesuits in Lower Louisiana (1700–1763)*. New Orleans: Loyola University.

———. 1985. "A Louisiana Poet-Historian: Dumont *dit* Montigney." In *A Jean Delanglez, S.J. Anthology*, ed. Mildred Mott Wedel. New York: Garland Publishing. Reprint from *Mid-America* 19, no. 1 (1937): 31–49.

Densmore, Frances. 1943. *Choctaw Music. Anthropological Papers, No. 28,* Smithsonian Institution Bureau of American Ethnology Bulletin 136 (1943): 101–88. Reprint, Brighton, MI: Native American Book Publishers, 1990.

DeRosier, Arthur H. Jr. 1970. *The Removal of the Choctaw Indians.* Knoxville: University of Tennessee Press.

Devens, Carol. 1992. *Countering Colonization: Native American Women and Great Lakes Missions, 1630–1900.* Berkeley: University of California Press.

Drechsel, Emanuel J. 1994. "Mobilian Jargon in the 'Prehistory' of Southeastern North America." In *Perspectives on the Southeast,* ed. Patricia B. Kwachka, 25–43. Athens: University of Georgia Press.

Du Pratz, M. Le Page. 1774. *The History of Louisiana.* Translated and edited by Joseph G. Tregle Jr. Baton Rouge: Louisiana State University Press, 1975.

Eggan, Fred. 1937. "Historical Changes in the Choctaw Kinship System." *American Anthropologist, n.s.,* 39:34–52.

Emerson, Thomas E. 1982. *Mississippian Stone Images in Illinois.* Circular no. 6. Urbana-Champaign: Illinois Archaeological Survey, University of Illinois.

———. 1989. "Water, Serpents, and the Underworld: An Exploration into Cahokian Symbolism." In *The Southeastern Ceremonial Complex: Artifacts and Analysis: The Cottonlandia Conference,* ed. Patricia Galloway, 45–92. Lincoln: University of Nebraska Press.

———. 1997. *Cahokia and the Archaeology of Power.* Tuscaloosa: University of Alabama Press.

Ferguson, Bob. 2002. "About the Choctaw Indian Fair." Available from Choctaw Vision, Choctaw Culture, Community Celebrations at www.choctaw.org.

Foreman, Grant. 1932. *Indian Removal.* The Civilization of the American Indian Series, vol. 2. 2d ed. Norman: University of Oklahoma Press, 1989.

Fortier, Alceé. 1904. *History of Louisiana.* Vol. 1, *Early Explorers and the Domination of the French 1512–1768.* New York: Manzi, Joyant and Co.

French, B. F. 1846. *Historical Collections of Louisiana Embracing Many Rare and Valuable Documents.* Part 1. New York: Wiley and Putnam. Reprint, vol. 1, New York: AMS Press, 1976.

———. 1853. *Historical Memoirs of Louisiana.* Historical Collections of Louisiana Series, part 5. New York: Lamport, Blakeman and Law. Reprint, vol. 5. New York: AMS Press, 1976.

———. 1857. *Historical Collections of Louisiana, Embracing Translations of Many Rare and Valuable Documents.* Part 3. New York: D. Appleton and Company.

Galloway, Patricia. 1982. "Henri de Tonti du Village des Chacta, 1702: The Beginning of the French Alliance." In *La Salle and His Legacy: Frenchmen and Indians in the Lower Mississippi Valley,* ed. Patricia K. Galloway, 146–75. Jackson: University Press of Mississippi.

———. 1985a. "The Barthelemy Murders: Bienville's Establishment of the *Lex Talionis* as a Principle of Indian Diplomacy." In *Proceedings of the Eighth Annual Meeting of the French Colonial Historical Society, 1982,* ed. E. P. Fitzgerald. Lanham, MD: University Press of America.

———. 1985b. "Choctaw Factionalism and Civil War, 1746–1750." In *The Choctaw Before Removal*, ed. Carolyn Keller Reeves, 120–56. Jackson: University Press of Mississippi.

———. 1986. "The Direct Historical Approach and Early Historical Documents: An Ethnohistorians's View." In *The Protohistoric Period in the Mid-South, 1500–1700: Proceedings of the 1983 Mid-South Archaeological Conference*. Archaeological Report 18. Jackson: Mississippi Department of Archives and History, 14–23.

———. 1987. "Talking with Indians: Interpreters and Diplomacy in French Louisiana." In *Race and Family in the Colonial South: Essays*, ed. Winthrop D. Jordan and Sheila L. Skemp, 109–29. Jackson: University Press of Mississippi.

———. 1989. "'The Chief Who Is Your Father': Choctaw and French Views of the Diplomatic Relation." In *Powhatan's Mantle: Indians in the Colonial Southeast*, ed. Peter H. Wood, Gregory A. Waselkov, and M. Thomas Hatley, 254–78. Lincoln: University of Nebraska Press.

———. 1991. "Formation of Historic Tribes and the French Colonial Period." In *Native, European, and African Cultures in Mississippi, 1500–1800*, ed. Patricia Galloway, 57–75. Jackson: Mississippi Department of Archives and History.

———. 1994. "Confederacy as a Solution to Chiefdom Dissolution: Historical Evidence in the Choctaw Case." In *The Forgotten Centuries: Indians and Europeans in the American South, 1521–1704*, ed. Charles Hudson and Carmen Chaves Tesser, 393–420. Athens: University of Georgia Press.

———. 1995. *Choctaw Genesis: 1500–1700*. Lincoln: University of Nebraska Press.

———. 1998. "Where Have All the Menstrual Huts Gone? The Invisibility of Menstrual Seclusion in the Late Prehistoric Southeast." In *Reader in Gender Archaeology*, ed. Kelly Hays-Gilpin and David S. Whitley, 197–211. London: Routledge.

Gayarré, Charles. 1879. *History of Louisiana*. Vol. 3, *The Spanish Domination*. New Orleans: James A. Gresham. Reprint, New Orleans: Armand Hawkins, 1885.

Giraud, Marcel. 1953. *A History of French Louisiana*. Vol. 1, *The Reign of Louis XIV, 1698–1715*. Paris: Presses Universitaires de France. Reprint, translated by Joseph C. Lambert, Baton Rouge: Louisiana State University Press, 1974.

———. 1987. *A History of French Louisiana*. Vol. 5, *The Company of the Indies, 1723–1731*. Revised and translated by Joseph C. Lambert. Baton Rouge: Louisiana State University Press, 1991.

Gregory, Jack, and Rennard Strickland. 1971. *Creek Seminole Spirit Tales: Tribal Folklore Legend and Myth*. Muskogee, OK: Indian Heritage Association.

Haag, Marcia, and Henry Willis. 2001. *Choctaw Language and Culture: Chahta Anumpa*. Norman: University of Oklahoma Press.

Habig, Marion A. 1934. "The Franciscan Pere Marquette: A Critical Biography of Father Zenobe Membre, O.F.M. La Salle's Chaplain and Missionary Companion 1645 (ca.)–1689." *Franciscan Studies* 13 (June). New York: Joseph F. Wagner.

Halbert, H. S. 1900. "Funeral Customs of the Mississippi Choctaws." *Publications of the Mississippi Historical Society* 3:353–66.

———. 1902a. "Bernard Romans' Map of 1772." *Publications of the Mississippi Historical Society* 6:415–39.

———. 1902b. "Story of the Treaty of Dancing Rabbit." *Publications of the Mississippi Historical Society* 6:373–402.

Hall, Gwendolyn Midlo. 1992. *Africans in Colonial Louisiana: The Development of Afro-Creole Culture in the Eighteenth Century.* Baton Rouge: Louisiana State University Press.

Hann, John H. 1988. *Apalachee: The Land Between the Rivers.* Gainesville: University of Florida Press and Florida State Museum.

Hardcastle, David. 1978. "Swiss Mercenary Soldiers in the Service of France in Louisiana." *Proceedings of the Fourth Meeting of the French Colonial Historical Society, April 6–8, 1978,* ed. Alf Andrew Heggoy and James J. Cooke, 82–91. Washington, DC: University Press of America.

Hertz, Robert. 1909. *Death and the Right Hand. L'Annee Sociologue,* 1907, and *Revue Philosophique.* Presses Universitaires de France. Reprint, translated by Rodney and Claudia Needham, Aberdeen, Scotland: University Press of Aberdeen, 1960.

Higgenbotham, Jay, trans. and ed. 1969. *The Journal of Sauvole.* Mobile, AL: Colonial Books.

———. 1977. *Old Mobile: Fort Louis de la Louisiane, 1702–1711.* Museum of the City of Mobile, Alabama.

Hodge, Frederick Webb. 1907. *Handbook of American Indians North of Mexico.* Parts 1 and 2. Smithsonian Institution Bureau of American Ethnology Bulletin 30. Washington, DC: Government Printing Office.

Hodgson, Adam. 1823. *Remarks During a Journey Through North America in the years 1819, 1820, and 1821, in a Series of Letters.* New York: J. Seymour. Reprint, Westport, CT: Negro Universities Press, 1970.

Holmes, Jack D. L. 1978. "The Failure of French Immigration to Louisiana, 1700–1765: A Comment." In *Proceedings of the Fourth Meeting of the French Colonial Historical Society, April 6–8, 1978,* ed. Alf Andrew Heggoy and James J. Cooke, 67–69. Washington, DC: University Press of America.

Howard, James H. 1968. "The Southeastern Ceremonial Complex and Its Interpretation." *Memoir Missouri Archaeological Society* 6.

Howard, James H., and Victoria L. Levine. 1990. *Choctaw Music and Dance.* Norman: University of Oklahoma Press.

Hudson, Charles. 1976. *The Southeastern Indians.* Knoxville: University of Tennessee Press.

Jacobs, Wilbur R., ed. 1954. *Indians of the Southern Colonial Frontier: The Edmond Atkin Report and Plan of 1755.* Columbia: University of South Carolina Press.

JR. 1896–1901. *The Jesuit Relations and Allied Documents: Travels and Explorations of the Jesuit Missionaries in New France 1610–1791.* Edited by Reuben Gold Thwaites. Cleveland: Burrows Brothers Company.

Kenton, Edna, ed. 1925. *The Jesuit Relations and Allied Documents: Travels and Explorations of the Jesuit Missionaries in North America (1610–1791)*. New York: Albert and Charles Boni.

Kidwell, Clara Sue. 1995a. "Choctaw Women and Cultural Persistence in Mississippi." In *Negotiators of Change: Historical Perspectives on Native American Women*, ed. Nancy Shoemaker, 115–34. New York: Routledge.

———. 1995b. *Choctaws and Missionaries in Mississippi, 1818–1918*. Norman: University of Oklahoma Press.

Kilpatrick, Jack F., and Anna G. Kilpatrick. 1964. *Friends of Thunder: Folktales of the Oklahoma Cherokees*. Dallas, TX: Southern Methodist University Press.

Klein, Laura F., and Lillian A. Ackerman, eds. 2000. *Women and Power in Native North America*. Norman: University of Oklahoma Press.

Kniffen, Fred B., Hiram F. Gregory, and George A. Stokes. 1987. *The Historic Indian Tribes of Louisiana from 1542 to the Present*. Baton Rouge: Louisiana State University Press.

Kriefall, Andreas. 1998. "Ethics of Polyphony: The Example of *Black Elk Speaks*." *Western American Literature* 33, no. 2 (Summer): 178–203.

Kwachka, Patricia B., ed. 1994. *Perspectives on the Southeast*. Athens: University of Georgia Press.

Larson, Lewis H. Jr. 1972. "Functional Considerations of Warfare in the Southeast During the Mississippi Period." *American Antiquity* 37, no. 3 (July): 383–92.

Le Maire, M. 1985. "Documents: M. Le Maire on Louisiana." In *A Jean Delanglez, S. J., Anthology*, ed. Mildred Mott Wedel. New York: Garland Publishing. First published in *Mid-America* 19, no. 2 (1937): 124–54.

Lincecum, Gideon. 1861. *Traditional History of the Chahta Nation*. Part 1. Austin: University of Texas Library (March 1932).

Martin, Joel W. 1991. "Before and Beyond the Sioux Ghost Dance: Native American Prophetic Movements and the Study of Religion." *Journal of the American Academy of Religion* 59, no. 4 (Winter): 677–701.

———. 1994. "Indians and the English Trade in Skins and Slaves." In *The Forgotten Centuries: Indians and Europeans in the American South, 1521–1704*, ed. Charles Hudson and Carmen Chaves Tesser, 304–24. Athens: University of Georgia Press.

McLoughlin, William G. 1986. *Cherokee Renascence in the New Republic*. Princeton, NJ: Princeton University Press.

McWilliams, Richebourg Gaillard, trans. and ed. 1981. *Iberville's Gulf Journals*. Alabama: University of Alabama Press.

Mereness, Newton D., ed. 1916. *Travels in the American Colonies*. New York: Macmillan Company.

Merrell, James H. 1989. "'Our Bonds of Peace': Patterns of Intercultural Exchange in the Carolina Piedmont, 1650–1750." In *Powhatan's Mantle: Indians in the Colonial Southeast*, ed. Peter H. Wood, Gregory A. Waselkov, and M. Thomas Hatley, 196–222. Lincoln: University of Nebraska Press.

Middleton, John. 1982. "Lugbara Death." In *Death and the Regeneration of Life*, ed. Maurice Bloch and Jonathan Parry, 134–54. New York: Cambridge University Press.

Milford, Louis LeClerc de. 1956. *Memoir or A Cursory Glance at My Different Travels and My Soujourn in the Creek Nation*. Translated by Geraldine de Courey, edited by John Francis McDermott. Chicago, IL: R. R. Donnelley and Sons.

Minet. 1682. "Voiage fait du Canada par dedans les terres allant vers le sud dans l'anne 1682, 1684–85." Reprint, trans. Ann Linda Bell, "Voyage Made from Canada Inland Going Southward during the Year 1682." In *La Salle, the Mississippi, and the Gulf: Three Primary Documents*, ed. Robert S. Weddle. College Station: Texas A&M University Press, 1987.

Mooney, James. 1900. *Myths of the Cherokee and Sacred Formulas of the Cherokees*. Nineteenth Annual Report of the Bureau of American Ethnology, Washington, DC: Government Printing Office, 1900; and 1891, Seventh Annual Report of the Bureau of American Ethnology, Washington, DC: Government Printing Office. Reprint, Nashville, TN: Charles and Randy Elder-Booksellers, 1982.

———. 1982. "The Cherokee River Cult." *Journal of Cherokee Studies* 7, no. 1 (Spring): 30–36.

Morgan, Lewis H. 1877. *Ancient Society*. Edited by Leslie A. White. Reprint, Cambridge, MA: Belknap Press of Harvard University Press, 1964.

MPA:FD. 1927. *Mississippi Provincial Archives, French Dominion*. Vol. 1. Edited and translated by Dunbar Rowland and Albert G. Sanders. Jackson: Press of the Mississippi Department of Archives and History.

———. 1929. *Mississippi Provincial Archives, French Dominion*. Vol. 2. Edited and translated by Dunbar Rowland and Albert G. Sanders. Jackson: Press of the Mississippi Department of Archives and History.

———. 1932. *Mississippi Provincial Archives, French Dominion*. Vol. 3. Edited and translated by Dunbar Rowland and Albert G. Sanders. Jackson: Press of the Mississippi Department of Archives and History.

———. 1984. *Mississippi Provincial Archives, French Dominion*. Vols. 4–5. Edited and translated by Dunbar Rowland, Albert G. Sanders, and Patricia Galloway. Baton Rouge: Louisiana State University Press.

Munro, Pamela, and Catherine Willmond. 1994. *Chickasaw: An Analytical Dictionary*. Norman: University of Oklahoma Press.

Nicklas, T. Dale. 1994. "Linguistic Provinces of the Southeast at the Time of Columbus." In *Perspectives on the Southeast*, ed. Patricia B. Kwachka, 1–13. Athens: University of Georgia Press.

Noley, Grayson. 1985. "The Early 1700s: Education, Economics, and Politics." In *The Choctaw Before Removal*, ed. Carolyn Killer Reeves, 73–119. Jackson: University Press of Mississippi.

Ogg, Frederic Austin. 1904. *The Opening of the Mississippi: A Struggle for Supremacy in the American Interior*. New York: Macmillan Company.

Oklahoma City Advocate, November 1973.
Parker, Sara Gwenyth. 1991. "The Transformation of Cherokee Appalachia." Ph.D. Diss., University of California, Berkeley.
Payne, John Howard. N.d. Papers. Vol. I. typescript. Ayer Collection, Newberry Library, Chicago.
Pénicaut, Andre. 1953 [1723]. *Fleur de Lys and Calumet: Being the Pénicaut Narrative of French Adventure in Louisiana*. Translated and edited by Richebourg Gaillard McWilliams. Baton Rouge: Louisiana State University Press.
Penman, John T. 1977. *Archaeological Survey in Mississippi, 1974–1975*. Jackson: Mississippi Department of Archives and History.
Perdue, Theda. 1979. *Slavery and the Evolution of Cherokee Society, 1540–1866*. Knoxville: University of Tennessee Press.
———. 1985. "Southern Indians and the Cult of True Womanhood." In *The Web of Southern Social Relations: Women, Family, and Education*, ed. Walter J. Fraser Jr., R. Frank Saunders Jr., and Jon L. Wakelyn. Athens: University of Georgia Press.
———. 1998. *Cherokee Women: Gender and Culture Change, 1700–1835*. Lincoln: University of Nebraska Press.
Pesantubbee, Michelene. 1994. "Culture Revitalization and Indigenization of Churches Among the Choctaw of Oklahoma." Ph.D. Diss., University of California, Santa Barbara.
———. 1999. "Beyond Domesticity: Choctaw Women Negotiating the Tension between Choctaw Culture and Protestantism." *Journal of the American Academy of Religion* 67, no. 2 (June): 387–409.
Peyser, Joseph L., trans. and ed. 1992. *Letters from New France The Upper Country, 1686–1783*. Urbana: University of Illinois Press.
Prentice, Guy. 1986. "An Analysis of the Symbolism Expressed by the Birger Figurine." *American Antiquity* 51, 2:239–66.
Rangel, Rodrigo. 1933. "Account of the Northern Conquest and Discovery of Hernando de Soto." Translated and edited by John E. Worth. In *The De Soto Chronicles: The Expedition of Hernando De Soto to North America in 1539–1543*. Vol. 1., ed. Lawrence A. Clayton, Vernon James Knight Jr., and Edward C. Moore. Tuscaloosa: University of Alabama Press.
Reid, John Phillip. 1970. *A Law of Blood: The Primitive Law of the Cherokee Nation*. New York: New York University Press.
Roberts, Lillie. 2002. *Chahta Anumpa* Internet course. Spring class, www.choctawnation.com.
Romans, Bernard. 1775. *A Concise Natural History of East and West Florida*. Vol. 1. New York. Reprint, New Orleans: Pelican Publishing Company, 1961.
Schlarman, J. H. 1929. *From Quebec to New Orleans*. Belleville, IL: Buechler Publishing Company.
Searcy, Margaret Zehmer. 1985. "Choctaw Subsistence, 1540–1830: Hunting, Fishing, Farming, and Gathering." In *The Choctaw Before Removal*, ed. Carolyn Keller Reeves, 32–54. Jackson: University Press of Mississippi.

Senate Executive Document 512. 1833. *Correspondence on the Subject of the Emigration of Indians.* 23d Cong., 1st sess., vol. 3.

Sharp, Henry S. 1995. "Asymmetric Equals; Women and Men Among the Chipewyan." In *Women and Power in Native North America*, ed. Laura F. Klein and Lillian A. Ackerman, 46–74. Norman: University of Oklahoma Press.

Shea, John Gilmary. 1855. *History of the Catholic Missions Among the Indian Tribes of the United States, 1529–1854.* New York: Edward Dunigan and Brother. Reprint, New York: Arno Press and the *New York Times*, 1969.

———. 1861. *Early Voyages Up and Down the Mississippi, by Cavelier, St. Cosme, Le Sueur, Gravier, and Guignas.* With introduction, notes, and index by John Gilmary Shea. Albany, NY: Joel Munsell.

Speck, Frank G. 1907. "Notes on Chickasaw Ethnology and Folk-lore." *Journal of American Folklore* 20:50–58.

Stubbs, John D. Jr. 1982. "The Chickasaw Contact with the La Salle Expedition in 1682." In *La Salle and His Legacy: Frenchmen and Indians in the Lower Mississippi Valley*, ed. Patricia K. Galloway, 41–48. Jackson: University Press of Mississippi.

Surrey, N. M. Miller. 1916. *The Commerce of Louisiana During the French Régime, 1699–1763.* Studies in History, Economics, and Public Law Series 70, no. 1: 1–400. New York: Columbia University Press.

Swanton, John R. 1911. *Indian Tribes of the Lower Mississippi Valley and Adjacent Coast of the Gulf of Mexico.* Smithsonian Institution Bureau of American Ethnology Bulletin 43. Washington, DC: Government Printing Office.

———. 1918. "An Early Account of the Choctaw Indians." *Memoirs of the American Anthropological Association* 5, no. 2:53–72.

———. 1928a. *Aboriginal Culture of the Southeast.* Forty-second Annual Report of the Smithsonian Institution Bureau of American Ethnology. Washington, DC: Government Printing Office.

———. 1928b. *Social Organization and Social Usages of the Indians of the Creek Confederacy.* Forty-second Annual Report of the Smithsonian Institution Bureau of American Ethnology 1924–25. Washington, DC: Government Printing Office.

———. 1928c. *Social and Religious Beliefs and Usages of the Chickasaw Indians.* Forty-fourth Annual Report of the Bureau of American Ethnology 1926–27. Washington, DC: Government Printing Office, 169–273.

———. 1929. *Myths and Tales of the Southeastern Indians.* Smithsonian Institution Bureau of American Ethnology Bulletin 88. Washington, DC: Government Printing Office.

———. 1931. *Source Material for the Social and Ceremonial Life of the Choctaw Indians.* Smithsonian Institution Bureau of American Ethnology Bulletin 103. Washington, DC: Government Printing Office.

———. 1946. *The Indians of the Southeastern United States.* Smithsonian Institution Bureau of American Ethnology Bulletin 137. Washington, DC: Government Printing Office.

Tonti, Henri. 1985. "Documents: Tonti Letters." In *A Jean Delanglez, S.J., Anthology*, ed. Mildred Mott Wedel. New York: Garland Publishing. Originally published in *Mid-America* 21, no. 3 (1939): 209–38.

Usner, Daniel H. Jr. 1992. *Indians, Settlers, and Slaves in a Frontier Exchange Economy: The Lower Mississippi Valley Before 1783*. Chapel Hill: University of North Carolina Press.

Vitry, Pierre. 1985. "The Journal of Pierre Vitry, S.J." In *A Jean Delanglez, S.J., Anthology*, ed. Mildred Mott Wedel. New York: Garland Publishing. Originally published in *Mid-America* 28, no. 1 (1946): 30–59.

Weddle, Robert S., ed. 1987. *La Salle, the Mississippi, and the Gulf: Three Primary Documents*. College Station: Texas A&M University Press.

Welter, Barbara. 1966. "The Cult of True Womanhood: 1820–1860." *American Quarterly* 18, no. 2, pt. 1 (Summer): 151–74.

Westward Expansion. 1983. British Public Record Office: Colonial Office, Class Five File—Westward Expansion, 1700–1783 (University Publications of America), Western History Collections, University of Oklahoma, Norman.

Wetmore, Ruth Y. 1983. "The Green Corn Ceremony of the Eastern Cherokees." *Journal of Cherokee Studies* 8, no. 1 (Spring): 46–55.

White, Richard. 1983. *The Roots of Dependency: Subsistence, Environment, and Social Change Among the Choctaws, Pawnees, and Navajos*. Lincoln: University of Nebraska Press.

Wiegers, Robert P. 1988. "A Proposal for Indian Slave Trading in the Mississippi Valley and Its Impact on the Osage." *Plains Anthropologist* 33, no. 120 (May): 187–202.

Woods, Patricia Dillon. 1980. *French-Indian Relations on the Southern Frontier 1699–1762*. Ann Arbor, MI: UMI Research Press.

Wright, Alfred. 1828a. "Choctaws. Religious Opinions, Traditions, Etc." *Missionary Herald*, June, 178–83.

———. 1828b. "Choctaws. Religious Opinions, Traditions, Etc." *Missionary Herald*, July, 214–16.

Wright, J. Leitch Jr. 1981. *The Only Land They Knew: The Tragic Story of the American Indians in the Old South*. New York: The Free Press.

York, Kenneth H. 1982. "Mobilian: The Indian *Lingua Franca* of Colonial Louisiana." In *La Salle and His Legacy: Frenchmen and Indians in the Lower Mississippi Valley*, ed. Patricia K. Galloway, 139–45. Jackson: University Press of Mississippi.

Zogry, Michael. 2001. "No Time Outs: Charting a Ritual History of the Cherokee Ball Game." Paper presented at American Academy of Religion Annual Meeting, Denver, Colorado, November 17.

Interviews

Anonymous. 13 July 1993. Interview by author. Tape recording, Dwight Mission, Sallisaw, Oklahoma.
Bobb, Bertram. 5 November 1990. Telephone conversation with author.
Farve, Linda. 10 January 2003. Telephone conversation with author.
Jackson, Charlotte. 6 May 2002. Telephone conversation with author.
Jefferson, Juanita. 6 May 2002. Telephone conversation with author.
Tate, Jack. 6 May 2002. Telephone conversation with author.

Index

Abihka, 41, 43, 183
Acolapissa, 16
Adair, James, 14, 148, 189
agriculture: corn, 22–23, 118–20, 124, 164; corn varieties, 124; development of, 22–23; and failure of crops, 128–31; and fertility, 24, 133; and French settlers, 89; and gender roles, 116, 124–25; and livestock, 136–37; and ritual, 27–28, 109; and slavery, 96–100; and trade items, 134–35. *See also* Green Corn Ceremony
Alabama, 16, 37, 49, 180
alcohol, 109–11, 128, 140
alikchi (medicine givers), 10, 44, 81–82
alliances, 40–41, 62–64, 106–7
Apalachee, 16, 65–66, 110, 183, 186
Arkansas, 184

baptisms, 61–62, 79–80, 100
Bartram, William, 148
Baudoüin, Father Michel, 61, 63–64, 66, 185
Bauers, Lu, 176
Bayogoula, 16, 180
Bekkers, Rev. B. J., 184
beloved: and Adair, James, 14; characteristics of, 2, 23–25, 168–69; and the Chickasaw, 14–15; and death, 80–82; funeral responsibilities, 160–67; holitopa, 14, 15; and politics, 4; and sacrifice, 85; and the soil, 124
Beloved Mother. *See* Nanih Waiya
Belvin, Edna, 176
Bernard, Jean Baptiste, 52
Biloxi, 16, 180
Birger figurine, 120–24, 152
Boisrenaud, Marie-Françoise de, 99
Bossu, Jean-Bernard, 148
Boulanger, Rev. Father, 185
British: and the Choctaw, 41–43; explorers, 35; and Indian captives, 54–56; and trade, 37, 39
Burial Urn people, 19–20
Burton, Lois, 176

Cadadoquis (Kadohadacho), 182
Caddo, 183
Cahayrohoua, 181
Cantrell, Deana, 176
captivity: and failure of crops, 130–31; and restitution, 39–40, 45–53; and slavery, 54–55; and torture, 57–58; and women's roles, 31–32, 36

Capuchins, 66
Cenis, 183
Chakchiuma, 16, 48, 180, 184
Chatenoqué, 71
Chatot, 183
Cherokee: and the Choctaw, 39; Corn Woman, 189; councils, 172; Green Corn Ceremony, 146; and slavery, 36
Chicacha Oulacta, 139
Chickasaw: beloved, 14–15; and the Choctaw, 20–22, 36–37, 39, 43–44, 55–56; and the French, 41–42; Green Corn Ceremony, 146; and slavery, 36
Chickasawhay, 66, 182
children, 10
Chitimacha, 110
Choctaw: in 1701, 38; and the Abihka, 41, 43; and African slaves, 98; and the Alabama, 37, 49; alliances, 40–41; and catastrophic change, 146–50, 172–74; and the Chickasaw, 36–37, 55–56; civil war, 42–43, 50–51, 130, 147; creation stories, 20–23; and the English, 41, 42–43; forehead flattening, 122–24; and French names, 70–71; and livestock, 136–37; and medal chiefs, 138–40; and missionaries, 67–69, 83–84; modern roles, 175–77; and the Natchez, 76–77; and population decline, 127–28; towns, 131; and trade, 49, 86; values, 150–51, 162, 165–67. *See also* Green Corn Ceremony
Chouacha, 187
Christianity: and Adair, James, 14; and death, 77–79; and indigenous restitution, 78; and medicine givers, 81–82; and slavery, 99–100; symbols, 64–65, 73, 82, 186; and the Tunica, 79
Colapissa, 180
Concha village, 44, 183
concubinage, 100–105
corn, 22–23, 118–20, 124, 164
Corn Woman (Ohoyo Osh Chisba), 22–23, 118–20, 189
Coroa, 185
Creek, 20–22, 36, 146, 188
Cushman, Horatio Bardwell, 149

dances, 28–30, 128, 162–65, 190
Davion, Father, 65, 66, 79
death: and ancestors, 47–48; and beloved people, 24, 80–82; and Choctaw values, 150–51; and Christianity, 77–79; and fertility, 151–52; mourning, 159–60; and restitution, 39–40, 45–53, 186; yaiya (funeral cry), 145, 154, 159, 166. *See also* mortuary practices
deserters, 51–52, 90, 93
disease: and Choctaw migration, 19–20; and French settlers, 88; and the Green Corn Ceremony, 131–32; and livestock, 137; and women, 108–9
Douay, Father Anastase, 65, 74
Doutreleau, Father, 185
Du Ru, Father Paul, 65, 185

economics, 5, 17–18, 108, 138
English: and the Choctaw, 41–43; explorers, 35; and Indian captives, 54–56; and trade, 37, 39
Erborie, Father Geoffry Thierry, 185
Etteacteala, 186

fanimingo, 105
Favré, Simon, 106
fertility, 24, 120–21, 133, 151–52
Foucault, Abbé Nicholas, 65
Franchimastabé, 71
French: and the Chickasaw, 41–42; and Choctaw leadership, 138–40; deserters, 51–52, 90, 93; early settlements, 87–91; and Indian captives, 53–56; and indigenous restitution, 51; and the Natchez, 41–42; perspectives, 12–14; populating the colonies, 91–96; and slavery, 96–100; and trade, 37, 39, 90–91; and warfare, 37–38

gender roles: and agriculture, 116, 124–25; and Choctaw values, 150–51; and Christian symbols, 73–74; complementary relations, 6; contemporary, 175–77; and division of labor, 5, 9–10; and economics, 138; and fertility, 24, 120–21; and French missionaries, 64; and funeral responsibilities, 159–67; and Jesuits, 82–83; and kinship, 57–58, 104–5; and slavery, 55; and trade, 46, 136–38; and travel, 19; Western concepts of, 4–5, 25, 112–14, 148–49

Gravier, Father Jacques, 65

Green Corn Ceremony: and alcohol, 140; and contributions of women, 125, 130–34; eighteenth-century, 117–18; and failure of crops, 128–31; and fertility, 151–52; its decline, 141–43; and modern harvest fairs, 117; and other indigenous groups, 146, 188; and politics, 138–40, 172; and population decline, 127–28; and trade, 134–40; and water purification, 125–26

Guedelonguay, 52–53

Hitchiti, 181
holitopa, 14, 15
Houma (Ouma), 73, 110, 182, 184
Hughes, Mary, 48
hunting, 19, 134–38
"Hunting Song", 164–65
Huvé, Alexandre, 65, 185

Iholitopa Ishki, 20–23

Jackson, Charlotte, 176
James, Harriet Wright, 176–77
Jefferson, Juanita, 175, 176–77
Jesuits: expulsion of, 67; and language, 70; and mission work, 66; and sexuality, 74, 83–85; and women, 82–83

Kaskaskia, 78
Keller figurine, *118*, *119*, 120–24
kinship, 10, 46–47, 57–58, 104–5
Kiraoueria, 78

Lady of Cofitachequi, 2
La Houssaye, Sieur de, 102
language: and caressing, 72, 74; holitopa, 14, 15; and interpreters, 105–6; and inter-tribal relations, 16–17, 180; and the Jesuits, 70; professional stratification of, 13–14

La Salle, Robert Cavelier de, 64, 87
Le Febvre, Father Nicolas, 66–67
Leflore, Greenwood, 1
LeMaire, Father, 185
Le Petit, Father Mathurin, 66, 83, 185
Limoges, Father Joseph de, 65
Loáche, 14

Mackey, Middleton, 2
marriages: Choctaw traditions, 102, 104–5; and inheritance, 106; intermarriages, 76, 85, 103–8; and sin, 75
medicine givers (alikchi), 10, 44, 81–82
Membré, Récollet Zénobe, 64
Mingo, Alibamon, 51–52
Mingo Hwoolatahoomah, 188
Mingo, Quikanabé, 63
Mingo, Tichou, 44
missionaries: and alliance building, 62–64; and the Apalachee, 65–66; and the Choctaw, 67–69, 83–84; documentation of, 60, 62; ineffectiveness of, 61–62, 67; long-term impact of, 68–69; and marriage, 75–76; and religious artifacts, 64–65, 72–73; and sexuality, 71–72, 74, 83–85; and sin, 77; and women, 62, 64, 68, 74, 174
Mississippi Valley, Lower, 6, 15–19
Mobilian, 16, 180
Moctoby, 182
Mongoulacha (Mugulasha), 185
Montigny, Father de, 65
Morand, Father, 67
mortuary practices: bone-gathering, 154–57; and Choctaw values, 162, 165–67; dances, 162–65; pole-pulling, 158–59; temporary burials, 153–54; women's roles, 160–67

Naniaba, 16, 180
Nanih Waiya, 20–23
Natchez: and the Choctaw, 17–18, 76–77; and female suns, 2; and the French, 41–42; Green Corn Ceremony, 188; and missionaries, 70; and slavery, 36
Nowabbi, Billie, 175

Index

Ofogoula, 184
Ohoyo Osh Chisba (Corn Woman), 22–23, 118–20, 181
Okeoulou, 183
Ouacha, 180
Ouma (Houma), 73, 110, 182, 184

Pascagoula, 16
Pensacola, 182
"Pleasure Dance Song", 164
Poisson, Father Paul du, 185
politics: and beloved people, 4; and the Green Corn Ceremony, 138–40, 172; and women, 25–27, 73–74, 169–74, 176–77

Quapaw, 184
Quinipissa, 87, 185

Ramey Incised pottery, 121
Red Chief, 51–52
Red Path, 190
Red Shoe, 106, 184
religion: according to Swanton, 10–11; artifacts, 64–65, 73, 82, 186; and slavery, 99–100. *See also* Christianity
restitution, 39–40, 45–53, 78, 186
rituals: agricultural, 27–28, 109; and alcohol, 128, 140; dances, 28–30, 128, 162–65, 190; and French explorers, 25–27; menstrual houses, 24, 121; and population decline, 127–28; and sacrifice, 80–82, 152–53, 186; and warfare, 28–30; water purification, 125–26. *See also* Green Corn Ceremony
Romans, Bernard, 148
Roulleaux, Father, 185

sacrifice, 80–82, 85, 152–53, 186
sagamite, 124
Saint-Cosme, Michel Buisson de, 65
sexuality, 71–72, 74, 83–85
Shawnee, 41, 183
siente hitkla (snake dance), 128
slavery: and captivity, 45–53; and concubinage, 100–105; and the English, 35–36; and French settlers, 96–100; and women, 53–56, 96–100

Soto, Hernando de, 35
Souel, Father John, 185
Spanish, 35, 57–58, 99
St. Alexis, Father Charles de, 66
Sullivan, Lillian, 176
Swanton, John R., 149

Taensa, 16, 80–82, 181
Tallapoosa, 43, 183
Tamaroa, 185
tanch hiloha, 128
tan fula, 128, 188
tan hlabo, 128
Tatoulimataha, 106
Tattoed Arm, 76
tattoos, 31
Tawasa, 183
Tchanke, 187
Testu, Father John Daniel, 185
Tohomé, 16, 180
Toubamingo, 52
Toupaoulastabé, 44
trade: and alcohol, 109–10; and the Choctaw, 49, 86; and civil war, 42–43; and concubinage, 100–105; and the English, 37, 39; and the French, 37, 39, 90–91; and the Green Corn Ceremony, 134–40; and language, 16–17; and slavery, 46, 48–49; and women, 137
Treaty of Dancing Rabbit Creek, 1–2, 169–170, 171, 172
Tunica, 16, 79, 110, 180, 182

Unknown Woman, 22–23, 118–20, 181

Varlet, Father Dominic, 185
Victorin, Father, 66
violence: and alcohol, 109–11; and the Green Corn Ceremony, 132–34; and troop deployment, 107; and women's domain, 38–39, 40–41, 45. *See also* warfare
Ward, Nancy, 2
warfare: and the alikchi, 44; and alliance building, 40–41, 106–107; and beloved people, 24–25; and captives, 31–32,

45–53; Choctaw civil war, 42–43; dances, 28–30; decision-making, 46; and failure of crops, 130–31; French attention to, 37–38; and restitution, 39–40; and slavery, 98–99; stickball, 190; and troop deployment, 107; and weapons, 39; the wounded, 29. *See also* violence

War Women, 24

water purification, 125–26

women. *See also* Green Corn Ceremony; and agriculture, 124–25, 133; in battle, 30–31; and captives, 31–32, 36; and cultural values, 174–77; and fertility, 24, 133, 151–52; fireclay sculptures, 120–24; French, 91–94; funeral responsibilities, 160–67; and hunting, 19, 134–38; and kinship, 57–58, 104–5; menstrual houses, 24, 121; and missionaries, 62, 64, 68, 74, 82–83, 174; and politics, 25–27, 73–74, 138–40, 169–74, 176–77; postmenopausal, 23; and sacrifice, 80–82; and slavery, 53–56, 96–100; and trade, 137; and violence, 38–39, 40–41, 45, 107–8; and yaiya (funeral cry), 145, 154, 159, 166

yaiya (funeral cry), 145, 154, 159, 166, 189
Yazoo, 182, 184
Ymatahatchitou, 184
Yowani, 182

www.ingramcontent.com/pod-product-compliance
Lightning Source LLC
Chambersburg PA
CBHW031436160426
43195CB00010BB/750